TOWARDS KNOWLEDGE PORTALS

Information Science and Knowledge Management

Volume 5

The titles published in this series are listed at the end of this volume.

TOWARDS KNOWLEDGE PORTALS

From Human Issues to Intelligent Agents

by

BRIAN DETLOR
McMaster University,
Hamilton, Ontario, Canada

KLUWER ACADEMIC PUBLISHERS
DORDRECHT / BOSTON / LONDON

A C.I.P. Catalogue record for this book is available from the Library of Congress.

ISBN   978-90-481-6584-1 (PB)
ISBN   978-1-4020-2079-7 (e-book)

Published by Kluwer Academic Publishers,
P.O. Box 17, 3300 AA Dordrecht, The Netherlands.

Sold and distributed in North, Central and South America
by Kluwer Academic Publishers,
101 Philip Drive, Norwell, MA 02061, U.S.A.

In all other countries, sold and distributed
by Kluwer Academic Publishers,
P.O. Box 322, 3300 AH Dordrecht, The Netherlands.

Printed on acid-free paper

For my son, Ben Detlor, who makes all things worthwhile.

Contents

List of Figures

List of Tables

Foreword

It was over a half-century ago, when Vannevar Bush published his critically-acclaimed visionary writing "As We May Think" in the *Atlantic Monthly*, with its fantasy of a personal desk-size information machine called Memex (Burke, 1994; Bush, 1945). There, Bush described how Memex would function as a bibliographic machine for personalized indexing and retrieval allowing convenient access to knowledge accumulated throughout the ages. Moreover, the machine would liberate knowledge seekers by allowing them to add, categorize, and create new associations between information items and documents at their own discretion. In Bush's view, each desk would become an individualized knowledge base, which in turn could be used to create and leverage new knowledge.

Fast forward to the beginning of the 21st century and there is evidence of Bush's vision turning into reality. Today, we live in a world where people have immediate access to quasi-Memex machines in the form of personal computers (PCs) and hand-held digital assistants (PDAs) connected to the Internet and the World Wide Web (WWW).

Organizations have been quick to realize the potential of this new technology to foster and promote the acquisition, creation, packaging, application, and reuse of knowledge across the firm. As such, many organizations have implemented enterprise portal systems to provide a gateway or launch pad for employees to find and reutilize the information they need and to help firms better know what they know. Such companies recognize the potential of an enterprise portal to capture, share, and grow organizational knowledge assets. Many view portal systems as being pivotal for the success and future wellness of their organizations.

This book acknowledges the knowledge-leveraging power of enterprise portals. Its primary purpose is to provide a novel, rich and comprehensive discussion on the factors affecting the design and utilization of enterprise portals for knowledge work. Somewhat boldly, the book puts forth a narrative of knowledge portals that moves beyond their design and delivery as mere information retrieval systems. Instead, a knowledge portal is viewed as a shared information work space that facilitates communication and collaboration among organizational workers, in addition to supporting the browsing, searching, and retrieval of information content.

By embracing an informational perspective towards knowledge work, the book provides an in-depth investigation of how enterprise portals can promote knowledge creation, distribution, and use. From an information vantage point, the book uniquely explores the "human issues" surrounding portal adoption and use, as well as the utilization of "intelligent agents" to ameliorate the utilization of portals for knowledge-based tasks. The result is a holistic and balanced examination of this relatively-new type of information system found in organizations today.

The motivation behind this writing was the author's own personal desire to produce a well-reasoned and empirically-valid account of enterprise portals and their use for knowledge work in organizations. After many years of consulting, reading, researching, and teaching about portals, it was time to put down in writing observations and insights about this new phenomenon of interest. The hope is that other academics and industry practitioners will find these insights useful in spurring on new avenues of research and building better, more robust, portal designs—ones that avidly promote the active creation, distribution, and use of knowledge across the enterprise.

Doing so may lead us one step closer towards realizing the promise of Vannevar Bush's Memex machine.

Preface

One of the goals and hopefully benefits of this book is to offer new suggestions and unique insights on portals and their utilization in organizations as knowledge management tools. To facilitate this, discussion is grounded on the author's own personal research and consulting experience. Theoretical contributions are drawn across three varied, but complementary, literature backgrounds: Information Systems, Knowledge Management, and Information Studies. As such, the book covers a wide range of inter-related topics, including information behaviour, intelligent agents, knowledge work, information environments, information design, information seeking, participatory design, and technology acceptance. Underlying the discussion, however, is the relevance of these topics to knowledge portals, yielding a comprehensive and holistic examination into the design, adoption, and use of these systems in organizations today.

In terms of content and layout, the book consists of seven individual chapters, each pertaining to a unique but important perspective of knowledge portals.

Chapter 1, *Portals and Knowledge Work,* sets the stage for discussion. It provides a definition and overview of portals, describing what they are and why they are important. Adopting an information orientation to knowledge management, the concept of knowledge work is defined. This leads to a general description of how portals can facilitate knowledge work in organizations, and more importantly, into a working definition of knowledge portals. From there, the reader is introduced to various models of information behaviour, gleaned from the past 50 years of Information Studies research, and the application of these models to the design and use of knowledge portals in organizations. The intent of this chapter is to 'ramp up' the reader towards having a good grasp and understanding of portals and knowledge work from an information perspective.

Chapter 2, *The Knowledge Portal Framework*, gets down to business. It presents a three-entity model of the major factors affecting the development, adoption, and use of enterprise portals for knowledge work. Specifically, these factors are: 1) users; 2) the information environment; and 3) a portal's information design. A detailed account of the theory comprising the composition of this framework is given. From there, an in-depth research investigation conducted by the author is described, one which utilizes the framework as a conceptual lens to examine the various factors which impede or promote the use of the portal for knowledge work. Triangulation of both qualitative and quantitative data collection and analysis methods yields an in-depth exploratory empirical assessment of organizational knowledge portal use.

Chapter 3, *Users and Knowledge Portals*, discusses in detail the user component of the Knowledge Portal Framework. Case study results are reported. Discussion involves: the functional role of users; their passion or interest in portals; the perception of users in terms of the capabilities of portals to promote knowledge generation, sharing, and use; and the importance of motivating users to learn as a means of fostering the active use and exploration of portal systems. Specific attention is paid to the role portals can play in facilitating communities of practice within organizations, as well the factors which promote end user adoption with Web-based portal systems. The chapter's mantra is its call for a participatory design approach to portal development—a technique that advocates the active engagement of end users in portal design. A case study of a government portal development project showcases the effectiveness of having users actively engaged in the design of a portal interface. Lessons learned are described. A theoretical model of a participatory design approach to portal development is also proposed.

Chapter 4, *The Information Environment and Knowledge Portals*, talks about the information environment construct of the Knowledge Portal Framework with respect to an information environment's influence on the development, design, and adoption and use of knowledge portals in organizations. The information environment can be considered the information context of an organization. This includes factors such as: the information politics surrounding portal development; the information system development process itself; and the degree to which information is readily shared, valued, and controlled across the organization. Case study results are again reported.

Chapter 5, *Information Design and Knowledge Portals*, discusses the knowledge portal interface of the Knowledge Portal Framework in terms of a portal's information design. This includes the ability of a portal to support the tailorability or personalization of what information is displayed; the quality of this information; the organization of this information; the presence of collaborative tools; and the engagement of these systems in providing interactive and attractive interfaces. Case study results are described. Other Human-Computer Interaction (HCI) factors are discussed as well. This chapter emphasizes the need to display information on the knowledge portal interface to support different modes of user information behaviour (for example, search vs. browse activity). Of primary consideration is the need to present information in ways that signal the value of information to users and that support their modes of information seeking activity.

Chapter 6, *Intelligent Agents and Knowledge Portals*, introduces the concept of intelligent agents and their capacity to facilitate knowledge work in portals. This chapter defines intelligent agents and describes their benefits and challenges. The Semantic Web is discussed and its potential to provide an agent-based infrastructure for organizational knowledge work. Agent toolkits are also described. Much of the chapter is devoted to the potential application of intelligent agents in knowledge portal design. It is shown that agents can be deployed in many ways which satisfy the information needs of individual knowledge workers, their information seeking behaviours, as well as their uses of information obtained from the portal. The chapter concludes with an agent-based architecture for knowledge portals.

Chapter 7, *Knowledge Portals and Digital Workers*, puts it all together. This is the capstone chapter of the book. Drawing upon the details presented earlier, this chapter summarizes, refines, and reflects on the role of knowledge portals in relation to the digital worker. Here, the digital worker is both the "human" organizational participant and the automated software agent (i.e., digital assistant) who works on behalf of a user or group of users.

The book's primary audience would be faculty and students in masters and doctoral programs in schools and departments specializing in Information Systems, Information Studies, and Knowledge Management. Consultants and organizations designing and implementing enterprise-wide portal solutions or those spearheading knowledge management initiatives would find the book useful in providing research-based insights on the design of enterprise portals for knowledge work.

Acknowledgements

There are several people to whom I owe a debt of gratitude in terms of the production and publication of this monograph. Their assistance has greatly enriched my thoughts and ideas surrounding the utilization of enterprise portals for knowledge work. Any mistakes or misrepresentations found within the text, however, are utterly my own.

First, I would like to thank Dr. Chun Wei Choo from the Faculty of Information Studies (FIS) at the University of Toronto. His encouragement and support to embark on this book project is greatly appreciated. A notable thank you also goes to my former professors, associates and classmates at FIS who helped formulate my initial grounding and interest in the fields of knowledge management, information seeking, and Web information systems in general.

Next, there are numerous colleagues at my new home, McMaster University, who have contributed to this project in a variety of ways resulting in a stronger final product. I would like to thank my friends involved with the McMaster eBusiness Research Centre (http://merc.mcmaster.ca), especially Dr. Khaled Hassanein, Dr. Milena Head, and Dr. Maureen Hupfer, for their encouragement and insightful comments. To my doctoral students, Allan Harold, Alexander Serenko, and Umar Ruhi, for their ideas and questions. To the Innis (Business) Library staff, namely Vivian Lewis and Ines Perkovic, for providing terrific reference support. To Linda Mirabelli, area secretary, for her good humour and practical commentary. And to Heather Wylie, for serving as a research book assistant.

Last, but not least, I wish to thank those involved in the publication aspects of this monograph, namely Melissa Smith for providing exacting indexing services and Robbert van Berckelaer from Kluwer Academic Publishers.

The research presented in this monograph was supported in part by grants held by the author over several years: a grant from Bell University Labs at the University of Toronto; a doctoral fellowship from the Social Sciences and Humanities Research Council of Canada; and a research grant from the Natural Sciences and Engineering Council of Canada. The hiring of a research assistant to help conduct a preliminary literature review was made possible through a start-up grant from McMaster University. The indexing of the final manuscript was supported by a scholarly publications grant from the Arts Research Board at McMaster University.

Brian Detlor
McMaster University
January 2004

1. PORTALS AND KNOWLEDGE WORK

1.1 Knowledge Work

Many reports and books attest to the recent shift in society towards the new knowledge-based economy—one driven by the creation and dissemination of information, best-practices, and shared insights rather than the production of tangible, manufactured goods. One of the first observations of this change was made back sometime around 1960 when Peter Drucker (1993), in his essay on post-capitalist society, denoted the transformation in society towards a more service-oriented, information-based economy. Emphasizing the importance of knowledge in the modern organization, Drucker (p. 7) acknowledged that "the basic economic resource" is no longer capital, natural resources, or labour, but *is and will be knowledge.*" He went further to suggest that organizations, in response to this shift, must learn to adapt to continuous change and build systematic practices for managing such transformations.

Others agree that the future belongs to organizations which focus on knowledge. Toffler (1990) states that knowledge is the ultimate replacement of other resources and is key to the power shift in the new economy. Quinn (1992) posits that the economic power of a modern corporation lies in its intellectual capabilities rather than in traditional assets such as land and capital. Prusak (2001) identifies three primary drivers propelling organizations to manage and capitalize on their knowledge assets: globalization; ubiquitous computing; and an emerging knowledge-centric view of the firm.

1.1.1 Knowledge

Here knowledge is described as a powerful organizational resource. But what exactly is knowledge? It is an elusive construct. It is more than data (facts and figures). It is more than information—data organized for a particular purpose (Drucker, 1988). Quinn, Anderson and Finkelstein (1996) describe knowledge as professional intellect, which falls in line with Blair's (2002) view that only a person can possess and exercise knowledge. Nonaka and Takeuchi (1995, p. 58) adopt the traditional philosophical definition of knowledge as 'justified true belief.' Davenport and Prusak (1998) note that knowledge is both fluid and formally structured, neither neat nor simple; they offer a working definition of knowledge as a

"fluid mix of framed experience, values, contextual information, and expert insight that provides a framework for evaluating and incorporating new experiences and information. It originates and is applied in the mind of knowers. In organizations, it often becomes embedded not only in documents or repositories but also in organizational routines, processes, and norms" (p. 5).

From this definition, knowledge in organizations is viewed as a dichotomous construct that exists both *tacitly* in the minds of people and *explicitly* in formal products and procedures. This distinction is recognized and discussed by Nonaka and Takeuchi (1995) in their classification of two types of knowledge: explicit knowledge, that which can be partly expressed in formal, systematic language and transmitted to individuals easily; and tacit knowledge, that which is personal, context-specific, and difficult to articulate formally (Polanyi, 1966). Others re-label explicit and tacit knowledge to be hard and soft respectively, whereby hard knowledge is that which is codifiable and soft knowledge is that which is less codifiable, incorporating people's internalized experiences, skills, and domain and cultural knowledge (Hildreth, Wright and Kimble, 1999; Hildreth and Kimble, 2002).

1.1.2 Knowledge Management

Though agreement on the nature and being of knowledge has sparked many an academic debate over the years, knowledge and the desire to leverage it for organizational success has given rise to a relatively new field on the subject: *knowledge management* (KM). As reflected by the extensive production of articles, books, and conferences on the subject, there has been an intense and overwhelming interest in knowledge management by organizations in the last decade across a variety of disciplines—one that indicates knowledge management is on its way to becoming an established field of study rather than a mere management fad (Ponzi and Koenig, 2002). At the root of this interest is "the view that knowledge, particularly as manifested in the creation of new products and services, has become the primary source of wealth creation and sustainable competitive advantage" (Cole, 1998, p. 18).

Varying definitions of KM exist (Hlupic, Pouloudi and Rzevski, 2002; Snyder and Wilson, 2002). Some view knowledge management as a new dimension of strategic information management (Ponelis and Fair-Wessels, 1998). Others suggest knowledge management is the purposeful and systematic management of vital knowledge along with its associated processes of creating, gathering, organizing, diffusing, using, and exploiting that knowledge (Skyrme, 1997). Smith and Farquhar (2000) describe the goal of KM to be the improvement of organizational performance by enabling individuals to capture, share, and apply their collective knowledge to make optimal decisions in real time. Thomas, Kellogg and Erickson (2001) call the need to augment the typical view of knowledge management as a problem of capturing, organizing, and retrieving information with a perspective that also acknowledges the role of human cognition in knowledge situated in social work contexts. King, Marks and McCoy (2002) recognize the strong role information technology plays in KM and identify key applications in this area which are based on existing information technology infrastructures: knowledge repositories; best-practices and lessons-learned systems; expert networks; and communities of practice (Hackbarth and Grover, 1999; McDermott, 1999; Zack, 1999).

In terms of this book, *knowledge management* is defined to be the systematic, effective management and utilization of an organization's knowledge resources (i.e., ones that contain or embody knowledge) and encompasses the creation, storage, arrangement, retrieval, and distribution of an organization's knowledge (Saffady, 1998). This includes the "methods and tools for capturing, storing, organizing, and making accessible knowledge and expertise within and across communities" (Mack, Ravin and Byrd, 2001, p. 925). It also includes the active management and support of human expertise (Blair, 2002).

In this sense, knowledge management deals equally with the acquisition, handling, and use of explicit knowledge as well as the management of tacit knowledge in terms of improving people's capacity to communicate and collaborate with one another (Al-Hawamdeh, 2002). There are a variety of ways in which organizations go about doing this. One recent field investigation of 12 private and public sector large-sized organizations identified eight distinct methodologies corporations undertake to manage both explicit and tacit types of knowledge: 1) communities of practice; 2) question and answer forums; 3) knowledge mapping; 4) expert databases; 5) knowledge databases; 6) news information alerts; 7) training and education; and 8) virtual collaboration (Bouthillier and Shearer, 2002). Similarly, Bhatt (2002) identifies four management strategies to promote KM within the firm: 1) the empowerment of employees; 2) the motivation and nurturing of individual expertise; 3) the fostering of self-organized teams and promotion of group social interaction; and 4) the storage and codification of rules and procedures in simple formats so that employees can easily access and understand these rules and processes.

By adopting such strategies, companies are bearing evidence of the importance of leveraging both explicit and tacit types of knowledge. In this sense, organizations are aware and recognize that their workers possess know-how, something in addition to the hard facts and tidbits of information stored in computer data files and electronic documents, and that both kinds of knowledge must be harvested in tandem to help the company identify and yield innovative products and services.

1.1.3 Knowledge Work

Emerging from the field of knowledge management is the new concept of *knowledge work*, which refers to the creation, distribution, and use of knowledge in the firm. It involves the act of "solving problems and accomplishing goals by gathering, organizing, analyzing, creating, and synthesizing information and expertise" (Mack et al., 2001, p. 925).

In terms of its underlying components, several references in the literature describe knowledge work as a process or a set of activities involving knowledge creation, distribution, and use. For example, a practical orientation to the discussion of knowledge work in organizations describes knowledge work as a series of activities, namely the acquisition, creation, packaging, application and reuse of knowledge (Davenport, Jarvenpaa and Beers, 1996). Alavi and Tiwana (2002) identify a similar set of three processes. The first, knowledge creation, refers to the development of new knowledge through the interplay of tacit and explicit knowledge at varying ontological levels (Nonaka and Nishiguchi, 2001). The second, knowledge codification, refers to the codification of tacit knowledge via mechanisms that formalize and embed it in documents, software, organizational routines and protocols. The third, knowledge application, refers to how knowledge is utilized or brought to bear on a problem at hand.

This view agrees with a comprehensive review on the topic by Choo (1998) who summarizes and identifies three broad similarities in the knowledge creation, distribution, and use processes described by Leonard-Barton (1998), Nonaka and Takeuchi (1995), and Wikstrom and Normann (1994). The first is that firms generate new knowledge which extends their capabilities by sharing and converting the tacit knowledge of organizational members. This requires employees to engage in face-to-face dialogue and work collectively together as a means of reflecting and solving the problems organizations face. The second is that organizations operationalize new concepts so that they can be applied to new or enhanced offerings and allow organizations to operate more efficiently. The third is that organizations diffuse and transfer new knowledge both within and outside the enterprise. This involves new knowledge spreading across organizational boundaries and peripheries, which in turn generates new cycles of learning.

This description points to how organizations *create* (i.e., generate), *distribute* (i.e., diffuse and transfer), and *use* (i.e., operationalize) knowledge. It is argued that these are the core processes involved in knowledge work. More importantly, given the close relationship between knowledge and information (Taylor, 1986, Checkland, 1995; Meadow, Boyce and Kraft, 2000), it is assumed that information plays a central role in these core processes. That is, due to its close association to knowledge, information is perceived to be a tangible conduit for knowledge creation, distribution, and use (Detlor, 2002). Moreover, information by itself is intrinsically meaningless (Miller, 2002) and carries only the potential for value (Taylor, 1986). Here, it is the person that creates, distributes, and uses knowledge who gives an information message its meaning and purpose. As such, information becomes knowledge at the moment of its human interpretation (Miller, 2002).

Consider the daily tasks of *knowledge workers*. These are the people who carry out knowledge-intensive tasks in organizations. Earlier definitions describe knowledge workers as a special class of white collar worker such as consultants, managers, technicians, and scientists (Wuthnow and Shrum, 1983; Quinn, 1992; Stehr 1994) and purposely exclude service workers, such as clerical and support staff, who deal with administrative and operational issues (Chamot, 1987; Davenport et al., 1996; Drucker, 1993). However, more recent investigations, as well as this monograph, rebuke the concept of knowledge workers as an elite, specialist group, and instead open up the definition to include any organizational participants actively engaged in knowledge work processes (Detlor, 2000b) where knowledge emerges from the interplay of actors and activities at many different levels (Suchman, 2000; Dourish, 2001). For example, knowledge workers often belong to communities of interest, where knowledge is shared and accumulated (Mack et al., 2001). Their work consists "largely of converting information to knowledge", where people for the most part use their own competencies and sometimes the assistance of suppliers of information or specialized knowledge (Sveiby, 1997, p. 19). In this sense, information becomes knowledge when it is processed in the minds of individuals and knowledge becomes information when it is articulated or communicated to others in the form of text, computer output, spoken or written words, or other means (Alavi and Leidner, 1999).

Adopting such an orientation, knowledge work can be viewed as a set of activities that use both tacit and explicit knowledge to produce outputs characterized by information content (Davis, 1991). As such, knowledge is actionable information (Nonaka, 1994) or "information transformed into capability for effective action" (Smith and Farquhar, 2000, p. 18) utilized in the knowledge work practices of organizational participants. A working definition of knowledge work offered by Hayman and Elliman (2000) emphasizes the critical role information plays. They suggest that the tasks of knowledge workers involves more than organizing information, that the worker enriches given information using his or her expertise to produce a response, and that the worker is informed by or learns from the information that is processed.

Such a view is shared by Stehr (1994), who extends one of the earliest descriptions of organizational knowledge work by Machlup (1962) to be the production and re-production of information. In this respect, the transmission of information is an active process where a worker's knowledge is applied to the information being transferred, thus changing the information in some way before it is communicated. Hence, there is a dynamic relationship between information and knowledge: information facilitates the development of knowledge; and knowledge facilitates the creation of new information (Swan et al., 2000).

A field investigation of organizational knowledge workers by Kidd (1994a, 1994b) finds evidence of the importance of information in knowledge work. The results of Kidd's study suggest that the defining characteristic of knowledge workers is that they are themselves changed by the information they process, and what distinguishes knowledge workers is that this is their primary motivation and the job they are paid to do. Of particular relevance is the discovery that information plays a significant role in the creation, distribution, and use of knowledge. Kidd's investigation highlights the extent to which knowledge workers see their value to the organization as being able to understand a body of knowledge and generate new information from this understanding which changes either the organization or its customer in a direct way. Findings demonstrate how information functions as a significant agent in the act of informing knowledge workers—enabling them to generate ideas, improve work practice, and create new products and services.

The above depiction of knowledge work concentrates on the knowledge work practices of individuals. The orientation of this book adopts a similar stance and perceives knowledge work from a participant vantage point. Thus *knowledge creation* is defined to be a knowledge work process in which an individual generates new knowledge, gains insight, or learns something new. *Knowledge distribution* is defined to be a knowledge work process in which an individual receives or disseminates knowledge. *Knowledge use* is defined to be a knowledge work process in which an individual uses knowledge to perform an action (i.e., create a report, make a decision), or where an individual utilizes his or her own know-how to perform an action.

Figure 1-1 provides a conceptual illustration of the four key points surrounding the concept of knowledge work described above. The first is that knowledge work comprises the three fundamental processes of knowledge creation, distribution, and use. The second is that humans, who are knowledgeable entities themselves, are central to these core processes. The third is that these processes draw upon both tacit and explicit types of knowledge. The fourth is that these processes involve the production and reproduction of information, often yielding information outputs utilized by knowledge workers in their daily routines and practices.

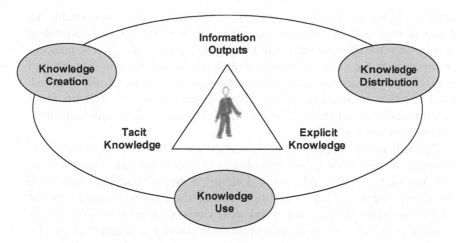

Figure 1-1. Knowledge work processes

1.2 Knowledge Portals

The above description points to the importance of supporting the information-laden processes of knowledge creation, distribution and use within the firm. Organizations have been quick to respond to this challenge by leveraging the use and deployment of Web-based technologies across the enterprise. Though knowledge management is not about technology, technology plays an important role in knowledge management (Al-Hawamdeh, 2002). Technology, especially those that are Web-based, can facilitate the process of transmitting and exchanging information (Zhang, 2002), as well as facilitate communication and collaboration between workers in organizations. By doing so, Web-based knowledge management systems foster the growth and exchange of explicit and tacit knowledge by providing organizational participants with access to both information content and collaborative technologies.

1.2.1 Web Information Technologies

The premier information technology utilized by employees in organizations today is Web-based technology—the technology underlying the infrastructure of the World Wide Web (WWW). Developed in 1991 to link physicists and engineers at remote sites to share ideas and aspects of a common project (Berners-Lee et al., 1994), the WWW utilizes standard communication and document publishing protocols such as the HTTP (HyperText Transfer Protocol), HTML (HyperText Markup Language), and XML (Extensible Markup Language) to exchange information across platforms. Adopting these core protocol standards, Web browsers enable the display of pages of text and graphics stored on Web servers and transmitted across a network of interconnected computers. As such, the WWW provides employees with the ability to browse and search for information regardless of the platform on which the information resides or where it physically is stored. Moreover, this information is accessible directly from the desktop via a standard, common interface, making the Web a convenient and frequently-utilized knowledge resource.

To facilitate knowledge creation, distribution, and use, many support the utilization of Web information technologies to systematize and expedite firm-wide knowledge work (Alavi and Leidner, 1999; Gottschalk, 2000). Of relevance is the technology's ability to reduce the costs associated with the transmission of much information and some kinds of knowledge (Cole, 1998). In fact, Web information systems support three primary redesign strategies for knowledge work processes: they change knowledge by reducing it to a unit that workers can reuse and access; they reduce the geographic distance between workers by providing access to information regardless of its physical location; and they create knowledge bases and enable telecommunications infrastructures to bolster knowledge work (Davenport et al., 1996).

Others note the dual role Web information systems can play in: 1) providing access to information content; and 2) supporting communication and coordination of activities between organizational participants. For instance, "Web-based infrastructures" are seen to possess the ability to provide firms with not only repositories of knowledge, that offer "knowledge bases of best practices" and search tools "that make the retrieval of the stored knowledge objects possible" (Schultze, 1998, p. 162), but also the ability to support narration, self-reflection, and multi-vocal dialogue (Boland and Tenkasi, 1995; 1994) as a means of helping communities within the firm understand one another's practices of knowledge creation, transfer, and use. In this way, Web-based information technology can function as a mechanism for augmenting and interconnecting both people and resources through the provision of a computer supported collaborative work space where knowledge can be created, organized, secured, distributed, and used, and where cooperative work can be enabled (Schmidt and Bannon, 1992; Snis, 2000). However, despite the recognition of this dual role, most Web information systems currently offer solutions that deal largely with explicit knowledge, such as search and classification of information, rather than with contributions to the formation and communication of tacit knowledge and support for making it explicit (Marwick, 2001).

1.2.2 Enterprise Portals

Enterprise portals are popular Web-based knowledge management solutions. Coined in a Merrill Lynch report,

> "enterprise information portals are applications that enable companies to unlock internally and externally stored information, and provide users a single gateway to personalized information needed to make informed business decisions." (Shilakes and Tylman, 1998)

This definition differentiates enterprise portals from intranets. An *intranet* refers to the underlying Web infrastructure upon which a portal resides. In this sense, an intranet can be thought of as a private internal network based on Internet standards operating within an organization where access is restricted to organizational participants only. Firewalls prevent access from external Internet users and allow information to be securely managed inside an organization (Hinrichs, 1997).

Using these definitions, one can think of an enterprise portal as a Web site operating over an intranet providing a path to all-encompassing content and services through one access point (Hagedorn, 2000). It provides secure, customizable, and personalizable access to dynamic information content wherever it is needed. It is in essence a launch pad or gateway to various information content and services for employees of an organization. It can be viewed as a single-point access vehicle to help orient employees to the information they need (Eckel, 2000). This information may be internal or external to the company and reference a variety of information sources such as internal departmental Web sites, external company Web sites, databases, and electronic documents (Detlor, 2000a). Moreover, an enterprise portal can be defined as a single point of access for the pooling, organizing, interacting, and distribution of organizational knowledge (Aneja, Brooksby and Rowan, 2000; Schroeder, 2000; Raol et al., 2002).

In fact, many companies implement and view enterprise portals as knowledge management solutions (Kotorov and Hsu, 2001; Davis, 2002). To promote a portal's utilization, organizations typically hard-wire the portal to be the default homepage that appears on an employee's personal Web browser when launched. The primary purpose of a portal is to navigate people; its secondary purpose is to provide unique content. This is in contrast to other types of Internet sites, such as external or departmental Web sites, where the primary purpose is to disseminate information and keep people at that specific site.

Other synonymous terms less frequently utilized to represent enterprise portals are *corporate portals* and *business portals*. For instance, Eckerson (1999) describes a business portal as an application that provides business users (i.e., employees) with one-stop shopping for any information they need inside or outside the enterprise. Here, a business portal is like a "shopping mall for knowledge workers" where organizational participants utilize the portal to find all the information they need instead of going to successive information resources scattered across different locations.

The excitement over enterprise portals by major corporations in recent years is due in large part to the success *Yahoo!* had with its 1996 launch of a personalized portal service called *MyYahoo!*, which allowed users to customize their own Web interfaces to filter and provide information that was relevant and meaningful to them (Plumtree, 1999). Corporations were quick to notice the success of this product in terms of its adoption and use by the general public and started to investigate ways to develop a similar view of corporate information.

Overall, enterprise portals are following a similar trajectory as consumer portals, though over much shorter time frames. First version portals containing referential links to information plus a search engine are quickly evolving into more complex, interactive gateways that embed applications to enhance personal and work group productivity, all within time periods as short as 12 months (Eckerson, 1999). Common elements contained within enterprise portal designs include an enterprise taxonomy or classification of information categories that help organize information for easy retrieval; a search engine to facilitate more specific and exact information requests; and hypertext links to both internal and external Web sites and information sources (Ouellette, 1999; Verity, 1999). More advanced portal features include access to work group productivity tools such as e-mail, calendars, work flow and project management software, expense reporting and travel reservation applications, as well as more specialized functions for transaction-based information processing where users can read, write, and update corporate data directly through the portal interface (Eckerson, 1999; Detlor, 2000a).

This view falls in line with Dias (2001) who identifies six major components of an enterprise portal. The first is a business information directory that provides an indexed catalogue of the organization's information. This directory controls user profiles which dictate the type of information that may be accessed by employees on an individual or group basis. The second are search engines which match user queries against the business information directory to help organizational workers locate the information they need, as well as, metadata crawlers which regularly scan Web servers (both external and internal to the enterprise) in search of new and relevant information for the business directory. The third is a publishing facility to enable users to load and index information into the portal. The fourth are import and export interfaces from the enterprise portal to other internal and external systems. The fifth is some sort of subscription facility which notifies and distributes on a regular basis information considered relevant to a user or a group of users. This can occur on demand or can be automatically routed according to user profiles contained in the enterprise portal or stored requests for information previously specified users. The last is an information assistant to tailor or present information on the Web interface. Both Dias' information assistant and subscription facility are agent-like components discussed in more detail in Chapter 6.

Yahoo! is a portal exemplar which contains the three basic elements of portals identified above, as well as more advance productivity tools such as e-mail, online chat, address books, maps etc. For example, the site provides a robust organization of information items via a taxonomy of subject categories, such as Arts and Humanities, Business and Economy etc. These categories are similar to subject categories one would see in a physical card catalogue in a library. They facilitate easy retrieval since the information contained in the system is pre-organized (i.e., indexed) prior to the formation of an information retrieval request in a manner users would prefer or most likely request that information. Further, the site contains a search box in which to facilitate a more formal information search than could be conducted through category browsing. As well, the site contains many hypertext links to information. In this way, the site functions as a transparent source of information to other resources rather than a supplier of information itself. In this respect, *Yahoo!* functions as a launch pad or gateway to information contained elsewhere. The more advanced productivity tools within *Yahoo!*, such as e-mail and calendar, provide incentives for users to visit the site. By comprising the three basic elements of portals in addition to more advance productivity tools, *Yahoo!* serves as a good example of what a portal should look like and how it should function.

1.2.3 Knowledge Portals

By viewing enterprise portals as rich virtual work environments, and not merely as simple information dissemination tools, enterprise portals can provide organizations with a shared information work space to facilitate the creation, exchange, retention, and reuse of knowledge (Choo, Detlor and Turnbull, 2000a). To accomplish this, enterprise portals need to comprise three distinct areas (see Figure 1-2): a *content space* to facilitate information access and retrieval; a *communication space* to support the negotiation of collective interpretations and shared meanings; and a *coordination space* to support cooperative work action and work processes (Detlor, 2000a).

As an information content space, enterprise portals can help organizations with improved information storage and retrieval. This can occur in a variety of ways, whether the information is pulled by users themselves, such as in browsing and goal-directed search, or pushed (filtered) to them directly via the use of intelligent agents.

In terms of a communication space, enterprise portals can help organizational users make better sense of the information they receive by providing users with channels and connections to other human experts. This can be accomplished through the provision of rich information channels, such as instant messaging environments or online discussion rooms, to help organizational workers engage in conversations and negotiations with others in the firm. In this way, new perspectives and innovation can result and be stored back in the portal's knowledge base for later re-use. In this regard, the portal functions as a repository of organizational memory.

As a coordination space, enterprise portals can give organizational participants the ability to coordinate work processes, gain access to work application software, and manage the flow of information necessary for cooperation between various organizational units. This necessitates the need for portals to have requisite functionality in their designs to automate work flows, coordinate routines, and manage projects, as well as signal the expertise of others in the organization and their availability for cooperative action.

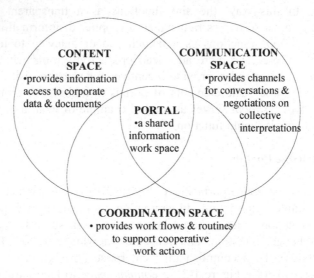

Figure 1-2. The portal as shared information work space (Detlor, 2000a, p. 93). Reprinted with permission from Elsevier Science.

By providing these three distinct spaces, enterprise portals can offer organizational participants the benefit of acquiring, distributing, interpreting, storing, and retrieving information in their daily work practice. Implied in these spaces is the concept of awareness (Stenmark 2001; 2002a) where organizational workers via the portal are made attentive to the existence and whereabouts of enterprise information resources, whether they be people or non-people based. According to Stenmark, such an intranet network feature is a prerequisite for community building and increases the likelihood of successful communication and collaboration opportunities.

Adopting such an orientation, a newer perspective of an enterprise portal as a *knowledge portal* has recently emerged, signifying the complexity and higher-level functionality available in enterprise portals today. In this sense, knowledge portals are a specific breed of enterprise portals which support the three main facets of information content storage and retrieval, organizational communication, and group collaboration.

One of the first utilizations of the term knowledge portal was by Murray (1999) who identifies four distinct types of portals: 1) enterprise information portals which connect people with information; 2) enterprise collaborative portals which provide a wide range of collaborative features for people to use to connect with one another; 3) enterprise expertise portals which connect people based on their experiences, abilities, and interests; and most importantly, 4) knowledge portals which combine all the previously mentioned features.

Mack et al. (2001) provide a healthy and robust description of the role of knowledge portals in organizations. They describe knowledge portals as information portals used by knowledge workers. In this capacity, the goal of a knowledge portal is to service the tasks performed by knowledge workers. This includes gathering information relevant to a task, organizing it, searching it, analyzing it, synthesizing solutions with respect to specific task goals, and sharing and distributing what has been learned with other knowledge workers. Of interest is their depiction and technical description of two knowledge management tools developed by IBM: the IBM Global Services K Portal and IBM's internal intellectual capital management AssetWeb Notes-based application. According to these authors, the two systems complement one another. K Portal is a totally Web-based, lightweight application focused on search and categorization. In contrast, AssetWeb incorporates collaboration and communication tools, as well as some level of work flow to manage information content. Of interest is the recognition of the need to offer the complementary components that each of these two applications possess to facilitate organizational knowledge work: namely, an information content space and collaboration and communication areas.

Grammer (2000) defines the concept of an enterprise knowledge portal (EKP) as an evolution of an enterprise information portal influenced by the goals of KM. Here, the EKP is an extension of the enterprise information portal which also captures tacit knowledge, integrates access to expertise, and embeds application functionality. Thus, the EKP not only provides the means for information access, but also lets organizational users interact with one another, and to link an individual's information with a company's shared collective insight, value, and experiences. In this way, an EKP combines acquired information and knowledge, and serves as a self-documenting centre of experiential learning.

Firestone (2000; 2001; 2003), responds to Grammer's description of the EKP, by providing a more comprehensive definition of the enterprise knowledge portal construct. In essence, Firestone describes an EKP as an enhanced enterprise information portal that is: 1) goal-directed towards knowledge production, knowledge integration, and knowledge management; 2) focuses upon, provides, produces, and manages information about the validity of the information it supplies; 3) provides information and meta-information about the organization's business; 4) distinguishes knowledge from information; 5) provides a facility for producing knowledge from information; and 6) orients the user towards producing and integrating knowledge rather than information.

Both Grammer's and Firestone's descriptions are important in that they recognize the role of information in knowledge work and position the (enterprise) knowledge portal as a more elaborate extension of the traditional firm-wide information portal. This view is also advocated by Collins (2002) in her depiction of enterprise knowledge portals as IT enabling platforms by which companies can implement their KM initiatives—a description which situates knowledge portals at the intersection of knowledge management and enterprise information portals. Collins explicitly describes enterprise knowledge portals as vehicles which bring together people, processes, and content. These three entities draw striking parallels to the communication, collaboration, and content spaces depicted in Figure 1-2. Moreover, Collins grounds the effectiveness of an organization's enterprise knowledge portal in facilitating knowledge work on the portal's ability to capture information, turn it into true knowledge, disseminate it, keep it up-to-date, and make it available all the time across the firm.

Adopting such a perspective, Collins offers a definition of an enterprise knowledge portal as:

> "A personalized interface to online resources for knowledge workers to organize and integrate applications and data. The solution allows knowledge workers to access information, collaborate with each other, make decisions, and take action on a wide variety of business-related work processes regardless of the knowledge worker's virtual location or business unit affiliation, the location of the information, or the format in which the information is stored." (Collins, 2002, p. 77)

In this way, all three works by Grammer, Firestone, and Collins help justify the need for content, communication, and coordination spaces in the formation of an enterprise-wide knowledge portal.

1.3 Information Behaviour

The two prior sections of this chapter provide insights into organizational knowledge work and the potential of Web-based knowledge portals to facilitate knowledge creation, distribution, and use across the enterprise. Of particular importance is the recognition that information-laden activities comprise knowledge work processes, and the potential of portals to support these activities through the provision of information content, communication, and coordination spaces. Utilizing these insights as a guide, it follows that if organizations wish to build portals that support knowledge work practice, then there is a strong need for enterprises, prior to systems development, to understand how workers behave with information in their daily activities. Such analysis would enable organizations to identify current information sources used and best practice scenarios and reflect upon enablers of and barriers to those sources and practices. This in turn would allow firms to utilize such findings to build knowledge portal systems that better address user information needs.

The Information Studies field offers a plethora of theoretical models and empirical findings on user information behaviour accumulated over the past 50 years (Paisley, 1968; Dervin and Nilan, 1986; Westbrook, 1993) upon which to glean insights for knowledge portal design. The discipline is concerned with the discovery and implementation of models and theories which focus on human information behaviour in context of social, institutional, or individual needs (Sonnenwald and Iivonen, 1999). Its literature area is strongly influenced from conceptual models and research results from the cognitive and psychological sciences. As such, the field offers a strong theoretical foundation to inform and guide information systems research, specifically studies concerned with the situated use of systems in particular contexts.

As defined by Wilson (1999, p. 249), *information behaviours* are "those activities a person may engage in when identifying his or her own needs for information, searching for such information in any way, and using or transferring that information." Over the past five decades, many models of information behaviour have been developed; some prominent ones include: Dervin's (1992) sense-making framework; Kuhlthau's (1991; 1993) affective orientation to the information search process; Ingwersen's (1996) cognitive model; Wilson's (1997; 1999) information seeking models; and Choo's (1998) general model of information use. Overall, these models provide pertinent insights on human information behaviour. They are examined briefly below, along with suggested implications of these models in terms of the design of portals for knowledge work.

1.3.1 Dervin's model

Dervin's (1992) sense-making framework comprises four basic elements: a *situation* in time and space defining the context in which information problems arise; a *cognitive gap* which identifies the difference between the contextual situation and the desired situation; an *outcome*; and a *cognitive bridge* involving some closing of the gap between the situation and outcome. In this model, the user is portrayed as moving through a situation in which he or she may experience a moment of discontinuity or gap.

To overcome or bridge that gap, a person invokes certain strategies to answer questions, form ideas, or obtain resources. This results in information use behaviour where the person receives some sort of help in bridging that gap.

A set of categories, labelled situation stops, describe the ways in which humans cognitively perceive their way ahead being blocked. These include: decision stops where the person sees two or more roads ahead; barrier stops where the person sees one road ahead but something or someone standing on the road blocking the way; spin-out stops where the person sees him or herself as having no road; wash-out stops where the person sees her or himself on a road that suddenly disappears; and problematic stops where the person sees him or herself as being dragged down a road not of his or her own choosing.

Dervin posits a set of help categories which explain how people utilize information to bridge these situation stops. These include creating ideas, finding directions, acquiring skills, getting support, getting motivated, getting connected, calming down, getting pleasure, and reaching goals.

In terms of knowledge portal design, it follows, or at least suggests, that portals should offer such functionality as described by Dervin in her help categories. By doing so, portals would give organizational workers the means to address cognitive gaps encountered when processing or seeking information in situated work contexts across time and space. Providing such mechanisms in portal design which allow people to generate new ideas, gain skills, gather support, obtain motivation, connect with other knowledge workers etc. would facilitate humans in their sense-making information behaviour.

1.3.2 Kuhlthau's model

While Dervin's model offers a cognitive approach to information seeking behaviour, Kuhlthau (1991, 1993), in a different yet similar vein, suggests an affective orientation to the information search process. In her model, information seeking is viewed as a process of construction in which users progress from uncertainty to understanding. Here, the information seeking process comprises six successive stages of gradual refinement of a problem area: initiation; selection; exploration; formulation; collection; and presentation.

During initiation, the user first recognizes a need for more information, where feelings of uncertainty and apprehension are common. In response, people relate the problem to past experiences and engage in discussing the situation with others in terms of possible topic and approaches.

During selection, the task is to identify and select the general area or topic to be investigated or the approach to be pursued. Feelings of uncertainty give way to a sense of optimism after a selection has been made. Actions involve seeking background information on the general area of concern.

During exploration, the user expands personal understanding of the general topic area. Feelings of confusion, doubt, and uncertainty frequently increase during this time. Actions involve locating information relevant to the general problem area and relating new information to what already is known.

During formulation, the turning point of the process, feelings of uncertainty diminish and confidence begins to rise. Thoughts become more clear and defined as a focused perspective on the problem is formed.

During collection, the emphasis is on gathering information pertinent to the focused problem and user confidence increases. The user is able to be specific and look for particular relevant information.

During presentation, the last stage, the user completes the search and resolves the problem. If the search goes well, a sense of relief is typical; if not, disappointment is common.

In terms of an impact on knowledge portal design, Kuhlthau's affective model suggests that a key challenge in designing information systems is to enable people to move from states of uncertainty towards states of understanding. The system must accommodate a non-linear path from initiation, where users experience symptoms of anxiety, confusion, frustration, and doubt, and progress towards presentation, where users experience feelings of confidence, relief, and satisfaction if the search goes well, and feelings of disappointment if the search goes awry.

Typically computer-based information systems assume a non-affective, indicative user mood and concentrate on the provision of information in terms of speed and specificity only. In reality, a user's mood oscillates during the information seeking process between periods of anxiety and doubt, and feelings of increased confidence. Therefore, knowledge portals need to provide functionality in their designs which assists users in their varying affective moods.

To do this, portals could offer assistance to users which minimize their level of anxiety, confusion, and frustration. This could be accomplished by suggesting possible subject topics, information sources, and search strategies to users during periods anxiety and doubt, or helping users connect with other individuals in the organization who can offer guidance, suggestions, and interpretations on search results received.

1.3.3 Ingwersen's model

Ingwersen (1996) presents a cognitive model of information retrieval. His model comprises several components: information objects consisting of knowledge representations, full text, semantic entities etc.; the information retrieval system which includes the search language, database structure and indexing rules; and an individual's cognitive space between the system interface and a user's social or organizational environment. It is in this space that users possess varying cognitive states of their work-related tasks, information needs, problems, and goals. Specifically, Ingwersen suggests that various cognitive transformations take place in this space from initial recognition of a new problem or goal (gap) to the situation where information objects are searched and useful objects are identified from the retrieval system.

Though Ingwersen's model pertains strictly to active search rather than broader information seeking behaviour, it possesses a "close family resemblance to other models of information seeking behaviour" (Wilson, 1999). In terms of knowledge portal design, his model raises awareness about the role user cognition plays in the information retrieval process and how environmental factors can influence how information retrieval is actually conducted.

1.3.4 Wilson's models

Over the years, Wilson presents several models of information behaviour. In 1997, he offers a revision to an earlier general model of information seeking behaviour that he first proposed in 1981 comprising three broad components. The first component is the information need context. Needs are described as subjective in nature and situated in a rich tapestry of personal, social, and environmental sub-contexts. For instance, in terms of a personal context, a person's self-interpretation of an information need is described as being affected by physiological, affective, and cognitive states. With respect to a social context, a person's role is said to influence and guide the types of information requested. In terms of the environment, other factors, such as the physical locality of a person or the organizational culture in which a person works, is described as limiting or biasing a person's need for information.

Further, Wilson describes a nested approach to these sub-contexts where an information need is shaped by a person performing a certain role within a specific environment.

The second component of Wilson's 1997 model are the barriers which impact the information seeking process. According to Wilson, various types of barriers exist. These again are described at personal, role-related, and environmental levels. For example, a person's knowledge of the existence and usefulness of possible sources of information may restrict the types of information sources examined to resolve a person's information need. A person's role in an organization may restrict access to certain information sources or bias the use of certain sources typically utilized in that role. A person's environment may physically deter access to information sources that are geographically inconvenient or financially expensive. Likewise, the culture of a person's work environment may value and promote the use of certain sets of information sources deemed worthy by that community which perhaps restrict a broader and more comprehensive information search.

The third component identified by Wilson is the information seeking behaviour elicited by people as they go about trying to satisfy their information needs. Wilson favours Ellis' (1989b; 1993) information seeking stages or features to describe the varying types of information behaviour activities exhibited by people. These are: starting (the means utilized by a person to begin seeking information (such as asking a knowledgeable colleague); chaining (following footnotes and citations in known material); browsing (semi-structured or semi-directed searching); differentiating (using known differences in information sources as a way of filtering the amount of information obtained); monitoring (keeping up-to-date); extracting (selectively identifying relevant material in an information source); verifying (checking the accuracy of information); and ending.

In 1999, Wilson offers an overhaul to his 1997 model that draws upon research from a variety of fields beyond Information Studies, such as decision-making, psychology, innovation, health communication, and consumer research. In essence, the basic framework of the 1997 model persists. First, the person in context remains the focus of information needs.

Second, barriers are represented by intervening variables. Here, the term 'intervening variables' replaces the term 'barriers' to suggest that outlying factors may prevent or promote information seeking (and not just inhibit such activity). The three original intervening variables (personal, role-related, and environmental) are expanded to consist of psychological, demographic, role-related/interpersonal, environmental, and information source intervening variables. For example, information sources characteristics of accessibility, credibility, and the type of information channel can impact, either in a positive or negative way, the likelihood of that information source being used or effective.

Third, information seeking behaviour is represented and expanded to contain more than 'active search' types of activity such as more passive, less-directed, and on-going types of search that those that are simply goal-directed.

In addition to these three similarities, Wilson adds a new component labelled "information processing and use" to his 1999 model. This addition is a significant improvement to the previous model in that the new component emphasizes the cyclical nature of information seeking behaviour. The model portrays how information needs can be reshaped as information seeking is carried out and how new information needs can be generated altogether during this process.

Thus, the 1999 model of information seeking portrays a cyclical process of information seeking behaviour where a person is situated in certain personal, role-related and environmental contexts from which information needs arise. To satisfy these needs, a person elicits information seeking behaviour which is constrained or enabled by mitigating intervening variables. As information is processed and used by the individual, his or her information needs are modified. Either they are resolved, become modified, or new ones are generated.

In terms of knowledge portal design, many lessons can be derived from Wilson's 1999 model. First, it suggests that designers need to understand the context in which information needs are derived and to build functionality in the design of portals which address user personal, role-based, and environmental situations. Second, it identifies how certain variables intervene in the information seeking behaviour of employees. The trick is to leverage the variables which promote seeking behaviour and remove, or at least minimize, those which detract or inhibit more successful and rewarding seeking behaviours. Third, Wilson's model hints at the need to handle more than active, goal-directed search behaviour in portal design, but also to support the browsing of information and on-going information search requests. Fourth, it suggests that portals need to recognize that information seeking is not a one interface session activity and that seeking behaviour can spur revisions to information needs or generate new ones. Thus portals should "remember" and ultimately leverage previous information seeking requests to handle future ones, and not treat information requests independently. Further, it suggests that portals should "learn" to what degree past information requests satisfied the information needs of users and remember these to service similar requests in the future by different users or different requests by the same individual.

Of interest to this discussion is Wilson's (1999) commentary on the problem solving nature of information seeking requests. He suggests that when users have information needs, they are in essence confronted with a *problematic situation*. Thus, "the solution of the problem, the resolution of the discrepancy, the advance from uncertainty to certainty (or at least some pragmatic solution to the problem) then becomes a goal of the person" (p. 265). En route to this goal, the individual moves gradually from a state of uncertainty towards a state of certainty. Further, there are distinct stages to this transition involving problem identification (stating that a problem exists), problem definition (describing exactly what the problem is), problem resolution (finding an answer to the problem), and solution statement (giving the answer to the problem). Wilson acknowledges that this process is not necessarily linear and most likely involves "feedback loops" or regressions to previous stages in the process. This is of relevance to knowledge portal design in that it suggests that such systems may need to designed as a problem-solving systems (rather than mere information retrieval systems) which support users in their progressions and regressions through the various stages from problem identification to solution statement. This again points to the need to capture and understand user needs in context of a user's situation and to build systems which help users resolve their information-based problems over time.

1.3.5　Choo's model

In a similar vein to Wilson's feedback loops and cyclical process of information seeking, Choo (1998) offers a general model of information use that comprises cycles of information needs, seeking and use activity. Based on Dervin's and Kulhthau's theoretical works, Choo's model recognizes an individual's cognitive structures and emotional dispositions, as well as the work/social setting in which the information needs-seeking-use cycle takes place (Taylor, 1991). The model examines information seeking and use behaviour at the level of the individual where individuals are portrayed as engaging in iterative cycles of activity comprising three discrete stages.

The first is *information needs* where individuals recognize gaps in their states of knowledge and in their ability to make sense of an experience. Once a clear understanding of these gaps is developed, individuals progress to the second stage, *information seeking*, where information needs are articulated as questions or topics that guide the choosing of and interaction with information sources in an information search. Upon completion of a scan of information sources, individuals move onto the third stage, *information use*, which involves the selection and processing of information. Here, individuals act upon the information selected. This can involve answering a question, resolving a problem, making a decision, negotiating a position, or making sense of a situation. As a result of this action, an individual's knowledge state is changed. If an individual recognizes gaps in this new knowledge state, then the needs-seeking-use cycle is iterated again. This cycle repeats until no (or an acceptable level of) gap is perceived by the individual.

In terms of knowledge portal design, Choo's model has certain implications. It suggests that such systems be built in a manner that handle these three unique modes of information activity. In the information needs stage, the knowledge portal may be required to present information in a way that helps users identify gaps in their current states of knowledge. This could entail presenting various perspectives on certain information topics deemed important to the user. This could be accomplished through the "pushing" of relevant content on pre-defined interest areas to users, and through the provision of chat and discussion areas where knowledge workers across the enterprise could offer personal interpretations and perspectives. Doing so would facilitate the questioning of currently held beliefs and would force users to make sense of new information received.

In the information seeking stage, the knowledge portal may have to facilitate robust ways of finding information. For example, employing the means to handle natural language query expressions would greatly facilitate the interpretation of user information needs and their translation into expansive search terms. Also, building knowledge portals to handle a wide range of seeking behaviour, from exploratory browsing to directed information search, would support users across a wide spectrum of seeking behaviour. This involves not only incorporating robust search engines within knowledge portal designs, but also rigorous and well-defined enterprise taxonomies of information categories to facilitate browsing. Additionally, through the provision of chat and discussion areas, portals could help people access subject area experts or learn about new sources of information on topic areas being investigated.

In the information use stage, knowledge portals could provide a tight integration between information sources and an employee's work tools. This could occur through intelligent summarizers of information content and the direct import of discovered information into a person's computer-based work applications. In this respect, a knowledge portal's content, collaboration, and coordination spaces would be highly integrated to provide a tightly-coupled shared information work space conducive to information use.

1.3.6 Implications for Knowledge Portals

Drawing upon the various theoretical models of information behaviour described above, several common ideas are shared. These include the cognitive and affective characteristics of users, problem-based tasks or goals which invoke user needs, the cyclical nature of information needs-seeking-use behaviour, and the situated environmental context in which this behaviour occurs.

Figure 1-3 provides an illustration of these common ideas elicited through the above review of information seeking models. The figure is loosely adapted from an earlier model proposed by the author (Detlor, 2003) that was utilized as a conceptual framework for an investigation of Internet-based information system use in organizations. That study found evidence of a core set of problem situations in organizations, as well as confirmation of an iterative cycle of information needs-seeking-use activity in firms with respect to Internet-based information system utilization.

In Figure 1-3, foremost is the identification of the information environment construct encapsulating the entire information needs-seeking-use cycle where users utilize a knowledge portal. The term "information environment" is used rather than just "environment" to signify and increase awareness of the information-oriented characteristics of the knowledge work context in which knowledge portals are utilized. Information environments are discussed in more detail in Chapter 4.

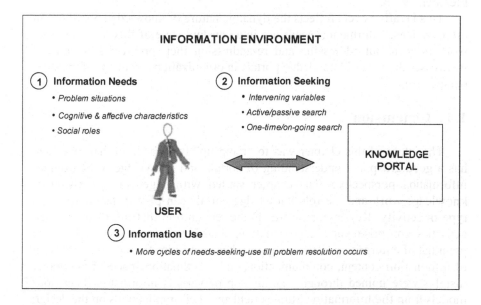

Figure 1-3. Knowledge portals and information-needs-seeking-use behaviour

Within the information environment, users are engaged in several iterations of an information needs-seeking-use cycle. Step 1 of this cycle refers to the information needs stage. Here, users are confronted with discrete problem situations typically faced in their work settings. What problem situations are perceived by users to be important and worth resolving is dependent on the cognitive and affective make-up of users and the social roles they play. In essence, users in this phase become aware of a gap in their knowledge to resolve the problem situation they face.

Step 2 is the information seeking stage where users turn to the knowledge portal to obtain the requisite information and knowledge to help resolve their problems. In this stage, several intervening variables (such as those that are psychological, demographic, role-related, environmental, and information source specific) may promote or inhibit information seeking. Further, several different types of seeking behaviour may occur ranging from active search, undirected browsing, one-time information retrieval activities, or on-going search requests.

Step 3 is the information use stage. This steps starts when the user has completed a scan of the knowledge portal's resources and processes the information and knowledge received. As a result of this action, the original problem situation is modified in some way. Either it is resolved, altered, or new problem situations become defined. These cycles of activities repeat until the problem situations become resolved in the minds of the user (Katzer and Fletcher, 1992).

This iterative cycle reflects the dynamic nature of knowledge portal use in organizations. Information needs are in a constant state of flux as knowledge workers go about addressing and re-addressing their problem situations. It showcases the role of knowledge portals in organizations from an information perspective.

1.4   Conclusion

The intent of this chapter was to "ramp up" the reader so that he or she has a good grasp and understanding of portals and knowledge work from an information perspective. The chapter started with a general discussion of knowledge work and the role knowledge portals can play in facilitating this type of activity. Key lessons were: 1) the recognition that information-laden activities comprise knowledge creation, distribution, and use; and 2) the potential of enterprise portals to support these activities through the provision of information content, communication, and coordination spaces. From there, insights were gained through examination of various information behaviour models from the Information Studies field and their implications on the design of knowledge portals. Based on a meta-analysis of these models, knowledge portals were shown to be: 1) situated within the information environment of the firm; and 2) employed in the on-going information needs-seeking-use cycle of knowledge workers as they go about resolving their problem situations.

The next chapter moves the discussion further. Specifically, various frameworks for the management of enterprise portals are described. Based on lessons learned, a new knowledge portal framework is put forth that depicts the major factors affecting the development, adoption, and use of enterprise portals for knowledge work.

2. THE KNOWLEDGE PORTAL FRAMEWORK

2.1 Introduction

The development and introduction of any enterprise-wide information system into a firm typically involves a change in current work practice and in existing ways of doing things. Due to an enterprise system's wide organizational reach, there is generally a higher risk of potential non-adoption and non-use by employees than with smaller, more localized systems. The challenge for designers of systems which span the corporation's user base is to introduce these systems in ways which offer the best chance for acceptance and which increase the likelihood of avid daily use.

This chapter examines and addresses this point in more detail in terms of the introduction of firm-wide knowledge portals. What factors should organizations be concerned with to increase adoption and use of such systems? Moreover, which factors are more salient in terms of increasing the probability of acceptance of systems designed to promote knowledge work?

To start this discussion, this chapter first looks to the literature on the design of technology to support expertise to gain insight on the deployment of knowledge portals. From there, an examination of the various barriers which impede the successful adoption and use of knowledge portals is given. Strategies companies can follow to implement knowledge portals are suggested. A three-entity conceptual framework of the major factors affecting the development, adoption, and use of enterprise portals for knowledge work is then presented. Specifically, these factors are: users, the information environment, and a portal's information design. From there, a research investigation is described, one which utilizes the framework as a conceptual lens to examine the various factors which impede or promote the use of the portal for knowledge work. Each of the three entities comprising the framework is expanded in more detail in subsequent chapters.

2.2 Expertise

According to Blackler (1993, p. 879), "the appropriate focus for an analysis of knowledge work is not knowledge or knowledge workers but expertise." Using this comment as a basis for investigation, the literature on designing systems to support expertise may offer suggestions on how to design portals for knowledge work. In that literature set, there is a recent call to support knowledge creation as well as knowledge access in the design of such technology.

The classical view of expertise derives from cognitive science which places emphasis on the individual and attempts to create formal models of cognitive systems as machines for information processing and logical reasoning (Feltovich, Ford and Hoffman, 1997). Cognitive scientists support a functionalist perspective to knowledge in that it is universal and objective, and the key task of the brain (or any other cognitive system) is to represent or model knowledge as accurately as possible (Von Krogh, 1998, p. 134). Under this paradigm, proponents of artificial intelligence delve into the development of computerized expert (i.e., knowledge-based) systems which can capture and replace human expertise in the form of rules and procedures. The goal of such systems is "to store large amounts of data (or *knowledge*) of a particular domain, organized in such a way as to enable them to solve problems and make inferences in that domain" (Shadbolt and O'Hara, 1997, p. 315). The goal is to produce expert systems that emulate human expertise.

Lately, there is a call to balance this orientation with an approach that extends expertise in various ways beyond that of the individual to include social and organizational factors as well (Feltovich et al., 1997). Adopting an interpretive perspective, cognition is not regarded as an act of representation but rather as an act of construction or creation. Here, knowledge is not universal. Though some is explicit, some is also tacit, highly personal, not easily expressed and thus not easy to share (Von Krogh, 1998, p. 134). As such, the development of systems to support expertise must give credence to "the surrounding social/physical/cultural context in which expertise is embedded... [and] try to model expertise in a way that is (more) sensitive to the interactions between the expert and the context that shapes and sustains his expertise" (Agnew, Ford and Hayes, 1997, p. 241). The goal is to provide computerized tools which help support human experts as they go about familiar tasks; this includes providing social networks to other experts as well as information to facilitate the exchange and creation of new ideas.

This move in the expert systems literature toward a more holistic understanding of expertise and the provision of knowledge management systems that reflect this new understanding gives support for the need for a similar orientation in the design of knowledge portals. Not only do such systems need to provide users with access to stored and codified knowledge, but they must also help facilitate the process by which knowledge is socially constructed by giving users ways to communicate shared understandings and coordinate activities with others in the enterprise. In this sense, the provision of content, communication, and coordination spaces within the design of knowledge portals, as introduced in Chapter 1, may be a viable method by which to enable the use of these tools for knowledge work.

2.3 Barriers to Knowledge Portal Adoption and Use

Despite the potential portals may have in facilitating organizational knowledge work, various barriers exist which can impede the successful adoption and utilization of these systems for knowledge creation, distribution, and use. For instance, Prusak (2000) cautions that technology is only an enabler and its introduction into an organization does not necessarily change people's behaviour. Thus, the "if we build it they will come" philosophy to system design is no guarantee for a technology's successful adoption and use. Cohen (1998, p. 27) agrees and succinctly points out in his commentary on corporations' experience in carrying out knowledge projects in organizations, that many firms discover information technology is not an answer, but rather a tool that can be effectively used only by people who understand its common purpose.

Though many recognize the healthy role that technology can play in facilitating knowledge work, O'Dell and Grayson (1998, p. 163) point out that the barriers to knowledge distribution and use are "really not technical." In their discussion on the success of implementing a knowledge repository of best practices in an organization, O'Dell and Grayson note that many companies are disappointed when they create technical solutions, such as internal electronic directories and databases, in that they are seldom utilized, despite these companies' best efforts to market the use of the new technology to organizational participants. In response, the authors recognize that culture and user behaviours are the key drivers and inhibitors of internal sharing, and recommend that organizations offer incentives and rewards to people to utilize and contribute to knowledge management systems.

Given this stance, O'Dell and Grayson identify several non-technical barriers to effective knowledge distribution and use in organizations. They state that the biggest barrier is ignorance of sources and recipients of knowledge: people do not know of others in the organization who have the knowledge they require or would be interested in the knowledge they have. The second biggest barrier is the absorptive capacity of recipients: many do not have the time, money, or human resources to monitor best practices nor implement them. The third barrier is the lack of relationship between source and recipients of knowledge which prevent people from listening to or helping out each other. Other factors identified by O'Dell and Grayson which deter the distribution, and use of knowledge in organizations include organizational structures that promote "silo" behaviour; organizational cultures that value personal technical expertise and knowledge creation over knowledge sharing; an over-reliance on transmitting explicit rather than tacit information; and, not rewarding people for taking the time to learn, share, and help each other outside of their local groups.

Von Krogh (1998, pp. 135-136) identifies four other barriers to the sharing and distribution of knowledge in organizations: 1) the need for a legitimate, common language across various groups; 2) stories of failed past attempts and ingrained routine habits; 3) formal procedures which stifle innovation; and 4) company paradigms. Von Krogh recognizes the latter category as being the most fundamental. Company paradigms include "a company's strategic intent, vision or mission statement, strategies, and core values" and may conflict and prevent individuals within the organization from sharing their knowledge if they hold values and beliefs not in accordance with those of the company.

Though Web-based portals have the potential to alleviate some of these barriers by providing organizational participants with access to information and social networks, it seems that other factors play an important role in determining the overall success of the system in facilitating knowledge work. Lessons from the field of Computer Supported Cooperative Work (CSCW) offer insights into this area. Coined in a call for participation for a workshop in 1984, CSCW grew out of a need to develop software to help groups increase their competence in working together and places particular emphasis on incorporating and emphasizing the social aspects of cooperative work settings (Bannon and Schmidt, 1991; Kuutti, 1996; Robinson, 1991).

According to the CSCW literature, numerous obstacles prevent or deter the successful introduction and use of organizational groupware systems (Zuboff, 1988; Perrin, 1991; Conklin, 1992; Harper, 1992; Orlikowski, 1992; Bowers, 1994; Grudin, 1994; Rogers, 1994). Some of the pertinent reasons why groupware typically fails are given by Grudin (1990; 1994): 1) they require some people to do additional work who often are not the ones who perceive a direct benefit from use; 2) they call for a critical mass of users to adopt the system; and 3) they lead to activity which may disrupt social processes, such as violations of social taboos, threats against existing political structures, or demotivations to crucial users. Similarly, Bowers (1994) comments on the difficulty in getting users to trust the system, share data, and be held accountable in their electronic communications to a larger community. He notes that the introduction of groupware can affect current work practice and require new ways of working.

Both Rogers (1994) and Perrin (1991) note the effect social and cultural factors can have that inhibit adoption and use of groupware. Conklin (1992) agrees and states the most challenging component in implementing any technological strategy is fostering an organizational culture that is committed to the use of the technology (p. 136). Likewise, Orlikowski (1992) identifies the impact organizational culture can have on facilitating the use of groupware by demonstrating how members of a competitive culture were reluctant to utilize a newly implemented groupware system, while those of a subgroup, who were not part of the competitive culture, were eager to share information and experiences with one another using the new technology. To aid the successful implementation of organizational groupware, she elaborates on the necessity of educating people on the benefits of new technology, changing organizational structural properties to induce norms or incentives for cooperating or sharing expertise, and anticipating how new technology will be received in the workplace by understanding current work practice. In a follow-up study, Orlikowski (1995) describes how organizations can benefit from the introduction of new groupware technology if they are accepting of the ideas of collaboration and sharing, and if they are willing to make changes to adapt the technology to user needs.

Newell, Scarbrough, Swan, and Hislop (1999), in their case study investigation of three separate intranet initiatives within a large global bank, offer empirical evidence on the difficulties in implementing Web-based information systems for knowledge work due to organizational structure and bureaucracy constraints. Though the authors recognize the potential of intranets in facilitating information sharing and collaboration across departments, the initiatives ironically reinforced existing structural and bureaucratic barriers to group collaboration and information sharing. Their study offers evidence that the introduction of Web-based technology alone does not facilitate organizational knowledge creation, distribution, and use, but rather the technology's success in facilitating knowledge work is dependent on the culture, structure and history of the firm.

2.4 Knowledge Portal Implementations

Davenport and Prusak (1998) offer insights into the role technology can play in facilitating knowledge work. They recognize that technologies such as portals and intranets are necessary ingredients in supporting knowledge creation, distribution and use but caution that a supportive organizational culture and structure are requirements as well, and perhaps more difficult to obtain:

> "Most firms make their first move with knowledge management in the domain of technology. They install Notes or an intranet Web, and then start searching for content to distribute with these tools. Throughout this book we've cautioned against a technology-centered knowledge management approach, but we've also argued that a technology infrastructure is a necessary ingredient for successful knowledge projects... [However] the knowledge behaviors you're seeking from users may be slow to emerge... Unfortunately, it's usually much harder to get organizational consensus for behavior change and new roles than it is for technology—and if you start with technology, the other necessary factors may never materialize" (p. 166).

To facilitate the use of technology to support knowledge work, Davenport (1997) suggests that the technology implementations possess the following characteristics if organizational participants are to utilize the technology for knowledge creation, distribution, and use: 1) a high degree of network interconnection; and 2) desktop access to internal information repositories such as databases and document repositories and external information sources such as the Internet. Davenport specifically recommends Web information systems, such as enterprise portals, as appropriate tools. He states that from a behavioural point of view, Web-based tools encourage user browsing and experimentation, and allows users to create their own links to information, thus supplanting the need to try to design a single technical interface that anticipates all the diverse information needs of a firm. Further, he values the Web's underlying document architecture in that it is "an information format that people feel comfortable with and understand" and hence are more inclined to adopt and use (p. 186).

It appears that leading portal vendors are following suit. A recent study by Raol et al. (2002) analysed more than 60 vendors and identified ten core functional characteristics and features of enterprise portals, ones which can be argued need to be included in the functionality of knowledge portals: 1) customization and personalization; 2) search; 3) collaboration and community; 4) security; 5) dynamic information behaviour; 6) extensibility and embedded work applications; 7) content management; 8) scalability and network functions; 9) administrative tools; and 10) ease of use.

Mack, Ravin and Byrd (2001) identify five key processes knowledge portals should support in their design. The first is the ability to facilitate the capture and extraction of knowledge. This involves knowledge work tasks such as submitting or linking documents to a document database, requesting information from colleagues, or modifying user profiles. The second is the need to support the analysis and organization of information. This entails organizing project artefacts in folders, and creating and organizing a project work space. The third is the ability to help organizational employees find information in the portal. This involves supporting knowledge work tasks such as searching for competitive information, browsing document archives, and searching for both people and documents on specific subject topics. The fourth is the need to create and synthesize information. This could entail creating budgets and project timelines, outlining issues, and drafting project proposals. The fifth is the ability to distribute and share knowledge. This involves sending e-mail requests for help; adding a project plan to a project workspace, organizing and scheduling teleconferences or organizing meetings and video conferences to review plans.

Firestone (2003) presents a conceptual framework for knowledge management having direct implications on the functionality supported by enterprise knowledge portal systems. The conceptual framework portrays a knowledge lifecycle composed of iterative cycles of knowledge production and knowledge integration. Knowledge production is initiated in response to problems introduced in the business environment and ends in the generation of organizational knowledge. Knowledge integration takes this organizational knowledge and integrates it within the firm, creating an enterprise-wide knowledge base. This knowledge base impacts the internal structure of the organization, and in combination with external events, generates new problems. This is turn initiates a new round of knowledge processing. Utilizing this conceptual framework for KM as a guide, Firestone calls for designers of enterprise portals to build functionality in these systems which support a series of *use cases* for firm-wide knowledge production and integration. A use case is defined as "a behaviourally related sequence of transactions performed by an actor in a dialogue with the system to provide some measurable value to the actor" (Jacobson, Ericsson and Jacobson, 1995, p. 343). To foster knowledge production, enterprise portals need to facilitate the use cases of: information acquisition; knowledge claim formulation; and knowledge claim validation. To leverage knowledge integration, enterprise portals need to facilitate the use cases of: searching and retrieving previously produced data, information, and knowledge; broadcasting; sharing; and teaching.

To accomplish such goals, Firestone (2003) identifies five distinct tasks and activities that enterprise knowledge portals must support to foster the firm-wide KM processes of knowledge production and knowledge integration. The first is that the portal must provide, produce, and manage information about the validity of the information it supplies. In this sense, knowledge is validated information and it is the role of the knowledge portal to highlight the validity of any piece of information through metadata. For example, the knowledge portal could record the full history of the discussions and interactions of organizational participants that transform certain bits of information into knowledge.

The second is that the knowledge portal needs to provide business information along with metadata to inform the user of the degree to which the validated information item is considered 'true, justified belief.' In this way, the business information provides a means of comparing the targeted knowledge claim to alternate knowledge claims. To support such activity, the knowledge portal could record the history of the competitive struggle around certain ideas (i.e., knowledge claims) put forward to solve problems across the enterprise.

The third is that the knowledge portal must distinguish knowledge from mere information. This is accomplished through the provision of metadata which signals the relative strength of ideas posted on the portal. By doing so, the portal can inform users which knowledge claims are stronger than others and thus which pieces of information should carry more weight in decision-making activities.

The fourth is that the knowledge portal needs to provide a facility for producing knowledge from information. This can be facilitated through the provision of services for knowledge claim formulation and validation, and from services which track and store the validation activities in knowledge claim objects. In this manner, enterprise-wide knowledge portals could support organizational workers in their production of validated knowledge claims from portal-based information.

The fifth is that the knowledge portal must orient users towards producing and integrating knowledge rather than only information. In this capacity, knowledge portals need to support the full cycle of knowledge generation and use through the provision of services such as individual and group learning, as well as knowledge validation.

To support these five tasks and activities, Firestone identifies certain functional requirements of an enterprise knowledge portal. These include a:

- "Knowledge worker-centric, knowledge workflow oriented, single point of access to enterprise data and content stores and to applications supporting knowledge production, knowledge integration, and knowledge management.
- Personalized desktop browser-based portal that with the assistance of an integrative, logically centralized, but physically distributed *artificial knowledge manager (AKM)*, composed of distributed *artificial knowledge servers (AKSS)* and *intelligent mobile agents*, is connected to all enterprise mission-critical application sources and data and content stores.
- Secure, seamless, single-logon capability for all network, application, and service resources" (Firestone, 2003, p. 258).

These suggestions are good ideas for the design of a portal's functionality geared to the promotion of knowledge creation, distribution, and use. At a more strategic (non-interface design) level, there are several steps or considerations corporations can follow to ensure smoother roll-outs and higher adoption rates of knowledge portal systems. For example, a detailed analysis of 11 case studies of successful knowledge portal initiatives at large corporations by Terra and Gordon (2003) yield several key lessons, including the need: to align the portal initiative with the organization's vision and mission; to be clear about the portal's value proposition and metrics to be used to measure its return on investment; to offer innovative rewards and recognition for avid and purposeful use of the portal; to treat portal initiatives as change management exercises requiring active support; to communicate and promote the benefits of the portal across the enterprise; to assign new roles and responsibilities to manage knowledge content in the portal; and to develop a due diligence process to select the most appropriate portal platform.

Kotorov and Hsu (2001) acknowledge two types of management

problems which have the potential to create risks and raise costs associated with enterprise portal projects: technical problems and content problems. To alleviate these concerns, the authors propose an integrated, strategic portal management model for organizations to follow. In their model, they propose that all members of the organization become involved in the process of portal information collection, processing, and presentation, and that upper management become responsible for establishing portal information standards. Kotorov and Hsu argue that engaging all members of the organization provides a cost-effective and efficient means to populate the portal with information content that is useful and beneficial to the enterprise. This reduces the risks associated with content. The authors also state that having management develop standards to populate and store portal content minimizes the risks associated with the more technical aspects of information storage, access, and retrieval.

King, Marks and McCoy (2002) conducted an extensive poll to more than 2,000 individuals holding job titles at a high level in KM or in general management which asked participants to identify and rate issues facing KM. In total, the results of their study identify eight key strategic management concerns, many of which can be applied to the rollout and success of knowledge portals. The first is providing strategic advantage. Knowledge portals must be linked to the organization's strategic vision and planning. The second is securing top management support. Knowledge portals need senior managers in the organization who understand KM and support the process of sharing knowledge throughout the organization. The third is motivating users to participate in sharing their knowledge, and creating incentives for them to do so. The fourth is sustainability. Knowledge portals need to be viewed and appreciated as an on-going and sustainable project requiring adequate and sufficient human, technical, and financial resources. The fifth is evaluating the chief technology officer. The person ultimately responsible for the successful adoption and use of the knowledge portal needs to be assessed in this regard. The sixth is fostering creativity and innovation. Knowledge portals must provide an organizational foundation for enhancing creativity and innovation across the enterprise. The seventh is the effect on organizational processes. Knowledge portals need to enhance knowledge sharing and thus will influence the way an organization operates. The eighth is organizational responsibility. Knowledge portals require an owner, either in top management or within the information systems department of the enterprise.

2.5 The Knowledge Portal Framework

The above description of expertise, barriers to knowledge portal adoption and use, and knowledge portal implementations provides an overview of the kinds of functionality and features knowledge portals should possess, as well as the strategic and organizational concerns that can affect the adoption and use of enterprise portal systems. In general, these can be summarized into a list of three core entities which impact the extent to which enterprise portals facilitate firm-wide knowledge creation, distribution, and use: 1) the knowledge portal's user population; 2) the information context or environment in which the knowledge portal is situated; and, 3) the knowledge portal's information design.

The identification of these three shaping entities is based loosely on a earlier conceptual model for intranet design proposed by the author coined the Behavioural/Ecological Framework (Choo, Detlor and Turnbull, 2000a; Detlor, 2000b), or BEF for short. BEF is a method for the design and evaluation of corporate portals and departmental Web sites that raises awareness for developers to understand the informational context in which such systems are utilized. BEF emphasizes the need to understand the contexts in which organizational participants access, search, collect, create, store, and use information. Overall, BEF suggests that an informational analysis of the use of Web-based information systems for knowledge work can occur from three perspectives: user; organizational; and interface.

From the user perspective, organizational participants exhibit information behaviours which refer to the practices and habits of individuals and groups as they go about obtaining and using information to resolve their work-related problem situations. To understand user information behaviours involves developing a clear understanding of whom the major sets of users are in terms of their information needs and preferences, their work-related problem situations, and how users seek and prefer information displayed and presented to them.

With respect to the organizational perspective, a corporation has an information environment comprising many interdependent social and cultural subsystems that influence the creation, flow, and use of information. This can include an organization's information system goals, information management plans, information culture, information politics, and physical setting.

From the interface perspective, information systems contain value-added processes which are functions or features with a Web information system's design that signal, amplify, and extend the value of information to the organization and its users. Ideally, Web information systems may be designed to support the information behaviours of users as they resolve their work-related problems, or improve the organization's information environment.

Adopting these three perspectives of orientation, BEF encompasses both top-down and bottom-up approaches to the investigation of Web-based information systems usage in organizations. It is top-down in the sense that it underscores an alignment of Web information system design with organizational (i.e., managerial) purpose and aspirations. It is bottom-up in the sense that it concentrates on the information behaviours and practices of individuals and groups whose Web use can turn or defy turning organizational aspirations into actuality.

Taking BEF into account, and the earlier theorizing described in Chapter 1, a Knowledge Portal Framework is proposed. The framework is grounded on several primary tenets. The first is that knowledge work activity is a set of knowledge creation, distribution, and use processes in which information plays a primary role. The second is that enterprise portals have the capacity to function as shared information work spaces which provide participants with access to information content, communication media, and coordination areas. The third is that designers of these systems need to look beyond technical constraints that inhibit adoption and use of enterprise portals for knowledge work, and also consider the social, cultural, and behavioural factors that play an active role in determining user system acceptance.

Taking these tenets into account, the Knowledge Portal Framework suggests that enterprise portal designers need to understand the organizational context and work practices of employees from an informational perspective if these systems are to be designed in a way to facilitate knowledge work. That is, since information plays an integral and fundamental role in organizational knowledge work activity, it is necessary that developers construct features and functions within enterprise portals that promote a supportive information context and address the information needs and uses of organizational participants. It is suggested that doing so can increase the likelihood of these systems in reaching their potential to support knowledge work.

Specifically, the Knowledge Portal Framework calls attention to three shaping entities of knowledge portals which impact organizational knowledge creation, distribution, and use: users, information environments, and the portal's information design. Figure 2-1 illustrates these three knowledge-shaping entities at work. Each of these are discussed extensively in more detail in the next three successive chapters of this monograph. The following is a short introduction to these concepts.

The *user* entity references the need for portal designers to identify and understand majors sets of users and their information needs and uses. This involves learning about the typical problem situations that sets of users confront in their daily work practice, and understanding the cognitive and affective factors impacting end user system adoption and use.

The *information environment* entity references the organization's physical setting, information culture, information staff, and information politics which can influence portal use. For example, an organization's physical setting can impose certain constraints and requirements on the availability of information and access to information on a portal. An organization's information culture can impact the degree to which information is valued, shared across organizational boundaries, and capitalized on in business processes. It determines the extent to which information overload exists. It also determines the strategy by which the organization goes about managing its information resources and building systems. It can do this in a controlled, centralized way or can encourage active participation and consensus among stakeholders. An organization's information staff can influence the quality of information displayed on an enterprise portal. Here, information staff includes both technical developers and content specialists—the people needed to distribute and interpret information to others in the company. The degree to which information staff can provide information that is accurate, timely, accessible, engaging, and applicable determines the extent others will use that information. An organization's information politics—the human struggle over the governance of organizational information—can impact the success of a knowledge portal system or knowledge portal strategy. For instance, the tensions between stakeholders can severely influence the functionality and information content available on a portal.

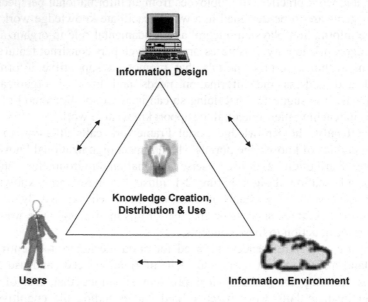

Figure 2-1: The knowledge portal framework

The *information design* entity references the need to create value-added processes, namely features and functions, within the knowledge portal which signal, amplify, and extend the value of information to the organization and its users. This involves delivering knowledge portal applications and services at three levels. The first is developing applications and services that directly support the information behaviours of organizational users as they go about resolving their typical work-related problem situations. The second is developing applications and services that promote a 'healthy' information environment. This can include the facilitation of information sharing, information filtering, a positive attitude towards information, or a negotiated consensus among portal stakeholders to the management and design of the knowledge portal. The third involves delivering applications and services that provide a shared information work space that allows users to move seamlessly between storing and retrieving content, engaging in communication, and coordinating work with others. It is suggested that doing so would promote the use of the enterprise portal for knowledge work.

These three entities of users, information environment, and information design, do not work in isolation. Rather, they influence and are influenced by one another. Figure 2-1 shows bi-directional relationships between these three shaping factors of knowledge work. These relationships suggest that these entities work in tandem to determine the extent to which the knowledge portal is utilized for knowledge creation, distribution, and use. For example, the features and functions offered within a portal's information design can impact the information behaviours of users and potentially alter the information environment. Likewise, the functional roles of users can influence the type of services offered with a knowledge portal design, while user perceptions, motivations, and personal information behaviours can help shape larger organizational attitudes towards the use and sharing of information. Similarly, the information environment of the firm can impact user adoption and use of a knowledge portal and directly influence the design and functionality offered within a portal's information design.

Overall, the Knowledge Portal Framework illustrates that many factors can shape and affect the development and use of knowledge portals in organizations. It suggests that Web designers and content developers need to concentrate on examination of the information environment, user characteristics, as well as the portal's information design when designing knowledge portals to foster knowledge creation, distribution, and use throughout the firm.

2.6 Research Investigation

The Knowledge Portal Framework outlined above presents a conceptual understanding of the dynamic complexities in designing and rolling out knowledge portals in organizations. Though insightful, the framework remains at a fairly high conceptual level. Empirical investigation is required to generate a more solid theoretical understanding of knowledge portal use. The following subsections delve into this foray where the author describes his own empirical investigation on the use of an enterprise portal by knowledge workers in a large organization. The first subsection elaborates on research questions which emanate from the workings of the Knowledge Portal Framework. The second subsection explicates the decision to employ the case study as a methodological approach. The third subsection describes the triangulation of qualitative and quantitative research methods. The last subsection looks to the research accuracy of the investigation. Portions of Chapters 3, 4, and 5 present findings from this research investigation.

2.6.1 Research Questions

Each of the shaping entities defined in the Knowledge Portal Framework suggests a certain subset of research questions for investigation.

In terms of users, what are the more salient characteristics of users which affect the degree to which knowledge portals are utilized? That is, what are the differences between organizational participants who utilize portals at higher and lower levels of intensity for knowledge work? From a user perspective, do users with greater familiarity with computers and the Internet utilize Web-based portals to a larger extent for knowledge work? Or are there other user characteristics at play that determine or influence portal use for knowledge creation, distribution, and use?

With respect to the information environment, what aspects or characteristics of an organization's information environment inhibit or promote the use and engagement of enterprise portals for knowledge creation, distribution, and use? From an organizational perspective, it is hypothesized that knowledge portals would need a healthy and supportive information environment to support knowledge work. Here, a healthy and supportive information environment is one that promotes consensus and negotiation among portal information stakeholders, facilitates access to both information content and experts, reduces information overload, and encourages the sharing and distribution of information among organizational participants. To do this, system developers may have to be aware of the situational contexts in which knowledge portals are utilized. This includes not only understanding the physical characteristics that impede information access and use via the portal (such as bandwidth), but also the political factors that deter the free flow of information between employees, and the culture of the organization that prevents information from being valued and shared in the company.

In terms of information design, how should a knowledge portal's interface be designed to facilitate and promote knowledge work? What features and functions offered by a knowledge portal's interface are utilized by organizational participants to conduct knowledge creation, distribution, and use? From an interface perspective, it is hypothesized that knowledge portals may need to provide a shared information work space that simultaneously functions as content, communication, and coordination spaces. Doing so may help employees gain access to the information they need, communicate with others to share insights and gain new perspectives, and support the coordination and collaboration of work activities between people dispersed throughout the firm.

2.6.2 Methodological Approach

To address these research questions, a case study investigation was conducted by the author with 20 knowledge workers at a large telecommunications company. These knowledge workers had a broad range of experience and comfort utilizing Internet-based information systems, and utilized the corporation's enterprise portal as part of their daily work The intent of the study was to investigate how organizational participants utilized an enterprise portal (and other Web-based information systems) for knowledge work in their day-to-day operations.

To set the boundaries of investigation, the Knowledge Portal Framework was utilized as a conceptual guide. It helped delineate the object under investigation—knowledge work activity via portal usage—by focusing analysis on users, the information environment, and the portal's information design. In essence, the framework provided a theoretical lens from which to glean insights and make discoveries.

In general, a case study involves the observation, description, or reconstruction of a phenomenon of interest (Williams, Rice and Rogers, 1988, p. 37). This phenomenon is bounded by time and activity (Creswell, 1994, p. 12) and can be "a program, an event, a person, a process, an institution, or a social group" (Merriam, 1988). Eisenhardt (1989, p. 534) defines a case study as "a research strategy which focuses on understanding the dynamics present within single settings." According to Yin (1994), case studies employ multiple methods of data collection, including direct observation and systematic interviewing, to gather information from people and organizations to examine a phenomenon in its natural setting. The boundaries of the phenomenon are not clearly evident at the outset of the research and no experimental control or manipulation is used. In this way, case studies are similar to naturalistic inquiries which utilize participant observation, unstructured interview, cultural informants, and personal documents to collect data in the field (Mellon, 1990, p. 39). Lincoln and Guba (1985) distinguish between naturalistic inquiry as a paradigm, and the case study as a means of reporting a phenomenon.

Benbasat, Goldstein and Mead (1987, p. 370) identify three reasons why case studies are viable strategies for information system research: 1) the researcher can study information systems in a natural setting, learn about the state of the art, and generate theories from practice; 2) the researcher can answer "how" and "why" questions to gain a better understanding of the nature and complexity of the processes taking place; and 3) the researcher can investigate an area in which few previous studies have been carried out. Further, Benbasat et al. discuss the applicability of case study research to certain types of problems: those in which research and theory are in their early formative stages (Roethlisberger, 1977); and "sticky, practice-based problems where the experiences of the actors are important and the context of action is critical" (Bonoma, 1983). The relative newness of knowledge portals in organizations and the Knowledge Portal Framework utilized in this study, which calls for the need to investigate the information environment, information design, and behaviours of portal users, would satisfy Benbasat et al.'s criteria for case study analysis.

Tesch (1990, p. 69) defines the traditional case study to remain "firmly within the domain of the qualitative researcher." In fact, the general methodological approach underlying this research investigation may be broadly be described as qualitative. Here, the word 'qualitative' is not synonymous for 'interpretive' as qualitative research may or not be interpretive, depending on the underlying philosophical assumptions of the researcher (Myers, 2003). For instance, case study research can be positivist (Yin, 1994), interpretive (Walsham, 1993), or critical. According to Creswell (1994, pp.1-2), a qualitative study is "an inquiry process of understanding a social or human problem, based on building a complex, holistic picture, formed with words, reporting detailed views of informants, and conducted in a natural setting." Moreover, it is "any type of research that produces findings not arrived at by statistical procedures or other means of quantification," applicable to research about persons' experiences, behaviours, as well as about organizational functioning (Strauss and Corbin, 1998, pp. 10-11).

Fidel (1993) identifies nine characteristics of qualitative research: it is non-controlling, holistic and case oriented, about processes, open and flexible, diverse in methods, humanistic, inductive, and scientific; and states that the qualitative approach "offers the best methods for *exploring* human behaviour... and is the best for investigating complex phenomena when very little is known about them" (p. 219). As such, an investigation of the use of an enterprise portal for knowledge work—a phenomenon dealing with an aspect of human behaviour which is relatively new—would be a suitable candidate for qualitative research.

Researchers that adhere to the qualitative paradigm emphasize theory generation over the proving of theory. In this sense, "theory isn't something you start with, it's something you build" (Palys, 1997). As such, qualitative studies are inductive rather than deductive in nature, with the goal of producing theory. This research study follows suit with the generation of a list of key elements or categories involved in the adoption and use of knowledge portals presented in Chapter 7.

Note that all research, whether quantitative or qualitative, is based on underlying assumptions about what constitutes valid research and which research methods are appropriate (Myers, 2003). Orlikowski and Baroudi (1991) outline three research paradigms: positivist, interpretive, and critical. Generally, positivists assume reality is objective and can be described by measurable properties independent of the researcher. Interpretivists assume reality is socially constructed through language, consciousness and shared meanings, where researchers attempt to understand the phenomenon under investigation through meanings that people assign to them. Critical researchers assume that reality is historically constituted and produced and reproduced by people; critical researchers recognize that the ability of people to change their social and economic circumstances are constrained by various form of social, political, and cultural domination.

For this research investigation, the underlying philosophical perspective may be considered largely interpretive. Research methods were used to investigate enterprise portal usage for knowledge work with the purpose of "producing an understanding of the context of the information system, and the process whereby the information system influences and is influenced by the context" (Walsham, 1993, pp. 4-5). Examples of in-depth interpretive case studies of information technology in organizations include Orlikowski (1991), Suchman (1987), Walsham (1993), and Zuboff (1988).

2.6.3 Research Methods

Being an interpretive research investigation, the study employed qualitative research methods as a basis for data collection and analysis. Data collection primarily involved the use of interviews and participant observations, which are typical techniques used by qualitative researchers to understand and explain social phenomena (Strauss and Corbin, 1998; Myers, 2003). To help organize and interpret the data, analysis predominantly involved the techniques of coding (Miles and Huberman, 1994) and constant comparison (Strauss and Corbin, 1994) of textual units contained in interview transcriptions and researcher field notes. The goal was to identify key categories and themes surrounding organizational portal use for knowledge work. As such, the study was interpretive in nature with emphasis on generating theory of enterprise portal use for knowledge work rather than proving one deductively.

However, the study did not strictly rely on qualitative research methods. Data were also collected utilizing quantitative means, namely questionnaires and the capture of portal use traffic in participant transaction logs. The tracking logs were useful in capturing and measuring significant episodes of portal activity and served as an interview prop to help participants recall and reflect on their portal use behaviour so that the author could gain an interpretive understanding of the context behind this usage. To analyze this quantitative data, descriptive statistics were generated from participants' portal tracking logs and questionnaires to help complement, support and strengthen the study's qualitative findings and triangulate research results. Utilizing multiple data gathering techniques, theoretical perspectives and analysis procedures can increase the depth of understanding an investigation can yield and facilitate a better, more substantial picture of reality of the object under scrutiny (Denzin, 1978; Miles and Huberman, 1994; Berg, 1998).

The importance of combining qualitative and quantitative methods as a means of triangulating research results is noted in the IS literature (Benbasat et al., 1987; Kaplan and Duchon, 1988; Lee, 1989; Orlikowski and Baroudi, 1991). For example, Orlikowski (1992; 1993; 1995; 1996) utilized interviews, observations, and document review in her case studies on the adoption and use of CASE tools and Lotus Notes applications in organizations. The author thought that the desire to investigate how participants utilized the enterprise portal for knowledge work would lend itself to inclusion of similar data collection methods.

Figure 2-2 outlines the study's data collection and analysis procedures. The research followed a three phase schedule to allow for an iterative approach between data collection and analysis.

In Phase A, individual, one-hour, semi-structured interviews were conducted to probe the information needs and uses of participants and their perceptions on the use of the enterprise portal for organizational knowledge work. The interview instrument comprised three sections: the first explored the participants' organizational information environment, typical problem situations, and information behaviours; the second delved into the participants' perception and use of the enterprise portal; and the third explored the extent to which the enterprise portal supported participants' personal areas of expertise.

After the interviews were transcribed, latent content analysis was used to gain an interpretive reading of the symbolism underlying the collected data (Berg, 1998). A textual analysis software package, was used to facilitate the discovery of common themes and patterns in the data. Specific techniques from grounded theory, such as open, axial, and selective coding (Strauss and Corbin, 1994; 1998), helped the researcher arrange, organize, and code data into categories, and explore relationships among these categories to develop "conceptually dense" descriptions or theories of enterprise portal usage for knowledge work in organizations.

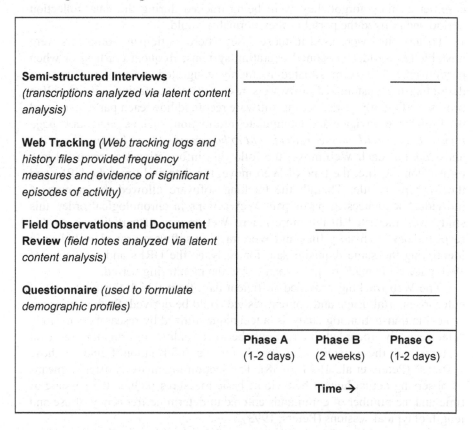

Semi-structured Interviews
(transcriptions analyzed via latent content analysis)

Web Tracking *(Web tracking logs and history files provided frequency measures and evidence of significant episodes of activity)*

Field Observations and Document Review *(field notes analyzed via latent content analysis)*

Questionnaire *(used to formulate demographic profiles)*

Phase A	Phase B	Phase C
(1-2 days)	(2 weeks)	(1-2 days)

Time →

Figure 2-2: Schedule of data collection and analysis

In Phase B, three data collection instruments were used: Web tracking, field observations, and document review.

Web tracking consisted of the use of history files and custom-developed software installed on participants' computers that ran transparently whenever a participant's Web browser was used during a two week monitoring period. The software, WebTracker, was developed by Ross Barclay under the direction of Dr. Chun Wei Choo at the Faculty of Information Studies, University of Toronto. For a detailed technical description of the WebTracker application, refer to Choo et al. (2000a, pp. 167-172). The decision to select a two-week time period was justified by the Choo, Detlor and Turnbull (1999; 2000b) study that tracked participants for the same length of time yielding ample data for analysis. The tracking was essentially invisible in that it worked behind the scenes. Participants' Web browser interface remained untouched and its operation was not affected. In this respect, the tracking was not expected to influence normal participant portal usage. Most participants commented they forgot they were being tracked during the data collection period and utilized the portal as they normally would.

History files were used in those cases where participant computers were unstable (e.g., older versioned operating systems; frequent crashes) or when participants' PCs were situated in highly congested network traffic areas degrading the customized software's response to interfacing with the Web browser efficiently. The tracking software recorded how each participant used the browser to navigate and manipulate information, such as *page back, page forward, open URL or file, reload, add to bookmarks, go to bookmarks, print*, and *stop*. For each Web move, the following information was recorded in a transaction log file: the type of Web move; the date and time; the URL; and the Web page title. Though the tracking software allowed the capture of individual sequences of participant Web actions in chronological order, this study was interested in the more macro Web moves of participants. In this respect, both the history files and Web tracking software proved sufficient in identifying the same requisite data for analysis: the URLs and frequency of Web page visits made by participants over the monitoring period.

The Web tracking provided sufficient data from which the frequency of enterprise portal usage and content visited could be derived. Such metrics are typical in transaction log analysis, a technique utilized by researchers to study "electronically recorded interactions between online information retrieval systems and the persons who search for the information found in those systems" (Peters et al., 1993, p. 38). Transaction log analysis offers a means of observing actual human behaviour; basic measures include the passage of time and the number of commands entered to determine frequency of use and length of typical sessions (Peters, 1993).

To analyze the Web activity captured in the history files, frequently visited Web sites were identified as being significant (i.e., representative of typical patterns of portal use). To analyze Web activity captured in the tracking logs, entries were grouped into major clusters indicating extended or frequent visits to particular sites. The logs were then re-examined to pinpoint significant episodes of information seeking. The selection of episodes was guided by evidence of the episode having consumed a relatively substantial amount of time and effort, or evidence that the episode was a recurrent activity. To avoid the misclassification of Web episodes which were short activities of use lengthened by long breaks in time, a 30 minute gap heuristic developed by Catledge and Pitkow (1995) was utilized to segment boundaries of Web activity by time. Gaps of over thirty minutes were assumed to indicate that participants were otherwise occupied, away from their desks, or utilizing their computers for other purposes. To identify such gaps, log files were reviewed manually to determine episode boundaries.

In terms of field observations and document review, the author immersed himself in close proximity to participants for the duration of the two week Web monitoring period. During this time, the author had access to a variety of corporate documents given to him by the participants, and was able to observe typical work practice and the informational context in which the participants were situated. Observations and insights were recorded using field notes. To analyze this data, the researcher's notes were transcribed, loaded into a textual analysis software package, and analyzed in the same manner as was done for the first set of interview data.

In Phase C, a second-round of interviews was conducted, as well as the administration of a questionnaire. The second-round of interviews was required to clarify the author's field observations and to add context to the significant portal usage episodes identified earlier from the tracking logs and history files. The author prompted the participants to discuss these events in sufficient detail so that the researcher could understand the motivating factors why the enterprise portal was used and the degree to which the participants were successful in using the portal to resolve their problems. The tracking logs and history files served as a useful interview prop to help participants recall and discuss their typical portal behaviour. As with the first set of interviews, the tapes from the second-round interviews were transcribed and analyzed in a textual analysis software package.

In analysing textual information, the text associated with each significant episode was classified according to theoretical attributes from the Knowledge Portal Framework (e.g., users, information environment, information design). The Web tracking information was referenced continually during this coding process. Though a large portion of the theoretical attributes were derived from the workings of the Knowledge Portal Framework, about half of the constructs were developed as the coding process progressed. The coding of significant episodes allowed for the development of a rich set of descriptive statistics on participant portal behaviour, namely the degree to which these systems were utilized, the types of problems that led participants to turn to portals for help, and the extent to which the portal supported organizational knowledge work. The generated coding attributes included:

- FEATURE / SITE (the feature utilized or site visited in each significant episode);
- PROBLEM TYPE (the general type of problem for which the portal was utilized in the significant episode);
- PROBLEM REASON (the more specific reason for utilizing the portal in the significant episode; separate lists of values were developed for each PROBLEM TYPE);
- KNOWLEDGE CREATION (a Boolean value set to TRUE if the participant in the episode—as identified and discussed during the

second interview session—utilized the portal to generate new knowledge, gain insights, or learn something new);
- KNOWLEDGE DISTRIBUTION (a Boolean value set to TRUE if the participant in the episode—as identified and discussed during the second interview session—used the portal to receive or disseminate knowledge);
- KNOWLEDGE USE (a Boolean value set to TRUE if the participant in the episode—as identified and discussed during the second interview session—uses knowledge obtained from or via use of the portal to perform an action (e.g., create a report, make a decision)).

Utilizing both the quantitative data captured in the Web traffic logs and history files, as well as the qualitative information recorded in the second interview transcripts helped provide a clearer understanding of participant enterprise portal usage than would have been possible had only one of those data sources been used. For instance, the Web traffic information helped to explain *what* actions participants performed within an enterprise portal, such as the specific applications used, the features utilized, and the Web sites visited. Meanwhile the participants' verbal descriptions of the significant episodes available in the second interview transcripts helped identify the *context* surrounding this activity, such as the types of problems which drew participants to use the enterprise portal, the portal-based information sources utilized to solve those problems, the way participants preferred this information packaged and displayed, and how participants used this information to help them resolve their problems.

A questionnaire was used in the later stages of the research to generate descriptive statistics on user profile characteristics of the participants being studied. Introducing the questionnaire in the later stages of the project was thought to be beneficial as questions at that time could be localized and asked in a language familiar to the workplace.

Overall, the data collection and analysis techniques described above allowed for the capture and understanding of a rich and comprehensive set of data. The goal was to obtain insights from this data on how enterprise portal systems were currently being used, the ways in which the portal supported knowledge work activity, and the differences in enterprise portal usage between participants.

It should be mentioned that data collection and analysis was an iterative process. As new insights and themes emerged from the analysis of the data, more data were collected to support or refute these findings. This occurred on three levels. The first involved the oscillation between data collection and analysis over time as different users joined and finished participation in the project at different stages. The second involved the author's own back and forth actions between data collection and analysis as the study was carried out. For example, after a participant interview or day spent in the field, the author would record and/or transcribe his notes, make reflections on emerging themes and use this knowledge to collect or probe ideas in the next set of observations and/or interviews. The third involved the back and forth activity between data collection and analysis when the author created progress and final reports to the case study organization and presented preliminary findings at conferences and speaking engagements; these forced the author to analyze data at various stages and to re-evaluate data categories and revisit emerging thoughts.

This iterative process is in accordance with Berg's (1998) spiral approach to qualitative research design. Rather than a linear progression of data collection to analysis to findings typically found in quantitative studies, Berg calls for an approach where the researcher does not follow a linear progression but rather spirals forward as the research is carried out. Thus, as a researcher,

> "you begin with an idea, gather theoretical information, reconsider and refine your idea, begin to examine possible designs, re-examine theoretical assumptions, and refine these theoretical assumptions and perhaps even your original or refined idea. Thus, with every two steps forward, you take a step or two backward before proceeding any further. What results is no longer a linear progression in a single, forward direction. Rather, you are spiralling forward, never actually leaving any stage behind completely." (Berg, 1998, pp. 17-18).

2.6.4 Research Accuracy

Steps were taken to ensure research accuracy. Ensuring the accuracy of the depiction of a phenomenon is a necessity in qualitative research (Kirk and Miller, 1986; Lofland and Lofland, 1995; Buchwald, 1999). Creswell (1994, p. 157) observes that though "qualitative researchers have no single stance or consensus on addressing traditional topics such as validity and reliability in qualitative studies", other reports from qualitative research investigators such as Lincoln and Guba (1985) and Erlandson et al. (1993) have established criteria such as trustworthiness and authenticity to counter the need to relate more traditional scientific criteria to procedures utilized in qualitative research.

For instance, Lincoln and Guba (1985) provide a list of procedures to establish trustworthiness in qualitative research. These include: keeping daily logs of activities, reflexive musings and methodological decisions to form a research audit trail; maintaining a prolonged engagement in the field to ensure research credibility; conducting persistent participant observation; and receiving feedback from key informants (also called member checks) of the study findings. Creswell (1994), allied with comments from Merriam (1988) and Miles and Huberman (1994), also identifies the need to triangulate or find convergence among sources of information, different investigators, or different methods of data collection as a way to ensure internal research validity (i.e., the accuracy of the study's findings and whether they match reality).

In terms of this research investigation, all these items were performed. Field notes of observed participant activities were created throughout the entire data collection period; insights and ideas on emerging themes and categories and methodological decisions were recorded directly into a textual analysis software package during data analysis. The author spent months in the field at the organizational site to learn and understand the firm's culture, build trust with the participants, and test for misinformation. Persistent observation occurred during this period to facilitate the identification of the characteristics and elements most relevant to the phenomenon of study. Progress and final reports were handed back to various organizational members to check the credibility of the study's findings. Interviews with key informants in the field were conducted in addition to participant interviews to help increase the credibility of the research findings. Triangulation of data collection methods, namely the use of both qualitative and quantitative techniques, was pivotal in helping achieve a more balanced perception of participant portal use activity and the context surrounding this usage.

There was accuracy in terms of the coding of the data. First, since the study occurred over many months, there was ample time for the author to reflect and oscillate between collection and coding of the data. Second, there were many iterations of constant comparison of the generated coding categories as several passes through the data occurred as the author identified, developed, combined, and rethought coding categories. Third, statement validity rules adapted from Miles and Huberman (1994) by Buchwald (1999) were used to assess the relative value of information provided by the participants: a statement was true if it was made by more than one informant and not contradicted by others; it was provided by a knowledgeable informant; it was a hard fact; or could be triangulated by independent sources.

In terms of validity, there was consistency with which the data were collected and analyzed as the author conducted all data collection and analysis procedures by himself. That is, one researcher interviewed all participants and took field notes, transcribed these into a textual analysis software package, and identified and coded emerging categories and themes.

There was also strong theoretical sensitivity on the part of the author to the phenomenon of study. Theoretical sensitivity refers to the personal qualities of a researcher which allow him or her to be aware of emergent categories found in the data. This awareness can be obtained through past experiences, such as reading, training, education, prior research, or through current dealings with present research. The ability to understand data and to identify its pertinent aspect aids a researcher in generating theory that is grounded, conceptually dense, and well-integrated. Strauss and Corbin (1998, p. 46) refer to theoretical sensitivity as "having insight into, and being able to give meaning to, the events and happenings in data. It means being able to see beneath the obvious to discover the new." The researcher brings over a decade of work experience in user systems design, several years of experience in the telecommunications field, and knowledge of the development and potential of organizational Web-based technology to the research process. Strauss and Corbin (p. 47) note that professional experience is a valuable potential source of sensitivity "as it can enable the researcher to move into an area more quickly because he or she does not have to spend time gaining familiarity with surroundings or events."

2.7 Conclusion

The predominant purpose of this chapter was to introduce the reader to the Knowledge Portal Framework. This framework, based upon a reflection of the literature on expertise, barriers to the adoption and use of knowledge management systems, and various knowledge portal implementation strategies, posited three key shaping entities that determine or influence the utilization of an enterprise portal for knowledge creation, distribution, and use: users, the information environment, and a portal's information design.

Taking an informational perspective, the Knowledge Portal Framework emphasizes the requirement to understand enterprise portal usage in terms of user problem situations and information behaviours within the context of an organization's information environment and with respect to the portal's information design. A research investigation was outlined where the author, utilizing the Knowledge Portal Framework as a conceptual guide, examined the various factors which could impede or promote the use of the portal for knowledge work. The investigation utilized both qualitative and quantitative research methods to hone its interpretation and analysis of the collected data.

The next three chapters of the book examine more closely each of the three shaping entities of the Knowledge Portal Framework. In each of these chapters, findings from the author's research investigation are described, along with additional opinions, anecdotes, and theory from related works.

Chapter 3 reports on the problem situations that confront sets of users in their daily organizational work practice that lead employees to utilize an enterprise portal. Salient characteristics of users which influence higher or lower levels of portal knowledge work behaviour are examined.

Chapter 4 delves into a detailed discussion on information environments and knowledge portals. Specifically, the chapter references how an organization's physical setting, information culture, information staff, and information politics can affect knowledge portal use.

Chapter 5 discusses knowledge portal interface design issues in more detail, specifically in terms of how to present and display information content to signal and highlight its potential value to users.

3. USERS AND KNOWLEDGE PORTALS

3.1 Introduction

This chapter devotes itself to the role users play in shaping the design and adoption of knowledge portals in organizations. It largely discusses the user entity of the Knowledge Portal Framework in detail. The goal is to explore, ponder, suggest, and find evidence of the more salient characteristics of users which affect the degree to which knowledge portals are utilized in the enterprise. Perhaps there are differences between organizational participants who utilize portals at higher and lower levels of intensity for knowledge work. If so, what characteristics distinguish or influence this behaviour? For example, do users with greater familiarity with computers and the Internet utilize Web-based portals to a larger extent for knowledge work? Or are there other user characteristics at play that determine or influence portal use for knowledge creation, distribution, and use? This is one of the goals of this chapter. To elaborate questions on this matter and probe at potential answers.

To start things off, results from the author's case study research investigation described in Chapter 2 are reported. Specifically, discussion involves: the functional role of users; their passion or interest in portals; the perception of users in terms of the capacity of portals to promote knowledge generation, sharing, and utilization; and the importance of motivating users to learn as a means of promoting the active use and exploration of portal systems.

From there, attention turns to the literature on communities of practice. Touted as an enabler and sufficient requisite for the sharing of tacit know-how between organizational workers, communities of practice are suggested to be an important facet in any knowledge portal design. The chapter strongly advocates that portals incorporate the necessary functionality and features to support the sharing of insights and best-practices between self-forming and prescribed groups of organizational participants. Doing so can enable enterprise-wide knowledge creation, distribution, and use through a portal-based communication space.

Emanating from this conservation is a discussion on the factors which promote end user satisfaction and technology acceptance with Web-based portal systems. The cognitive factors of users which lead to or promote information system adoption and use are explored. Specifically, the Technology Acceptance Model (TAM) is examined and applied to the acceptance and use of knowledge portals in organizations.

Last, the chapter calls for a participatory design approach to portal development—a technique that advocates the active engagement of end users in knowledge portal design. A case study of a government portal development project showcases the effectiveness of having users actively engaged in the design of a portal interface. Lessons learned are described. A theoretical model of a participatory design approach to portal development is also proposed.

3.2   Knowledge Portal Case Study Results

A total of 20 participants were recruited in the author's portal case study investigation described in Chapter 2. The first five participants were recruited through e-mail notifications and recommendations made by management; the remaining 15 were neighbours or associates of this initial group that were asked to participate by the researcher as data collection commenced. The recruitment of the additional 15 participants was random in nature, largely based on who was physically nearby.

3.2.1 Case Study Site

The case study site—a large telecommunications company—was chosen for several reasons. First, it was an early adopter of Web-based information systems and one of the first corporations in Canada to launch an internal enterprise portal to service the information needs and uses of employees. The purpose of the portal was to provide a mechanism for supporting not only information access and retrieval, but also to foster organizational communication and support the collaboration of work teams on projects. The corporate vision of the portal was that it eventually would become the internal on-line business environment that supported all employee work-related needs. Second, the company had a broad range of users familiar with information technology who utilized the corporate portal as part of their daily work. The need to have a diverse cross section of users was key in facilitating the comparison of participants who utilized the portal for varying amounts of knowledge work. Third, the portal was designed to support a variety of knowledge work related tasks, such as the gathering and sharing of information and the communication and collaboration of workers across departments and teams. Last, the organization was conducive to field research.

3.2.2 Participant Background and Web Usage

The 20 participants recruited formed a varied and diverse sample. In terms of functional roles, the participants comprised five distinct groups: administrative assistants, business analysts, middle managers, project managers, and system developers. Participants with primarily clerical and support duties were classified as administrative assistants. Participants who had no direct reports and primarily conducted analysis or wrote reports were deemed business analysts. Participants with direct reports who held senior positions were categorized as middle managers. Participants who had no direct reports and primarily managed projects or organized others into action were considered project managers. Participants whose primary responsibility was the development and maintenance of a computer application were classified as system developers.

On the whole, participants were found to be technically proficient and comfortable with using computers and Web-based technology in their day-to-day work. With respect to the general computer and Web background of participants as reported on the study's questionnaire, overall the participants collectively reported themselves at the intermediate/expert level in terms of their computer background and at the intermediate level in terms of their Web expertise.

Generally participants rated themselves lower in familiarity with the Web with respect to their familiarity with computers, however variations occurred across functional groups. For instance, project managers and business analysts rated themselves higher than the other two groups and reported a greater number of years of Web use; administrative assistants reported the least familiarity with using computers and the World Wide Web; system developers reported the highest familiarity with using computers and the World Wide Web (in fact, this was the only group where Web expertise outranked computer background); and middle managers reported higher familiarity with computers in relation to their comfort in utilizing Web technology, which may be indicative of senior staff's history and experience with using older computer technologies.

There was a high percentage of computer use reported across all functional groups. Overall, participants indicated that approximately two thirds of their time (67.8%) was spent using a computer. As may be expected, middle managers reported using a computer the least intensively in their jobs (52.6%), while system developers reported the highest (83.3%). This difference may be explained by the general nature of these two groups' functional roles. Middle managers, having a supervisory role, may generally have less time to engage in computer use and spend more time performing general managerial duties such as attending meetings and engaging in face-to-face dealings, which are non-computer intensive tasks. Meanwhile, system developers, whose primary purpose is the development of system software, may, as a result of their functional role, spend a very large percentage of their time in front of a computer.

In addition to this high frequency of computer use, participants reported a notable percentage of their time was spent utilizing the World Wide Web and corporate portal in their jobs. Interestingly, World Wide Web usage (11.2%) was roughly double that of the portal (6.9%). In terms of functional groups, the administrative assistants were the only group who reported a higher frequency of portal usage over the World Wide Web. Though no data were available on the system developers' frequency of World Wide Web usage (due to an earlier version of the questionnaire distributed to these members which did not pose that particular question), the other three groups indicated a greater frequency of use of the World Wide Web over that of the corporate portal.

In terms of analysis of the interview data and field notes, general patterns of portal and World Wide Web use were identifiable across functional groups. These patterns were derived from analysis of participant interview data and from observations recorded in the researcher's field notes.

Overall, administrative assistants tended to use Web information systems to keep abreast of general happenings both inside and outside the company, to use transaction-based Web applications to generate reports for their work, and to coordinate online calendar information. They primarily utilized Web-based work applications, such as PeopleSoft, and the Human Resources departmental Web site to find information pertaining to benefits, pension, and separation information; the corporate portal provided a direct link to the Human Resources site which participants used. This group accessed e-mail, document e-mail attachments, the phone, the Human Resources Web site and paper files as primary information sources. Their main problem situations were trying to synchronize calendar information, finding information in a timely fashion, generating transaction-based reports quickly, and utilizing unstable computer configurations. These users stated that both the enterprise portal and the World Wide Web did not play an active role in supporting their personal areas of expertise but found departmental Web sites and applications to be highly effective in this regard.

Business analysts tended to utilize the Web and enterprise portal the most frequently and intensely of all the functional groups. This group typically used search engines or frequented bookmarked sites pertaining to product, vendor, and competitor information, and utilized news from the corporate portal to stay abreast of the telecommunications industry. Their primary activity was that of searching and browsing a variety of information. Though some of this activity was to gather background information or keep abreast of external happenings, a large portion of their activity was monitoring and finding detailed, specific information primarily on company products, vendor services, and competitor information. In general, this group accessed e-mail, the phone, the World Wide Web, co-workers, a mainframe directory application, departmental Web sites and databases as primary information sources. Their main problem situations were tracking down people who have the information they need, finding out who in the company does what, and locating experts within the organization. Overall, this group of users was frustrated with having incomplete and inconsistent information, and slow report generation from Web-based transaction applications. Other areas of concern included trying to manage different versions of electronic documents and understanding client needs. Some business analysts indicated they used the Web to build up their own personal areas of expertise and indicated a desire for the corporate portal to improve in this area.

Middle managers utilized the Web and corporate portal to a varying extent. One manager searched the World Wide Web frequently on his own; the other had an assistant to process his information requests. This group utilized search engines and bookmarked sites for browsing/searching purposes. Overall, the middle managers tended to utilize Web information sources more often than the administrative assistants, but less frequently than the business analysts, project managers, and system developers. The middle managers also primarily used the Web for information browsing and searching purposes rather than for working or downloading software. In general, this group tended to access e-mail, teleconferencing phone calls, departmental Web sites, and World Wide Web information sources. The middle managers' problem situations typically involved gathering information for decision-making or knowledge-building purposes, and finding others in the organizations for cooperative action.

Project managers utilized the enterprise portal and the Web very frequently, but not as often as the business analysts. This group used the news from the corporate portal to keep up-to-date and also utilized search engines and bookmarked sites to find/locate sites pertaining to their areas of expertise. The primary activity of the project managers was more broad in nature than the business analysts. The project managers tended to use the Web to build up areas of expertise and keep up-to-date on happenings in the news rather than locating specific detailed bits of information. In general, this group accessed departmental Web sites, e-mail, the phone, the World Wide Web, shared documents, and other experts in the company as their primary information sources. Their main problem situations involved locating human contacts, managing frequent and large e-mail attachments, and keeping track of different versions of the same electronic document.

System developers utilized the enterprise portal and the Web in a unique way from other groups: it facilitated their day-to-day work which was primarily to design and construct a working Web-based application. Therefore, members of this group were heavy users of the Web, but primarily used this medium to test or check out the application being built. In fact, two of the system developers frequented the departmental Web sites and the corporate portal on a regular basis to 'steal' code to use in their own applications, rather than to search or browse for any particular piece of information. To a lesser extent, these users utilized the portal to track down the phone numbers of specific individuals or enter timesheet information. One frequented departmental Web site was the Information Technology department's home page used to obtain methodology guidelines for system development projects. The more technical users in this group used the World Wide Web to get answers to specific programming problems. This was done by visiting specific, previously-known computer-related sites. Members of this group also utilized the World Wide Web to maintain contact with other professionals in their area of expertise.

3.2.3 The Portal and Knowledge Work

Recall that significant episodes of activity were identified from the collected Web tracking logs and history files. Each episode was representative of several instances of Web behaviour; for instance, if a participant utilized the portal to distribute a document to colleagues twenty times, then those twenty occurrences were represented in one single 'significant' episode of activity. Each significant episode was an event that either took a substantial amount of time in relation to other activities in the logs or was a recurring activity. In total, 39 unique types of significant episodes of enterprise portal usage were identified from the Web tracking logs and history files of the 20 participants who took part in the study. This primarily involved participants utilizing the enterprise portal for browsing news information pertaining to the telecommunications industry, learning functions or seeing what features were available on portal Web pages, and searching for people or a specific Web site.

In terms of the extent to which the enterprise portal was utilized for knowledge work at the case study site, there were two predominant types of activity. The first predominant portal-based activity involved knowledge creation only. This occurred when participants used the portal to browse news to learn of events outside the company and keep abreast of happenings in the telecommunications industry, and to learn of functions available within the portal or see what new features were available. The second predominant portal-based activity involved no evidence of knowledge creation, distribution, or use. This occurred when participants used the portal to retrieve directory-based information on other workers in the organization or Web address information on the location of a particular intranet site, or to perform a transaction such as posting a vacation e-mail message or maintaining employee records.

With respect to the distribution of knowledge work patterns for the 39 portal-related significant episodes of activity across functional groups, all groups exhibited knowledge creation in a majority of their portal-related significant episodes. Both business analysts and project managers showed no evidence of portal usage for knowledge distribution or use. Meanwhile, system developers were the only group that utilized the portal for all three components of the knowledge work: knowledge creation, distribution, and use.

3.2.4 Key Knowledge Workers

The above findings indicate a rather low frequency of use for the portal for knowledge work by study participants—primarily for knowledge creation only. This low frequency was most likely due to the relative newness of the enterprise portal application at the time data were collected for the study. Since that time, several iterations of the portal have been introduced throughout the company (each with successively larger functionality and features) and users have become more comfortable in utilizing the system.

To further explore these findings, the author analysed and compared the extent to which these same 20 participants utilized other Web-based information systems (WIS) for knowledge work. These other systems included Web-based groupware systems, the World Wide Web, and departmental Web sites. Participants had used these other systems for a much longer time than the enterprise portal. The ability to compare and contrast knowledge work usage across these varying WIS types was largely due to the research methods employed in the study which facilitated the capture and analysis of significant episodes of activity across various types of WIS including that of the corporate portal. Incorporating these other Web information systems into the data collection set allowed for identification of 164 unique significant episodes of activity across the 20 participant sample for analysis. Utilizing this much larger data sample, it was found that user characteristics played a major role in determining the extent, intensity, and frequency of use of Web-information system technology for knowledge creation, distribution, and use.

This finding was based on a closer observation of the significant episodes of activity of key knowledge workers from the participant sample. Participants were identified who had seven or more significant episodes in their tracking logs of which at least a third involved a dual combination of knowledge creation, distribution, or use activity. The number of significant episodes per participant ranged between two and 14 episodes, with eight being the average number of significant episodes per participant. The idea to select those participants who had relatively higher frequencies of dual combinations of knowledge creation, distribution, and use activity was thought to be a viable means of focusing in on participants who utilized Web information systems for knowledge work more intensely. By utilizing these selection criteria, participants who were frequent users of WIS technology but did not utilize these systems heavily for knowledge work purposes, or participants who were non-frequent WIS technology users but did utilize these systems for knowledge work were not identified as key WIS knowledge workers.

Based on these criteria, eight of the 20 participants were identified as being key users of Web information systems for knowledge work. These users came from a broad cross section of functional roles: one administrative assistant; two business analysts; one middle manager; three project managers; and one system developer. The interview and field note data contained in the textual analysis software package were analyzed further to determine the factors or characteristics that distinguished these users from the other twelve participants who utilized Web information systems for knowledge work to a lesser degree.

Overall it was found that the eight key WIS knowledge workers differed from the other participants in the following three areas: 1) their interest in Web information systems technology; 2) their perception of Web information systems as viable tools for knowledge work; and 3) their general motivation to learn and keep up-to-date in personal areas of expertise.

These areas were identified from several iterations of the use open coding and axial coding techniques from grounded theory. As the data were simultaneously being collected and coded, literally hundreds of categories were created in the textual analysis software package. At several different stages, these were grouped together, re-categorized, and moved around as the author made sense of the findings and asking questions of the data. The three categories listed above were the ones that were predominant from this analysis process and best captured the distinguishing characteristics of those participants who utilized Web information systems frequently for knowledge creation, distribution, and use purposes.

In terms of *interest in Web information systems technology*, key WIS knowledge workers often stated that their primary information source was the World Wide Web while non-key WIS knowledge workers more often identified Web information systems as a secondary source of information, placing people or more traditional resources as their primary information sources. Consider the following two excerpts from the interview data. The first is from a non-key WIS knowledge worker who preferred traditional face-to-face communication over the use of the portal and departmental intranet sites to satisfy her information needs. The other is from a key WIS knowledge worker who regarded the Web and portal as primary information sources and who used these systems frequently. The juxtaposition of these statements highlights the interest key WIS knowledge workers have in utilizing Web information systems in their day-to-day activity:

*** NON-KEY WIS KNOWLEDGE WORKER ***

Participant: "The only time I'll go there [to the enterprise portal] is if I need a reply like ASAP and there's voice-mails and the other person's not there to give an answer."

Interviewer: "Why do you do that? Why do you prefer face-to-face?"

Participant: "Because the answer is given to you right away. That way you don't have to go searching."

*** KEY WIS KNOWLEDGE WORKER ***

Interviewer: "What do you use the portal for?"

Participant: "The biggest purpose for me is that I find it a major resource of information on anything on the company pretty well. And it's easy just for me to go and look. I don't have to run around and ask people and tell them what I'm up to or why I'm looking. Or call 4 or 5 people to get the same information when I could just sit there and read it myself. I prefer to work that way. There's probably others that prefer to pick up the phone and do it but I like to sit there and pick and choose what I want to read and when I want to read it. And I'm sure there's stuff in there I still haven't gone into even though I've been looking through it for a year or so."

A couple of key WIS knowledge workers displayed their interest in WIS technology through their involvement in the design of local WIS applications. For example, one key WIS knowledge worker, upon his own initiative, decided to create a Web-based project library for others in his team to use. Another WIS knowledge worker, who created a departmental intranet site in her previous job, still maintained an arms-length involvement in the site's design. Both participants discussed their plans and desires to enhance and evolve the design of their WIS applications in the near future. Also, key WIS knowledge workers were more likely to promote the benefits of WIS technology to others in the organization. For example, two key knowledge workers wrote white papers and reports on their views of how to utilize the corporate portal and other Web-based systems more effectively and passed these documents on to colleagues and managers.

In terms of a *positive attitude towards WIS technology*, key WIS knowledge workers often indicated that they saw tools such as the World Wide Web and departmental Web sites as facilitating the learning of events outside the company, the building of relationships with external experts, the creation of new ideas and ways of doing things, and the sharing of documents and insights throughout the company. For instance, most key knowledge workers saw the World Wide Web as pivotal in helping them gain different perspectives on topics of interest and a more international perspective on business-related issues:

> Participant: "[The Web] gives me access to a forum where I can go in and get not only articles but have conversations with people if you have a specific problem, which I have done on occasion. And I get an international perspective from people as well."

Further, key WIS knowledge workers explored departmental Web sites or the company's external Web site to learn what other departments and subsidiaries were doing and to gain a better understanding of the products and services that the company offers. Key WIS knowledge workers also identified the Web as a convenient and accessible method of learning and gathering information about competitors, products, and external happenings, and as a tool that helps them do their jobs.

> Participant: "I use the Web, [for] specifically going to vendors, like say I'll go to the Oracle site, or I'll go to Novell, or I'll go to the Netscape site. That's more for a project I'm involved with right now... So I'm doing a lot [of Web searches]."
>
> Interviewer: "So why do you go to the Web to look for that information?"
>
> Participant: "As opposed to calling them up [on the phone] and asking them to send that [information] in the mail?... it's faster; pretty much everybody has all their product information on their Web site now. I cut down on mailing time, talking time..."

In terms of internal Web-based systems, such as the corporate portal and departmental Web sites, key WIS knowledge workers were more likely to identify or recognize the potential of this technology in helping them connect with other team members (especially those who were distributed across the organization) and to share documents and best practices with their colleagues.

> Interviewer: "With respect to the Web-based project management tool you described to coordinate your project work with other team members... why do you use that?"
>
> Participant: "Mainly because it's an easy environment for us to capture all of our minutes, attachments, and our updates rather than having to send additional emails to people. We just route them to that site and they can view everything... one copy of everything... so it's good for editing... I think a lot of groups are trying to find new ways of sharing information without sending excess [e-mails] around... There are too many e-mails; too many attachments; too many versions [of project documents]."

In fact, because of their perception of what Web information systems can deliver, several key WIS knowledge workers were opinionated on the current functional design of the corporate portal and indicated a desire to enhance its functionality.

In terms of *motivation to learn*, key WIS knowledge workers showed evidence of a greater personal desire for continual learning, both inside and outside the company, over that of non-key users. For instance, several key WIS knowledge workers indicated that to keep up-to-date in their personal areas of expertise they took courses, read books and articles. In fact, one key WIS knowledge worker stated that she taught a course in her personal area of expertise at a local university to pass on her knowledge to others and to learn what other people who had similar interests in her area were doing in their organizations. Overall, key WIS knowledge workers identified the following as personal areas of expertise: technical writing; communications; data architecture; executive support; project management; computers; marketing; and information management. The following excerpts typify the general positive attitude of key WIS knowledge workers when asked how they kept abreast in these topics:

> Participant: "I take courses... I also belong to professional associations specific to Communications... The professional associations that I'm involved with have information seminar sessions, social sessions, that sort of thing, which gives you an opportunity to meet new people and sort of broaden your horizons a bit."

> ***

> Participant: "I read excessively. I have a lot of access to the literature."

> Interviewer: "What type of literature do you read?"

> Participant: "Mostly trade journals. Also Communications publication materials. That type of thing."

> ***

> Participant: "And also... coaching and development, training as well... we have had access to a lot of courses over the past couple of years. I've taken a ton of them."

Key WIS knowledge workers were also more inclined than non-key WIS knowledge workers to want to collaborate or discuss issues with other members of the organization in relation to their areas of expertise. Some of this activity was formal; most was ad hoc. Further, key WIS knowledge workers were more likely to extol the benefits of WIS technology in helping them maintain currency in their self-defined areas of expertise. This was done predominantly by visiting external Web sites, such as those set up by associations, relating to specific topics of interest. Participants utilized these sites for information gathering, obtaining news feeds, accessing on-line newsletters, downloading white papers, and communicating or connecting with other experts in their field through discussion forums.

Most of the activity by key WIS knowledge workers centred on frequenting external Web sites relating to the participants' areas of expertise. These users generally found it difficult to track down local experts in their areas of interest within their own organization. However, there was some indication that WIS technology had the potential to help organizational actors connect with other local experts.

Interviewer: "I noticed that your habit is to go to the World Wide Web to do this [search for LDAP information]. Do you see a need or a reason to do that within the company? Perhaps there's another LDAP person within the company."

Participant: "Exactly. That would be great."

Interviewer: "But you don't do that."

Participant: "I don't know how... I always go external, yes... I don't do it internally."

Interviewer: "I'm sure that there is somebody who you could call if you knew their phone number."

Participant: "Exactly... Well, [this Web-based groupware application] is a good example. I created a project called 'Implementing an LDAP directory'. I got a call out of that. Some guy saw that project name and said 'hey, I've been reading about that and I have an application that we should be talking [about]'. So there's an excellent thing [example]... it was just a fluke."

Of related interest are the reasons that non-key WIS knowledge workers gave for not utilizing Web information systems to a large degree. The two most common reasons for infrequent usage which pertained to all WIS types were: 1) the general lack of need to use these systems for daily work; and 2) the lack of time to explore the technology. In addition to these, non-key WIS knowledge workers also identified other reasons that pertained specifically to the corporate portal: the information desired was not available on the system; they had alternate (and generally more convenient) means of getting the same information; they needed training on the system; and they were not aware of the functionality offered on the portal.

3.3   Knowledge Portals and Communities of Practice

One of the key roles of knowledge portals posited in this book is that they are to help organizational participants communicate and collaborate with one another. It is believed that earlier technologies that concentrated solely on the retention, organization, and retrieval of explicit knowledge were limited in their extent to support knowledge management, and that providing environments for people to develop, nurture, and sustain knowledge through social interaction among members is needed (Thomas, Kellogg and Erickson, 2001; Hildreth and Kimble, 2002).

Users who share a common disciplinary background, similar work activities and tools, stories, contexts, and values are said to participate in a *community of practice*. As of late, there has been much research and interest in understanding how organizations can leverage communities of practice in their own firms to help foster knowledge creation, distribution, and use. With the advent of Web-based technologies, many groups of users are turning to Web-based portals to help facilitate their discussions and information exchange.

For example, Millen, Fontaine and Muller (2002, pp. 69-70) observe how user communities are "moving beyond face-to-face exchanges, to interact in online environments, shared Web spaces, email lists, discussion forums, and synchronous chats." In their qualitative investigation of seven diverse firms, these authors conducted over 60 semi-structured interviews with community members, leaders, and knowledge management personnel in organizations to gain insight on ways to promote healthy collaboration in communities of practice. From their analysis, Millen et al. discovered three distinct categories of community benefits at the individual, community, and organizational levels.

Individual benefits included: improved reputation; a better understanding of what others were doing in the organization; increased levels of trust; more interest in learning about new tools and methods; greater interest in on-going professional development; and increased access to experts and valuable information resources. These individual benefits together allow community members "to develop professionally, remain at the forefront of their own discipline, and gain confidence in their own expertise" (p. 71).

Community benefits involved: greater idea creation; increased quality of knowledge, advice, and problem solving; and the creation of a common context. Taken together, these benefits provide members with a mechanism for creativity and the free expression of ideas—enabling community members to think outside the box and share ideas.

Organizational benefits involved tangible business outcomes, namely in: successfully executed projects; increased new business; product innovation; and time savings in terms of improved operational efficiencies, such as not re-inventing the wheel on projects or solving problems that others in the community have already worked on or previously dealt with.

However, all these benefits do not come without their costs. According to Millen et al., there are four major categories of cost drivers for communities of practice in organizations: 1) the cost of the participation time for community members; 2) meeting and conference expenses; 3) technology costs; and 4) content publishing and promotional expenses. These results indicate that organizations interested in supporting healthy collaborations in communities of practice need to invest not only delivering robust technical solutions, such as knowledge portals, but also to cover expenses attributed to softer concerns. Interestingly, technology costs were viewed by 36 knowledge management professionals in Millen et al.'s study to run only 10% of the total expenses required to support such communities. People and meeting costs were considered to bear 52% and 32% of the community budget respectively.

3.3.1 What is a Community of Practice?

The communities of practice concept was coined by researchers studying organizational learning in the early 1990s. Two key works heavily referenced in this area are *Situated Learning: Legitimate Peripheral Learning* (Lave and Wenger, 1995) and *Communities of Practice: Learning, Meaning and Identity* (Wenger, 1998). The latter defines communities of practice as "groups of people who share a concern, a set of problems, or a passion about a topic, and who deepen their understanding and knowledge of this area by interacting on an on-going basis" (p. 4). The former describes how learning occurs in an active social context of a community of practice because this is how people develop real knowledge, insights, and behaviour. In this sense, a community of practice is an intrinsic condition for the existence and sustainability of a group's knowledge, not least because it provides contextual support for sense making and shared interpretations.

Certain characteristics differentiate communities of practice from other forms of community; the most important from a knowledge management perspective is that knowledge is self-generating and perpetuating, and the transfer of knowledge is an intrinsic aspect of the community's functioning (Adams, 2000; Blair, 2002). A review by Wenger and Snyder (2000) suggests that a community of practice draws its strength from the fact that it is informal, driven by the desire to share expertise, determines its own agenda and shape, and is sustained by the interest and passion of its members. Recent work by Davenport (2001a; 2001b) overviews three online community of practices and gives evidence of the ability of online technical infrastructures to support such groups' knowledge creation, sharing and use activities.

An often cited example of a community of practice exemplifying sound knowledge sharing activity, learning, and organizational memory is the Xerox service technicians story. Here the technicians at Xerox built a shared database of tips and best practices that were learned from trial and error over repeated repair situations; this knowledge was not available in company manuals or courses. The database and online front-end allowed technicians in the field to access up-to-the-minute tips and techniques to help find solutions to problems faced by technicians while on service calls. As a result of this technical infrastructure and the willingness of technicians as a group to share insights and best practices with one another, the length of service calls was shortened and customer satisfaction soared. In line with Millen et al.'s observation, Xerox's investment in technical infrastructure was relatively small compared to the profits and benefits resulting from implementation of the system which leveraged service technician's knowledge (Botkin, 1999).

3.3.2 How Can Knowledge Portals Help?

One of the goals of a knowledge portal is to provide a similar environment or context such as that exemplified in the Xerox story where organizational users share insights and learn from one another. Thomas et al. (2001) agree and believe that one of the most important aspects of a knowledge management system is to support knowledge communities by giving organizational workers a place where "people discover, use, and manipulate knowledge, and can encounter and interact with others who are doing likewise" (p. 881). In this way, knowledge portals become online environments for supporting knowledge management in its social context (Erickson and Kellogg, 2000; Erickson and Kellogg, 2002).

According to Thomas et al., a fundamental characteristic of a knowledge community is that it includes conversations, stories, and unguarded discussions among workers who know one another, share professional interests, and understand the contexts within which their remarks and comments are made. To facilitate this, Thomas et al. encourage the inclusion of techniques and features in the design of knowledge management systems, such as storytelling and scenarios, which enhance creativity and clarity (e.g., the use of metaphor) as well as support expressive communication. These authors put forth the claim that by incorporating such techniques into knowledge support systems, the result is organizational opportunities which build social capital, including trust and cooperation among colleagues. It follows that knowledge portals could benefit from the inclusion of these techniques and features too.

An example of an electronic environment to support virtual communities of practice is CommunitySpace (Muller et al., 1999). This tool provides community members with a structured organization for the community's collective knowledge, including a means of maintaining multiple perspectives of that knowledge. Common features to support a virtual community include electronic mail and discussion databases. Of interest, is Muller et al.'s identification of key factors which contribute to the successful launch and evolution of virtual communities, which are highly relevant to our discussion on knowledge portal implementation: 1) developing systematic processes that spur participation in communities; 2) creating an identifiable recognition system for participation, and tying organizational incentives to this recognition; 3) supporting new organizational roles such as moderators, cybrarians, and knowledge weavers; 4) giving community members the time and space to participate; and 5) providing flexible ways for communities to describe and find their knowledge resources, for example, through the implementation of multiple, community-defined taxonomy schemas in lieu of one corporate-wide classification structure.

Incorporating such suggestions in the launch and design of knowledge portals can help overcome constraints which impede knowledge sharing in virtual team settings. A set of four such constraints is proposed by Alavi and Tiwana (2002): restrictions on transactive memory; insufficient mutual understanding among team members; failure in sharing and retaining contextual knowledge; and inflexibility of organizational ties. Alavi and Tiwana propose several approaches to counteract these constraints in the design of knowledge management systems, which for our purposes can equally apply to knowledge portals.

To alleviate shortcomings in transactive memory, knowledge portals could include searchable repositories of codified knowledge and computerized 'yellow-pages' of employee skills and experience. To counter insufficient mutual understanding among team members, knowledge portals could offer: rich, multiple communication channels and a real-time collaboration area; support the rapid development and joint modifications of models and prototypes developed by the team; and encourage opportunities for frequent, rich communication to share uniquely held information. To reduce failure in sharing and retaining contextual knowledge, knowledge portals could: create notification profiles of users to disseminate local contextual knowledge to team members; maintain persistent individual identities and project involvements; incorporate trust-building mechanisms; offer peer-to-peer collaboration tools; and retain a temporally stable history of individual contributions. Last, to limit the constraint of inflexible organizational ties, knowledge portals could include feedback recording and access mechanisms in their design.

Other means of supporting communities of practice in knowledge portals are identified by Smith and Farquhar (2000). Their suggestions are based on their lengthy experience with the Schlumberger knowledge hub portal designed to foster a variety of communities of practice engaged in field activities across the firm, with foci such a geophysics, reservoir characterization, well engineering, and well simulation. Often community members ask each other questions, exchange ideas, and debate solutions to problems. According to the two authors, the Schlumbeger hub is one of the largest 'intranets' in the world and is essential to the company's business. A variety of applications comprise the hub: e-mail; bulletin boards; documents, such as training materials, product information, technical manuals, and policies; work flow; job-specific software applications and database systems; project archives where communities have access to current and past project information; an expertise directory; a best practices (lessons learned) knowledge store; news of interest; a help desk; and frequently-asked questions.

In utilizing the Schlumberger hub, community members adhere to a basic best practice knowledge management cycle. In the course of normal everyday activity, members apply current best practices. As new problem situations arise, either through dealings with customers or interaction with fellow community members, new practices are discovered and existing practices are discussed. New practices or enhancements to existing ones are submitted as best practice proposals. The community collectively validates the proposals whereby deemed valid ones are integrated back into the overall set of best practices stored in the knowledge hub for later re-use. Such a cycle is illustrative of the knowledge conversion cycle in organizations between tacit and explicit forms as defined by Nonaka and Takeuchi (1995).

In Nonaka and Takeuchi's model, there are four steps in this continuous cycle. The first is socialization (tacit to tacit) where the shared formation and communication of tacit knowledge between community members occurs. For instance, such an exchange can occur in team meetings and discussions. The second is externalization (tacit to explicit) where through conceptualization, elicitation, and articulation—typically in collaboration with others—some portion of a community member's tacit knowledge is captured in explicit form. For example, such activity occurs in dialogue among community members in response to questions posed to the team, or through the elicitation of stories. The third is combination (explicit to explicit) where explicit knowledge is shared among community members via documents, electronic mail, or through education and training. The fourth is internalization (explicit to tacit) where individuals comprehend explicit information and create their own insights and understanding. In this sense, the explicit information becomes actionable and thus represents a new form of tacit knowledge. Within this cyclical process, knowledge objects (codified explicit knowledge) form the knowledge base that can be referenced, community member experience (internal tacit knowledge) is exchanged, and productive inquiry (finding an answer to a question) is the catalyst which sets the cycle in motion (Saint-Onge and Wallace, 2003). Here, process and practice are at the heart of community building, with technology playing a supportive rather than dictative role in community member knowledge work behaviour (Wallace and Saint-Onge, 2003).

Marwick (2001) identifies several example technologies that can support or enhance the transformation of knowledge in each of the four steps of Nonaka and Takeuchi's model. It is suggested that these technologies are equally applicable for inclusion in a knowledge portal designed to support communities of practice at work. For tacit to tacit knowledge exchange, the portal can support electronic meetings and synchronous collaborations, such as chat. This is typically done through technologies such as groupware and expertise location systems. For tacit to explicit knowledge exchange, the portal can support the answering of questions and annotations. For explicit to explicit knowledge exchange, the portal can support text search and document categorization. Last, for explicit to tacit knowledge exchange, the portal can support visualization and browsable video and audio presentations. These foster the understanding and utilization of presented information.

3.4   Knowledge Portal Adoption and Use

It has been suggested that social influences, such as those found within a community of practice, as well as facilitating conditions, like user training and support resources, exert an effect not just on *whether* organizational employees adopt an information technological solution (Taylor and Todd, 1995), but also on *how* and *how much* employees utilize the technology in their work (Gallivan, 2000). This section explores this issue further with respect to describing the user-based factors that shape and influence the adoption and use of knowledge portals by organizational knowledge workers. What are the influencing factors from a user perspective which encourage or promote the utilization of firm-wide knowledge portals?

To help find an answer to this question, attention turns to the popular Technology Acceptance Model (TAM) originally developed by Davis (1989; 1993), and then later slightly revised (Venkatesh and Davis, 1996). TAM has received substantial theoretical and empirical support from literally hundreds of studies conducted over the last decade which verify the model's ability to explain and predict user acceptance of information technology at work. As such, TAM has become a generally-accepted and well-established cognitive model for predicting user IT acceptance found in the Information Systems literature. The argument is presented that it can also provide guidance to help understand the reasons why a knowledge portal may or may not be adopted and used by organizational employees for knowledge work.

According to TAM, there are two user belief variables which play fundamental roles in influencing computer acceptance behaviour in individuals: perceived usefulness and perceived ease of use. *Perceived usefulness* is defined as the extent to which a person believes that using an information system will enhance his or her job performance. *Perceived ease of use* is defined as the extent to which a person believes that using the system will be free of effort. Note both these variables are based on a user's cognitive perception of an information system, and not the extent to which the system actually can support work practice or is easy to utilize. From a user perspective, perception is reality.

Figure 3-1 illustrates the workings of the Technology Acceptance Model adapted to knowledge portals. TAM theorizes that the effect of *external variables*, such as system design features, system development process, and system training, on a user's intention to utilize an information system are mediated by perceived usefulness and perceived ease of use. TAM also puts forth the claim that perceived usefulness is influenced by perceived ease of use since the easier an information system is to use the more useful it would be. Applying these principles to knowledge portals, TAM theory would suggest that cognitive determinants (i.e., perceived usefulness and perceived ease of use) and affective determinants (i.e., attitude toward using) play a mediating role in determining the extent to which a knowledge portal is utilized for knowledge creation, distribution, and use purposes.

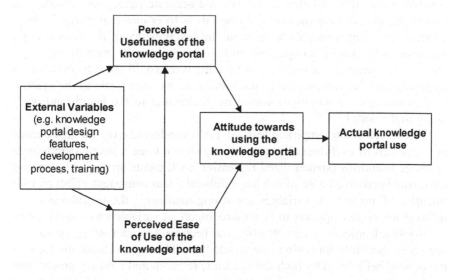

Figure 3-1: The technology acceptance model applied to knowledge portals

The ideas encapsulated in Figure 3-1 reaffirm earlier suggestions put forth in Chapter 1 where various information behaviour models incorporate affective and cognitive components in their descriptions. They also re-verify findings from the author's own case study investigation described in section 3.2.4 where user interest in and positive attitude towards Web information systems were differentiating characteristics between key and non-key WIS knowledge workers. The case study illustrated how user perception of Web information systems as viable tools for knowledge work was a factor differentiating those who did utilize WIS for knowledge creation, distribution, and use from those who did not.

The beauty of TAM applied to knowledge portals is that it provides a rationale for the flow of causality from external variables concerning knowledge portal design characteristics and development processes through user-based perceptions to attitude and finally to knowledge portal use. Organizations now have a causal model which highlights the role perception plays in determining whether or not portals are adopted and utilized. It appears that building robust, user-friendly knowledge portal systems is not enough. Equally important is the need for users to be made aware of the high functionality portals provide—functionality which avidly and actively supports users in their daily knowledge work practice—and the ease with which the portal facilitates these tasks. This suggests that organizations must pay respect to the role perception plays in end user portal adoption and consider ways of facilitating a positive and accurate perception towards the knowledge portal. One means of doing this is to ensure that portal budgets allocate sufficient resources to promote the functionality of the system (e.g., via internal marketing campaigns) and to demonstrate its ease of use (e.g., through user training sessions). These initiatives would have to occur on a sustained basis as enhancements and modifications were made to the system. Underfunding such initiatives would be detrimental to the health and well-being of the portal.

Across the many empirical tests of TAM conducted over the last decade or so, perceived usefulness has consistently shown to be a strong determinant of usage intentions (standardized regression coefficients are typically around 0.6), while perceived ease of use has exhibited a less consistent effect on user intention. Though both variables are strong mediators, the usefulness of an information system appears to be a more important variable and should not be overlooked. Ironically, more attention has been paid to addressing the ease of use component in information system adoption. The logic behind this focus is the general belief held by both the academic research and industry practitioner communities that the key to user acceptance is the lack of user friendliness of a system and that devising user interfaces which increase usability is pivotal to end user adoption.

This point is valid and discussed more in Chapter 5. However, TAM raises awareness of the need to address the usefulness of a system in promoting system adoption. This has significant implications to our discussion on knowledge portal acceptance. It suggests that end users would be more willing to tolerate a difficult knowledge portal interface in order to access its functionality, while no amount of ease of use could compensate for a knowledge portal system that did not perform a useful task. Though in an ideal world, both factors would be addressed, TAM suggests that organizations should concentrate efforts in, or at least pay more attention to, delivering (and marketing) functional knowledge portals over those efforts which deal with strictly raising the usability or user friendliness of the system.

Given the importance of perceived usefulness and its lack of attention, TAM was recently extended to TAM2 as a means of better understanding the determinants of this construct (Venkatesh and Davis, 2000). Other rationales behind this extension were the need to understand the types of interventions organizations could create which increase user acceptance and usage of an information system, and to investigate how the effects of those interventions change over time with increasing user experience with the system. Specifically, additional theoretical constructs spanning social influence and cognitive instrumental processes were added to the workings of TAM and empirically tested. The results showed that these new constructs significantly influenced end user acceptance of an information system. For our purposes, the results have direct implications for interventions organizations can devise which would raise the adoption of the use of knowledge portals in their firms.

In terms of social influence processes on IT usage behaviour, TAM2 identifies three influencing factors: subjective norm, voluntariness, and image. *Subjective norm* is defined as a person's perception that most people who are important to him or her think that the person should or should not perform the behaviour in question. The rationale here is that people choose to perform a behaviour (even if they are favourable toward the behaviour and its consequences) if they believe that one or more important referents think they should. In this respect, people internalize a referent's belief to utilize a system or not into their own belief structure. For knowledge portal adoption and use, TAM2 suggests that organizational workers are influenced by the attitudes of people important to them towards utilizing the portal for knowledge creation, distribution, and use activity. Organizations need to recognize this effect and perhaps target portal marketing campaigns on highly-placed individuals in the organization (such as senior managers), and perhaps recruit those individuals to become spoke-persons and champions of knowledge portal use in the firm.

Voluntariness refers to the degree to which a person is mandated to comply to using an information system. According to TAM2 theory, this compliance has a direct positive effect on a person's intention to use an information system when the compliance is perceived by the person to be mandatory, and no significant direct effect when compliance is perceived to be voluntary. With respect to knowledge portal adoption and use, TAM2 recognizes that mandating or forcing knowledge portal use will have a direct effect on portal usage, and thus may be one strategy organizations can implement to secure portal buy-in. This is not to say that voluntary usage of a portal leads to non-portal use, rather just that it has no direct effect. However, TAM2 cautions that the effect of mandating system use fades over time. That is, the direct effect of subjective norm on intentions to utilize a knowledge portal in mandatory contexts will be strong prior to implementation of the system and during early usage, but will weaken over time as increasing hands-on experience with the portal by knowledge workers provides a growing basis for intentions toward on-going use. So the effect of mandating system usage may be a short-sighted strategy for organizations to follow.

Image is the extent to which an information system is perceived to enhance one's status in one's own social system. The argument here is that if important members of a person's social group at work believe the person should perform a certain behaviour, then performing it will tend to raise his or her standing within that group. In terms of knowledge portal use, TAM2 suggests that if an individual perceives that utilizing a knowledge portal will enhance or elevate his or her image within one's one local work group or community of practice, then the person will be more inclined to adopt and utilize the portal. This suggests that organizations should rally support from key members of communities of practice within the firm about utilizing the portal. Doing so would place social pressure for others in those communities to adopt the system as well. Rallying such support may be more beneficial in promoting portal usage than the promotion of benefits to job performance attributable to portal use (such as working smarter and not re-inventing the wheel).

This is especially true over time and increased hands-on usage with the portal. TAM2 suggests that the direct effects of subjective norm on intentions to utilize a system subsides over time but that the direct effects of image on system use continue as long as a group's norms favour usage of the target system. That is, the direct effect of what senior management or other influential people in organization say about portal usage fades over time, but what those in one's own community of practice say has a lasting and sustained effect on portal use. Thus, organizations should initially find key champions in senior management to rally and promote portal acceptance and adoption in the portal's early implementation days, but more importantly, concentrate and sustain efforts in having respected members in communities of practice across the firm market the benefits and positive aspects of utilizing the portal for knowledge work on an on-going basis.

In terms of cognitive instrumental processes on IT usage behaviour, TAM2 identifies three additional influencing factors other than perceived ease of use: job relevance, output quality, and result demonstrability. These factors play a role in how people formulate perceived usefulness judgments with respect to how people cognitively compare what an information system is capable of doing with what people need to do to get their jobs done.

Job relevance is defined as an individual's perception regarding the degree to which a target information system is applicable to his or her job. Here, people possess and utilize insights and knowledge about their work tasks, which they utilize as a basis for determining what job-related tasks an information system can help perform. With respect to knowledge portal adoption and use, TAM2 theory suggests that job relevance has a positive effect on perceived usefulness. That is, if an employee perceives the portal as possessing the capacity to help facilitate knowledge works tasks the employee must perform in his or her job situation, then the employee will be more likely inclined to perceive the portal as being useful, which in turn positively influences a person's intention to use the system.

In addition to whether the a system possesses the capacity to help perform job functions, the degree to how well the system performs such tasks is referred to as *output quality*. This factor, according to TAM2, has a positive effect on perceived usefulness of a system. For our discussion, if a knowledge portal is perceived to perform knowledge work tasks well, it will be more greatly utilized and adopted in the workplace by organizational knowledge workers.

Result demonstrability refers to the degree to which the benefits or results of an information system is easily demonstrated to others. TAM2 stipulates that result demonstrability has a positive effect on perceived usefulness. In terms of knowledge portal adoption, it follows that the extent to which the benefits of utilizing the system for knowledge creation, distribution, and use can be demonstrated or showcased to others in the organization, would have a direct impact on the perceived usefulness of the system for knowledge work activity. For example, if it can be shown that utilization of the portal leads to positive job-related results, such as improved employee productivity, the creation of new innovations, the sharing of best-practices, or a tangible return on investment, then the greater the likelihood the portal will be perceived as a useful tool for knowledge work.

All three cognitive instrumental processes (job relevance, output quality, and result demonstrability) play an important role in determining the degree to which a person perceives a knowledge portal as being useful. Firms need to be aware of these cognitive processes and, in turn, take action to market the portal across the enterprise. Specifically, organizations need to promote how a knowledge portal is a critical and vital tool for helping workers perform their job-related knowledge work tasks. Doing so, would help promote end user adoption of these systems.

3.5   A Participatory Design Approach to Knowledge Portals

Previous research indicates that an effective way to increase user adoption of systems is to get users involved in the system development process (Tait and Vessey, 1988). It has been suggested that a participatory design may be an appropriate approach for promoting user involvement (Hahn and Subramani, 2000). By encouraging such involvement, the skills and experiences of organizational participants can help inform the design and implementation of computer systems and the work they support. It is argued that doing so will "help ensure a better fit between technology and the ways people (want to) perform their work" (Kensing and Blomberg, 1998, p. 168).

3.5.1   What is Participatory Design?

Participatory design (PD) is a method of systems design that falls under the larger umbrella of design approaches labelled *user-centered design* (Blomberg and Trigg, 2002; Vredenburg et al., 2002). The field has its origins with the seminal work of Norman and Draper (1986). User-centered design is more than usability testing or software engineering. It is an philosophical approach to system design which calls for the active involvement of users to gain a clear understanding of user needs and task requirements, and which is iterative and multi-disciplinary in nature (Vredenburg et al., 2002). According to a survey to usability practitioners on mailing lists of human-computer interaction groups conducted by Hudson (2000), the most commonly used methods for conducting user-centered design include: informal usability testing, user analysis/profiling, evaluating existing systems, low-fidelity prototyping, heuristic evaluation, task identification, navigation design, and scenario-based design.

Participatory design differs from these common user-centered design methods in that it calls for a more radical approach to the active involvement of users in terms of eliciting user requirements and having users play a lead role in the decision-making process. That is, "the people destined to *use* the system play a critical role in *designing* it" (Schuler and Namioka, 1993, p. xi). By doing so, the traditional designer/user relationship is reversed: users are viewed as "the experts – the ones with the most knowledge about what they do and what they need – and the designers as technical consultants" (p. xi). Here, users participate in negotiations over how system projects are organized and what outcomes are desired. According to Kensing and Bloomberg (1998), users can take an active part in: 1) analyzing needs and possibilities; 2) evaluating and selecting technology components; 3) designing and prototyping new technologies; and 4) facilitating the organizational implementation.

The roots of PD originate from system projects conducted in Scandinavia in the 1970s and 1980s, such as UTOPIA, where there was, and continues to be, an explicit commitment to workplace democracy through the direct and effective participation of workers in design activities and decision-making (Kuhn and Muller, 1993; Spinuzzi, 2002). Over the years, especially in North America, the method has been less associated with a grassroots social movement concerned with worker's rights and has attracted attention to all players in organizational settings concerned with building systems which help workers perform their jobs better, which ultimately is good for everyone in the company. Thus most PD projects today involve the participation of management and other non-union personnel. A strong argument can be made that some degree of cooperation between workers and management has been necessary for the success of many PD projects (Kensing and Blomberg, 1998).

Greenbaum and Kyng (1991) provide a thorough and notable discussion on designing computer systems in collaboration with users in their edited book *Design at Work*. There, they stress the need for users to become "full partners in a cooperative system design process where the pursuit of users' interest is a legitimate element" (p. ix). This is crux of PD. It views the active participation of intended users, as well of those indirectly affected, as a precondition for good design that increases the likelihood of systems being useful and well-integrated into the daily work practices of the firm. Greenbaum and Kyng suggest the following ways to facilitate cooperative action in design: 1) create opportunities for mutual learning between users and traditional designers; 2) utilize design tools and language familiar to participants; 3) facilitate events where users can envision future situations of working with the final system—this would allow users to experience how emerging design may affect their lives in practice; and 4) start the design process with the current practice of users—that is, understand how users currently conduct activities that the future system will help users perform, and use that knowledge as a springboard for determining ways to make improvements.

There are a variety of techniques available to aid the participatory design process. In essence, these techniques employ informal ways of engaging users and system designers to contemplate about the relationship between technology and work, and where designer and user can learn from each other. PD techniques for needs identification include workshops, questionnaires, interviews, and ethnographic observations of work practice. PD techniques geared more towards system analysis include the use of scenarios, mock-ups, future workshops, design games, case-based prototyping, and cooperative prototyping (Kensing and Blomberg, 1998).

Ehn and Sjogren (1991, p. 247), two contributing authors to *Design at*

Work, provide sage advice for promoting successful PD in practice based on Russell Ackoff's (1974) concept of idealized design of social systems: it makes a difference for participants; implementation of the results are likely; and it is fun to participate. The first two points refer to the political side of having users participate in design. The project must make a difference for participants. If they perceive the system as having little benefit or relevance to their daily lives, the likelihood of engaging users actively in the project is unlikely. Further, if participants perceive their inclusion in the process as only a gesture of goodwill, then participants will not buy-in. Participants need to feel their contributions are meaningful and will be put into action, not just recorded and put aside. The last point concentrates on the design process itself; it must be fun for users to participate. To secure the active engagement of users in design, steps must be taken to overcome obstacles of hard work and boredom that is inherently part of any systems project.

3.5.2 Implications for Knowledge Portals

In terms of knowledge portals, this book views participatory design as a robust and comprehensive method by which to secure a useful and well-utilized portal system. It bases this claim on three factors. The first is the complex and intricate nature of organizational knowledge work. Identifying how users go about creating, distributing, and utilizing knowledge in the workplace and positing ways of doing these activities better is difficult for systems designers to do in isolation. User participation is required to secure ways of identifying and improving knowledge work activities across the enterprise. The second is the reach of portals across the firm. These systems are not situated in small, localized environments. Rather they span the enterprise and ideally contain the entire organizational population base. As such, a method of system development is required that ensures representatives from all stakeholder groups in the organization are awarded an opportunity to express their needs and concerns. The third is the portal's pervasiveness and capacity to change organizational processes. The portal is an enterprise-wide application that will affect the daily work routines of organizational participants. To ensure and secure buy-in from as many of these users as possible, organizational workers require a critical role in the design and implementation of the final portal product to help increase the chance of firm-wide acceptance.

A PD approach is advocated by Vaughan and Schwartz (1999) who laud the utilization of participatory design techniques to facilitate the building of Web-based community networks. Their work draws on the paradox in the design of community information networks where the person who is intended to benefit most from the system, the average citizen, is least involved in the process. Typically the work of design in delegated to a select computer-literate few who assume what the information needs of the community are. Most common is the implementation of an electronic city metaphor (e.g., post office, newsstand, public square) on the developed community Web page. Toms and Kinnucan (1996) report that this basic design is wrong and that in fact community members prefer everyday language over that of the electronic city metaphor. Vaughan and Schwartz (1999) suggest incorporating a more user-centered design philosophy to community network building would have prevented such erroneous design implementations. Specifically, the authors feel confident in recommending a PD process as a viable means to jumpstart the design of community-based networks.

A model of a participatory design approach to knowledge portal development is shown in Figure 3-2. The model is based on work by Finn and Detlor (2002a) who purport a PD-based orientation to the design of electronic government Web sites.

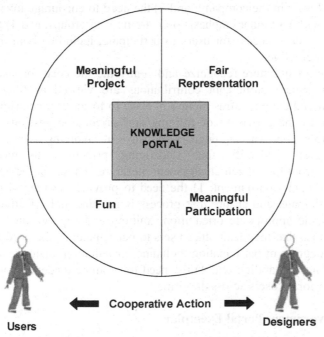

Figure 3-2: A participatory design approach to knowledge portal design

Finn and Detlor's model incorporates three basic PD tenets (meaningful project; fun; cooperative action) with two generally-accepted principles of citizen engagement (fair representation; meaningful participation) to produce a holistic approach to electronic government design. These tenets and principles are adapted to the design of knowledge portals in organizational settings.

The PD literature contributes the need for a *meaningful project* where participants believe the resulting system will serve a benefiting purpose in that it will make a difference to their daily lives. It also contributes the need to promote *fun* or playfulness in design and some initial methods by which *cooperative action* between users and technical developers can be achieved.

The principles of citizen engagement offers the need to maintain *fair representation* across constituents in terms of both recruitment and involvement of a diverse and representative set of users, and universal access to those user groups through various means. In essence, there are four underlying principles to fair representation which can be applied to an organizational setting: 1) the need to strive for a recruitment process that reflects the diversity of the user population; 2) the need to provide opportunities for user involvement across various jurisdictional and hierarchical levels in the company; and 3) the need to encourage involvement of all users, with particular emphasis on marginalized groups; and 4) the need to provide universal access for users to participate, including both in-person and virtual interaction.

Both sets of literature recognize and contribute the need for *meaningful participation* where participant contributions are viewed as likely to be implemented and there is infrastructure in place to foster user contributions to design such as the provision of training and orientation sessions, and an acceptance to support varying degrees and ways of involving users in design. Finn and Detlor identify four underlying principles to meaningful participation from the citizen engagement literature. These can be applied to the organizational environment: 1) the need to provide meaningful roles for users to participate, and ensure that process is genuine and effective; 2) the need to provide appropriate orientation, training and supervision for users, especially those that may lead other users to participate; 3) the need to allow for varying degrees of participation including consultation, dialogue, decision making and accountability; and 4) the need to promote leadership and skills development for all users across the firm.

3.5.3 A Government Portal Exemplar

The tenets and principles showcased in Figure 3-2 were used to assess the effectiveness of adopting a PD approach to portal design for a particular electronic government project. That project involved the active engagement of young Canadians in the design and development of the Government of Canada's youth portal. The portal, coined YouthPath (www.youthpath.ca), is a centralized Web site launched in spring 2002 which contains a comprehensive offering of youth-related government information. Over 400 youths between the ages of 15 and 24 from across Canada participated in the project via a secure online workspace. The idea to include end users in design was seen by the Canadian government as a viable means of identifying and implementing a portal that presented youth-related information in a manner that was easy to access and targeted to youth. To date, no other federal organization in Canada has attempted to engage such a large number of its citizens in the development of a product in this manner.

This particular government portal initiative is noteworthy since it showcases the benefits of adopting a PD approach to portal design and also highlights key learnings about utilizing this approach based on a real-life practice. More detailed information concerning the specifics of the project, including screenshots of the virtual workspace where youth citizens engaged in design activities, can be found in Finn and Detlor (2002a; 2002b). For a description of the history, success factors, and strategic considerations surrounding the implementation of YouthPath in context of the larger Canadian government online presence, see Detlor and Finn (2002).

One of the strong points of the project was its focus on securing *fair representation*. This was illustrated through broad calls for participation across the country over various print, Web-based, and face-to-face mediums. This included recruitment through a network of local youth serving agencies, career and information fairs at community colleges and universities, and a call for participants via a Web site dedicated to the project. Two types of calls were made: one for a Core Team and one for a Virtual Team. The Core Team comprised 19 individuals situated in the National Capital region of Ottawa. The role of this team was to act a team leaders to Virtual Team members. Each Core Team member was responsible for leading a specific subset of the Virtual Team composed of roughly 20 youth citizens who were geographically scattered across the country. A limitation on the call for participants was the need to constrain recruitment of Core Team members to the National Capital region of Ottawa; however this was primarily for logistical reasons. Of relevance was the purposeful recruitment of a diverse group of participants: those with and without technical interests in the Web; those reflecting the multi-cultural nature of Canada; those from both French and English parts of Canada; and those representative of marginalized groups. Universal access of participants was reflected through the acquisition of computers and Internet access by the Government of Canada for those Youth Team members who did not have the available means themselves to participate.

Another strength was the project's focus to ensuring *meaningful participation*. Youth participants segmented into Core and Virtual Teams had very clear roles to play in design. Moreover, these roles were purposeful and added value to the final design. The activities directed to youth participants clearly translated into the layout and functionality of the portal interface. In terms of engaging youth in design, the Government of Canada provided sufficient training to Core Team members to increase the likelihood of Virtual Team members' effective participation in the online environment. Further, tasks and activities were developed which were not dependent on one another; this allowed for varying degrees of participation to occur. Last, the project contributed to participant skill development. For example, utilization of the Virtual Workspace environment increased participants' familiarity with the Web; participation in an electronic government project increased participant knowledge of government workings and introduced many of the youth to their first experience with Web site design.

The project also exhibited clear instances of supporting *fun* and playfulness in design. First, the online tool which participants utilized was innovative and offered a creative workspace through which to design. The environment facilitated social interaction, both project and non-project related. Second, there was tolerance in allowing flexibility in youth participation. No ramifications resulted for those who participated in bursts of activity. Third, there was ample rewards (e.g., prizes) and offerings of praise and recognition to youth participants. All these contributed towards supporting aspects of fun in design which in turn helped sustain participant engagement in the long run.

Good effort was also expended in fostering *cooperative action* between users and civil service project team members. For example, to facilitate cooperation, a two-tier structure of users (Core and Virtual Teams) was created whereby intense interaction between Core Team members and government employees could occur due to the relatively small number of Core Team members and their close proximity to the National Capital area. This interaction included opportunities for Core Youth Team members to learn about the project purpose through on-site orientation sessions and attendance at various government meetings. Further, since Core Team member were youth themselves, they could easily relay assignments and tasks in language familiar to the other youths in the Virtual Teams. This concept was also evidenced in the provision of a Virtual Moderator—a government employee who was a youth himself—who was responsible for answering questions online posted by youth participants and for providing technical assistance on a continuous basis. By hiring a youth employee to play this role, the Canadian government thought that such a person could more easily relate to youth team members. The use of the Virtual Workspace was a good example of the use of a familiar design tool (the Web), one in which the majority of youth participants would be comfortable in engaging. Other examples of cooperative activity included the provision of regular information postings on project updates to youth members, as well as the creation of activities where youth could brainstorm on the functionality of the portal. The latter provided opportunities for youth to envision future situations of working with the system. Despite these good efforts, some improvements in this process could have been made in the area of cooperative action, namely by providing more opportunities for government employees to learn about youth participant perspectives on government operations and focusing initial design on youth's current practice and experience in utilizing federal government information services.

In terms of being a *meaningful project*, YouthPath exhibited sizeable strength. The recruitment blitz, extensive effort to engage youth citizens (particularly those of the Core Team), and provision of a secure online work space, all strengthened participants' belief that their input indeed was valued and needed. Further, through regular updates and access to project status information, participants could directly see the impact of their contributions on the design of the portal. This validated participant importance and heightened the meaningfulness of the project to those youth involved as implementation of their ideas seemed likely.

From this analysis, the YouthPath project was found to be an exemplary case study site exhibiting many of the fundamental components outlined in the Figure 3-2. Recall that the figure was derived from major tenets of participation design and citizen engagement principles. Overall, the YouthPath project dealt with specific issues surrounding user engagement in portal design: fair representation; meaningful participation; cooperative action; meaningful project, and fun in design. As such, the project is a good candidate to be used as an example for other portal design initiatives that wish to engage representatives from their user base in the design process.

3.6 Conclusion

So what have we learned in this chapter about users, portals, and knowledge work? Many things. Recall the main purpose of this chapter was to report findings of the author's case study research investigation described in Chapter 2. One of the main findings of that study was that though the functional role of users had an important impact in determining the problem situations and information needs of users which led to utilization of the portal, in terms of knowledge work, the degree and extent to which the portal was used was based on a distinct set of user characteristics. These characteristics were a person's interest in portal technology, a user's perception of the portal as a viable tool for knowledge work, and a person's self motivation to learn and keep up-to-date in personal areas of expertise.

These findings can be utilized to draw implications on ways to improve the development and use of knowledge portals in firms. For example, it appears that greater emphasis should be placed on marketing the portal to organizational workers, and training users on its strategic advantage. Doing so could help showcase the functionality available in the portal, facilitate a more accurate perception of the features available for use, instil a greater interest or passion in use of this technology on a daily basis, and increase potential utilization of the portal in maintaining currency in personal areas of expertise.

The need for marketing was substantiated by the chapter's application of the Technology Acceptance Model to knowledge portals. Specifically, showcasing the usefulness of a portal to organizational workers, in addition to demonstrating its ease of use, job relevance, output quality, and result demonstrability, was seen as a viable way to foster a positive attitude toward the portal and increase the likelihood of actual portal use. Another suggestion emanating from the author's case study investigation would be for firms to hire or recruit organizational workers that are motivated to learn and/or have an interest in Web-based portal technology. Such workers appear to possess a predisposition to utilizing Web information systems to a greater extent for knowledge creation, distribution, and use. Hiring such employees may compensate for any deterrent obfuscating portal acceptance.

Other key learnings from the chapter were derived. The application of TAM2 theory to knowledge portals raised awareness of the significance of social influence on portal adoption. Key insights included the need to find champions within communities of practice to promote and sustain adoption of the technology by other community members. Mandating use may only be a successful strategy in the early stages of a portal's implementation history, despite whether a senior manager promotes the technology or not. The discussion on communities of practice raised the importance of incorporating requisite functionality in knowledge portal design to connect community members together. Doing so could help support knowledge generation in terms of socialization, externalization, combination, and internalization processes. Last, the examination of following a participatory design approach to portal development was shown to be a novel and effective way of promoting end-user adoption. By actively engaging user representatives across the firm in the design and implementation of a portal, particularly through principles of fair representation, meaningful participation, fun in design, meaningful projects, and cooperative action between designers and the user community, increased adoption and utilization of portals can be secured.

In summary, this chapter delved into an exploration of the user-based factors which affect and shape the way knowledge portals are utilized in organizational work practice. In the next chapter, attention turns towards a focus on the informational context in which knowledge portals are used.

4. THE INFORMATION ENVIRONMENT AND KNOWLEDGE PORTALS

4.1 Introduction

In contrast to the prior chapter, which discussed user concerns in the design and adoption of knowledge portals in organizations, this chapter focuses on the informational context in which portals are utilized. Doing so allows for a unique and insightful perspective on the design and adoption of enterprise portals in terms of their ability to support organizational knowledge work—defined in Chapter 1 to be a set of information-laden activities comprising knowledge creation, distribution, and use.

The goal is to investigate and ponder the aspects or characteristics of an organization's information environment which inhibit or promote the utilization of enterprise portals for knowledge work. From an organizational perspective, it is hypothesized that knowledge portals would need a healthy and supportive information environment to support knowledge creation, distribution, and use. A healthy and supportive information environment would be one that promotes consensus and negotiation among portal information stakeholders. It would also be one that facilitates access to information content and knowledge experts. Additionally, it would help reduce information overload, and encourage the sharing and distribution of information among organizational participants.

To start things off, a detailed description is given on the information environment construct, a theoretical concept which has gathered growing interest and acceptance by both academics and practitioners alike.

From there, results from the author's case study research investigation described in Chapter 2 are reported. Results indicate that certain factors of a firm's information environment can influence the development, design, and adoption and use of knowledge portals in organizations. These factors include the information politics which surround portal development, the information system development process itself, and the degree to which information is readily shared, valued, and controlled across the organization.

Recommendations are made to incorporate such insights into the design and deployment of knowledge portal systems. The chapter's call is for portal system designers to become aware of the situational information contexts in which knowledge portals are utilized, and to use these insights to devise ways of fostering healthy and supportive information environments that promote portal adoption. This includes not only understanding the physical characteristics that impede information access and use via the portal, but also the political factors that deter the free flow of information between employees, and the culture of the organization that prevents information from being valued and shared.

4.2 Information Environments

4.2.1 Information Ecologies

Perhaps the most popular literature on organizational information environments to-date is given by Davenport (1997) in his holistic description of the information ecology of organizations. Here, Davenport describes how the information environment lies at the core of a firm's organizational environment (i.e., the company's overall business situation, technical infrastructure, and physical arrangement) and focuses on people and their information behaviours. Such behaviours include the degree to which information is easily shared across the enterprise, and how well information is filtered and presented in engaging ways to encourage the recognition and use of the right information by employees.

According to Davenport, there are six critical components of an organization's information ecology: strategy, politics, behaviour/culture, staff, processes, and architecture.

Information strategy refers to the high-level intent of an organization concerning items such as information content, common information, information processes, and new information markets.

Information politics "involves the power information provides and the governance responsibilities for its management and use" (p. 35). Davenport, Eccles and Prusak (1992) identify five information political models: 1) technocratic utopianism, a belief that technology can solve all problems of information governance; 2) anarchy, where individuals manage their own information, often at their own peril; 3) feudalism, where business units define their own information needs and report limited information back to the corporation; 4) monarchy, where a central person dictates information management policies on behalf of everyone else; and 5) federalism, where there is consensus and negotiation among business units on the use of information.

Information culture comprises a firm's information behaviours and determines "how much those involved value information, share it across organizational boundaries, disclose it internally and externally, and capitalize on it in their businesses" (Davenport, 1997, p. 35). Information behaviours include: information sharing which requires the removal of various political, emotional, and technological barriers to encourage the exchange of information between organizational participants; handling information overload which requires the filtering of information and information engagement (i.e., the communication of information in compelling ways to encourage the recognition and use of the right information); and dealing with multiple information meanings which requires consensus and cooperation among organizational workers if multiple meanings need to be controlled.

Information staff are the people in the firm needed to provide and interpret information to others in the organization. These include both technology specialists and information professionals. The primary goal of such staff is to make information meaningful and valuable; this can be accomplished by pruning information, adding to its context, enhancing its style and choosing the right medium.

Information processes consist of "all those activities performed by information workers" (p. 36) and include the determination of information requirements, information capture, distribution, and use.

Information architecture is a "guide to the structure and location of information within an organization" (p. 36) and can include pointers to people and incorporate both computer and non-computer based information sources.

Nardi and O'Day (1999) provide a different description of information environments that also utilizes the metaphor of ecology. These authors define an information ecology to be "a system of people, practices, values, and technologies in a particular local environment" and emphasize that "the spotlight is not technology, but on human activities that are served by technology" (p. 49). In their description, an information ecology is a complex system of parts and relationships which exhibit diversity, experience continual evolution, and has a sense of locality. By utilizing the metaphor of ecology, Nardi and O'Day are able to emphasize the sense of urgency in fostering healthy information ecologies (i.e., if environmental destructive forces are left unchecked they can cause ecological failure) through participant engagement and collective participation in socially shared and valued activities. Acknowledging that "healthy information ecologies take time to grow, just as rain forests and coral reefs do" (p. 58), Nardi and O'Day encourage the active involvement of people in the evolution of their own information ecologies, specifically in terms of the shape and direction of the technologies that people use and the settings in which they are utilized. This is similar to the call for a participatory design approach to knowledge portal development described in Chapter 3.

4.2.2 Information Processing Contexts

A related description of the information environments of organizations is given by Huber and Daft (1987). These authors recognize that organizations follow both a rational information processing approach to reducing uncertainty through formal activities of acquiring and internally distributing information, and an interpretive approach where organizational participants give meaning to information through self-interpretation and shared interactions with others.

Huber and Daft refer to the rational information processing approach as information logistics. "Organizations purposefully acquire and internally distribute information in order to carry out the critical functions of decision-making and control" (p. 145). That is, organizations offer routinized procedures for the acquisition of information to reduce uncertainty. This occurs in two forms: scanning and probing. These are done primarily to identify problems and opportunities, as well as to fulfill information procurement and reporting responsibilities; other reasons include legitimating decisions or developing personal information banks. In terms of the internal distribution of information, Huber and Daft note two ways in which organizations can reduce information load: by routing information messages to relatively few organizational units; and by summarizing messages which reduce message size while reproducing its meaning.

In terms of the interpretive approach to information processing, Huber and Daft recognize the role symbolic interactionism and communications media richness play in reducing information equivocality in organizations. With symbolic interactionism (Stryker and Statham, 1985), the organization is viewed as a web of human interactions where, through communication between organizational participants, symbols such as language and behaviour evolve and take on meaning; here, symbols are used to interpret information from the environment. Taking a symbolic interactionist point of view, information ambiguity is reduced as organizational members create meaning through social interaction and discussion. In terms of communications media richness, Huber and Daft note a continuum of media richness where richness is defined as a medium's capacity to change understanding. The authors suggest richer information mediums be used when information ambiguity is high.

By incorporating these two opposing views in their discussion of organizational information environments, Huber and Daft recognize the importance of both perspectives. Together they can explain how organizations respond to varying degrees of environmental information uncertainty:

"when environmental situations are routine or well understood... information acquisition and transmission are sufficient to make organizational choices that solve problems or exploit opportunities. However, novel and unexpected external events cannot be handled in the same way because existing meanings tend to be less adequate for interpreting the information received. When the equivocality of the environment is high, the problem... is to interpret and know the world." (Huber and Daft, 1987, p. 152)

4.2.3 Information Use Environments

The above descriptions of information ecologies and organizational information processing contexts help describe the theoretical construct of firm-wide information environments and give support for the existence of such constructs in organizations today. This chapter recognizes the existence of an organization's information environment and suggests that such contexts play an important role in determining the extent to which enterprise portals are potentially utilized for knowledge work. Thus the chapter calls for the need to examine knowledge portals in context of the firm-wide information environment in which these systems are situated as a means of devising ways to promote a healthy information environment which will leverage portal adoption and use.

To better understand the workings of information environments, attention turns towards the Information Studies field which provides its own pertinent and descriptive account of the theoretical components comprising information environments. This account includes the development of a theoretical model of the information use environment or IUE by Taylor (1986; 1991), later expanded by Katzer and Fletcher (1992), and then by Rosenbaum (1993; 1996; 1999; 2000).

In his writings, Taylor offers a definitive conceptualization of the information environment construct. Taylor defines the IUE as "the set of those elements that (a) affect the flow and use of information messages into, within, and out of any definable entity; and (b) determine the criteria by which the value of information messages will be judged" (1986, pp. 3-4). Moreover, he describes four categories of the IUE: sets of people, their problems, typical settings, and problem resolutions (Taylor, 1991).

Katzer and Fletcher's (1992) model of the information environment of managers is explicitly based on Taylor's concept of the IUE. Using the context and the person as two fairly fixed starting points, Katzer and Fletcher formulate a model based on the characteristics of Taylor's IUE, namely people (i.e., managers), their organizational settings, their typical problems, and their range of acceptable resolutions. Central to the model is the notion that managers, as they attend to their information environments, are confronted with problematic situations. It is through this concept of problematic situations that the IUE and information behaviours are linked. During the resolution of problematic situations, managers exhibit information behaviours, which are actions that contribute to the usefulness of information. In doing so, managers determine "whether or not to seek information, what information to seek, where to seek it, how to seek it, how much to seek, how to interpret it, how to assess it, and how to use it" (Katzer and Fletcher, 1992, p. 233). Furthermore, as managers exhibit information behaviours, problematic situations change over time. That is,

> "new uncertainties and concerns may emerge, different activities or roles become
> dominant, and other dimensions increase in importance. As long as the (revised)
> problematic situation remains unresolved, additional information behaviors will
> emerge. These, in turn, are influenced by the manager's current definition of the
> situation and current 'choice' of activities, roles, and dimensions. This process
> continues until the problematic situation becomes resolved... in the mind of the
> manager." (Katzer and Fletcher, 1992, p. 233)

The significance of Katzer and Fletcher's model is that it attempts to explain how the IUE influences information behaviour, a topic largely left ambiguous in Taylor's writings. It does this through the concept of problematic situations which provides a mechanism for relating the organizational setting to managerial information behaviours. Though their model suggests one-directional causal relationships between the IUE and information behaviours, Katzer and Fletcher caution that this is "an oversimplification; most likely some of the links are bi-directional" (p. 231).

Rosenbaum's (1993; 1996) model addresses Katzer and Fletcher's concerns by suggesting a bi-directional relationship between information behaviours and the IUE. Specifically, he rejects "the determinative and generative powers... attributed to IUEs [by Taylor], including the abilities to generate problems, create information needs, and produce information behaviors" (1996, p. 81). He also refutes Taylor's (1991) definition of information behaviour as being a product of the four elements of the IUE (i.e. set of users, problems, settings, and problem resolutions) in that it suggests a unidirectional influence of structure over behaviour, and does not recognize a possible counter-influencing effect of information behaviour on the IUE. Additionally, Rosenbaum (1996) does not agree with the inclusion of sets of people in the IUE itself.

Rather, Rosenbaum suggests that the IUE is structural in nature and comprised of rules, resources, problems, and problem resolutions. Here, the IUE "has virtual existence until instantiated in action" and is "routinely produced and reproduced through the social practices or information behaviors of users" (1996, p. 112). Information behaviours are depicted as action-oriented, existing outside of the structure of the IUE. They "can be grouped together and seen as social practices which exist in the world" (p. 112). Moreover, "information behaviors are not generated or produced by an IUE, although they can certainly be constrained, shaped, and enabled by an IUE" (p. 113).

An interesting aspect of Rosenbaum's framework is that it offers an explanation for the persistence of information behaviour in organizations over time. This happens as users attempt to solve problematic situations and engage in information behaviours; they draw upon the rules, resources, problems and assumptions of problem resolutions of the IUE. Though users can choose not to be influenced by the components of the IUE, they tend not to, and, as a result, end up unintentionally re-verifying the structure of the IUE. This explains how the same information behaviours of managers, namely the producing, gathering, filtering, and sharing of information, are replicated across time and space in organizations.

In more recent writings, Rosenbaum refines the IUE concept by introducing the construct of the digital information environment or IE to be a subset of the IUE. Specifically, he describes the IE as

"the social context within which ICTs [information and communication technologies] are designed, implemented, and used and digital information is created, accessed, manipulated, stored, disseminated, and use. It is a subset of the information [use] environment and has similar elements. Although it is a social space, as is the information [use] environment, it is more structured because of the explicit work done by people to create, recreate, maintain, and change it; examples include interface and Web page design; two activities which add a degree of rigidity to the digital IE. Understanding the digital IE is a key to understanding how people work, play, and interact as they use ICTs and digital information." (Rosenbaum, 1999, p. 706)

Applying the IE concept to electronic business activities, Rosenbaum (2000) identifies three information imperatives for the firm. The first is that information generated by a firm's activities must flow rapidly and effectively throughout the entire organization. For example, organizations can develop policies and procedures to manage digital information flows. The second is that the firm has a responsibility to manage this information carefully. They can, for instance, concentrate on preserving the security and integrity of digitized information. The third is that the firm must be involved in a continual effort to build and maintain trust between business stakeholders involved in these activities. As organizations go about doing these three things, they can expect to experience adjustments and alterations in the way their firms operate. This occurs because a digital IE is dynamic and changes in response to new rules and resources within it. Thus, as a result of implementing and promoting a digital IE, organizations can expect changes in its information culture, information processes, technological infrastructure, and its internal information structure in terms of consolidation of information silos or islands, and the creation of new information staffing roles such as managers, technologists, and information content specialists (Rosenbaum, 2000).

Choo, Detlor and Turnbull (2000a, pp. 115-117) provide a detailed review of the three models of information environments depicted by Taylor, Katzer and Fletcher, and Rosenbaum, along with Davenport's information ecology construct. From this review, several recurring themes on the structure of a firm's information environment and its relationship to user information behaviours are identified: problem situations constitute a central component of the information environment construct; information behaviours play a central role; there is a relationship between the information environment and information behaviours; there is a need to present information in engaging ways to help people resolve their problems (see Chapter 5 on information design); and an organization's information culture and setting (e.g., structure, style, and politics) are influential in determining employee attitudes toward information, employee information behaviours, and the firm's information architecture and information processes.

4.2.4 Implications for Knowledge Portals

So what does all this mean for knowledge portals? Basically three things. First, knowledge portals, people, their problem situations, and information behaviours are situated in information environments. That is, people in organizations are situated in contexts where they are confronted with problem situations. To resolve these problems, people may turn to the knowledge portal for information. This activity may solve the problem or redefine it, leading to cycles of knowledge portal use till the situations become resolved or eventually abandoned. This cycle of knowledge portal use is similar to the information needs-seeking-use cycle depicted in Figure 1-3.

Second, a firm's information environment comprises several entities. These include an organization's information culture, information systems development processes, and information politics. *Information culture* refers to the degree to which information is readily shared, valued, and filtered across the company. *Information systems development processes* are the procedures in place in a firm which dictate how information systems (such as portals) are developed and maintained. *Information politics* refers to the human struggle over the management of information, in this case the management of portal content and applications.

Third, how well people utilize the knowledge portal to access, create, share, find, browse, create, and use information to help resolve their problem situations is constrained or enhanced by these information environmental components. Here, an organization's information culture, system development processes, and politics play important roles in determining the extent to which employees utilize the portal to resolve their problem situations.

Figure 4-1 illustrates the influencing effect of information environments on portal utilization. In a three-step cyclical process of portal use, the figure shows how organizational users are confronted with problem situations, which in turn inspires them to elicit information behaviours via the knowledge portal, leading to problem resolutions (i.e., redefinitions of problem situations). As users cycle through this three-step process of interaction with the portal, they do so within a situated context of the organization's information environment.

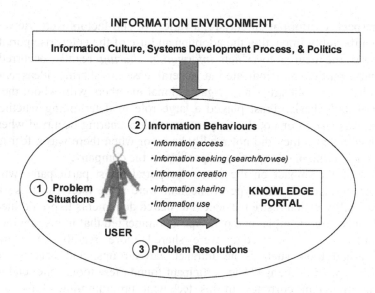

Figure 4-1: The effect of information environments on knowledge portal use

Figure 4-1 suggests that this context has an influencing effect on how and to what extent the portal is utilized. To further explicate the effect of information environments on portal use, the next subsection reports on the author's case study findings.

4.3   Knowledge Portal Case Study Results

Recall the author's case study described in Chapter 2 which investigated the use of an enterprise portal by 20 organizational workers. One of the mandates of that investigation was to delve into and explore the extent to which an organization's information environment promoted or deterred the use of the firm's enterprise portal. Specifically, field notes and interview data obtained from participants and key informants in the organization were analyzed to determine the more salient characteristics of the information environment that affected portal adoption and use for knowledge work.

In general, several broad categories were identified: the information culture of the organization; the system development process by which the portal was maintained; and the information politics surrounding portal design and development. Detlor (2001) provides a initial report on how these factors impacted the design, adoption, and use of the organization's enterprise portal.

The findings are elaborated and extended below.

4.3.1 Information Culture

With respect to information culture, a variety of sub-factors were viewed as being significant in impacting the adoption and use of the enterprise portal. Foremost was the degree to which *information sharing* readily occurred. Overall, most participants indicated a general ease of sharing ideas and documents between colleagues and organizational members with whom they worked on a daily basis. Trust played a large role in determining whether information was shared or not. Participants noted less sharing occurred when it was with colleagues they did not readily know or when there was a fear of protecting one's domain of expertise or position in the company.

In terms of the impact on the enterprise portal, most participants who were willing to share via this type of medium were more likely to do so if there was a facility which restricted access to shared documents to pre-defined individuals only. For example, one participant commented that in his previous job, information and knowledge were shared more readily since the organization had tools such as an intranet, newsgroups, and listservs to facilitate this type of exchange. The participant found these tools beneficial in helping him maintain currency in his technical programming skills and wished that his current company would provide a similar means of knowledge exchange within the firm. Another participant commented on the general desire of employees to share knowledge, but stated the need for the company to provide a means of facilitating that sharing.

> Participant: "It's not that people don't want to share it, it's just that... it's not made available in a sharing... the environment doesn't make it available in a sense. There is no central repository that provides you any context about what information is available. And I see that as a huge impediment to sharing. And especially... even if the stuff is all out there, there's none of the things that seem to be generally available on the Web... where if you have a Web site and you've got all these documents and everything... like you have a Memex [refer back to this book's Foreword for a description of Vannevar Bush's 1945 vision of a desktop personal information machine]... you can search that thing. You should be able to search this stuff and find things. So that's an impediment. No repository. We don't know what information is out there. It's bad."

> ***

> Participant: "It becomes difficult at times to get information to find out where it's housed, that sort of thing. System-wise, I think we're lacking in that way. We don't necessarily have a central archives capability. And I think generally we

don't have the manpower to be able to do the education and management of that."

Of interest was that some participants reported an unwillingness to contribute documents and ideas to a public space for fear of reprisals. Many participants advocated the need for the organization to support a safe sharing environment which facilitated a convenient electronic means to do so and a context free of repercussions and critical judgements.

Participant: "And hoarding does go on. And I mean that in the sense that... project per project... it's sort of like that you want to watch your butt and you don't want to let a document out there, for example a technical document, until people have approved it. And someone might want it, and for all intensive purposes it's ready for them to look at but you don't want to commit or you don't want it out there floating around, exposing yourself. Someone might pick it up and say 'hey, that's not right'. In that way, there's hoarding. I can have something ready and my manager will say 'don't share it with the world just yet'. So I would say only hoarding goes on with non-authorized documents."

Whether participants felt comfortable sharing documents or not, many commented on the need for the company's help in reducing *information overload*. For example, few had time to examine external Web sites or portal pages recommended by colleagues or digest information pushed at them through e-mail. Many participants voiced their frustration in trying to search for information within the portal. Typically, participants indicated that the portal search engine lacked robustness and returned irrelevant hit list items that were unwieldy to sort through. Several participants spoke of the difficulties in filtering their own information from these sources.

Another concern dealt with the company's desire to *control information* presented and displayed on the enterprise portal. Two groups in the firm had responsibility for portal development: the IT division concerned itself with the portal's technical infrastructure; and the Communications group had mandate over the portal's information content. Both of these groups indicated they wanted to rationalize the enterprise portal, though from different vantage points. Communications wanted to standardize the portal's look and feel (e.g., the use of corporate colours, standard fonts, and the placement of the company logo at the top of departmental Web sites' main pages) as well as the portal content. The IT group wanted to standardize the portal's technological design (e.g., the use of standard-approved Web page development tools, the inclusion of standard buttons on departmental Web sites back to the portal home page).

The extent to which these two groups wanted to standardize the portal was evident in a recent policy change to encourage the registration and linkage to departmental Web sites from the portal. Previously, there was a portal policy in place for organizational Web sites to comply to certain guidelines before these sites could be registered. Many people refused to change their Web site designs and hence did not register, leaving the portal to be a skeleton of the true organizational Web site structure. In the hope of swaying people to identify their Web sites and eventually comply to company deemed standards, the requirement for sites to comply to guidelines before they could be registered was dropped. In effect, this relaxation of standards was a softer approach in trying to persuade employees to conform to company portal standards.

> Informant: "There are, depending on whose numbers you believe, 800 to 3,000 intranet sites within the company. The CIO's office calls them *undernets* because in a lot of cases they're just one guy whose written it in FrontPage and is running it off his NT machine at his desk. Or himself, or his little group, or his department or whatever. There's also larger sites that are more corporate sanctioned and things like that. So, as a result, a lot of those intranet sites, we don't even know exist. They haven't done it through any official process because we didn't have an official intranet policy in place for many years. So they just went ahead and did it on their own. So we don't know about them... In the new portal, unlike the old, we have absolutely no criteria for registering your site. If your site is about your own personal ski club for six people in your department and running it off your own computer, fine we'll register your site."

> Interviewer: "Why the change in philosophy?"

> Informant: "Because we figured if we put in a rationalization or guidelines for whether or not you could list your site, then we would lose all those sites we don't know about. So what we figured out right now is that we would gather the information. We'll get everyone to list their site. That way we know they exist and we can start gently and gradually re-moulding them and reshaping them and rationalizing the kind of sites and letting the company know what is appropriate and what isn't appropriate. But we can't do that until we know about them."

> Interviewer: "So it's a way of getting them in?"

> Informant: "Right. We have IP addresses... the CIO's office has IP addresses for most of the intranets that are out there and they are beginning to craft a strategy that will have them rationalize those sites. But at this point, we're not there yet."

According to both the IT and Communications groups, control over Web design and content was a necessary means for coordinating and developing a cohesive company gateway to information.

> Informant: "There always has to be a centralized point... with a limited number of people, that have to take ownership at the end of the day with the ultimate responsibility."

Interviewer: "Why do you feel that that is required?"

Informant: "Because if you don't have some form of an owner at the end of the day, then there is no control as to how things get done. It's just like throwing a bag of candies into a room of kids. You could tell them 'okay, divide it up fairly and evenly'. You know they're never going to do it unless someone is orchestrating the process."

There was mixed reaction from users on the control over Web site design. Some participants saw the necessity of setting standards.

Participant: "This is the whole thing with me. We should be standard... A lot of things are not consistent, and we don't follow standards. We should have a standard look, feel. Then you know it always works this way."

***

Participant: "Yeah, we need a standard... we need to standardize for costing savings and whatever else."

***

Participant: "I appreciate the requirement and necessity for standards and so I appreciate where it's coming from, I think it's probably to have a central place where people can go to".

However, several participants were vocal in their opposition to the company's control over Web design. One participant was frustrated by her attempt to create a departmental Web site. She had commissioned the work of hosting the site to another group and ran into trouble when trying to get this done since her subordinates who developed the site utilized non-standard software. The participant had to make certain aesthetic changes to the site as well as convert the site to FrontPage (the company's deemed standard software for Web site design). The participant was frustrated that she had to convert her site to a package she saw was more inferior to the one that was previously utilized. In essence, she saw the standards as being myopic in terms of not being flexible enough to consider improvements or changes in deemed standards.

Interviewer: "I'm trying to find out why they reject certain sites. Are they trying to follow corporate standards?"

Participant: "They are. And what's very interesting about that... well we can get into that when I tell you about how the Web site went... but there's a struggle between doing things right and doing them quickly and efficiently. Okay? And that's always the one. Well, I developed this site and I did most of the work myself but I needed someone to actually clean it up because I was an amateur but someone else to post it to an existing host. And it never occurred to me that they wouldn't follow company standards. As it turned out they didn't on the software, and it caused us big problems."

Interviewer: "Did you know what the standards were?"

Participant: "No, but I relied on them to make sure they knew the standards. Yeah, I knew what the standards were and I bought the standard, which was FrontPage, and that's what I created it in, and I gave it to these guys and said 'okay, please post it to this host' and clean it up or do whatever because I had problems with links. But anyway, I said 'please post this for me' and they said 'oh, did you know that they changed some things?'. They specifically said to me on the phone 'your company logo or company icon or whatever was not standard.' They changed that. I said 'okay, right, fine… they know what the standards are.' Well they came back and they used software that wasn't FrontPage. So they used non-standard software. So when it came back to the team that was to maintain the site, Corporate Purchasing wouldn't let us buy the software that we now needed to run the site. We converted it back to FrontPage, but I'll tell you it was like 18 headaches in the meantime trying to convince these people 'look, just give me some software, okay?… I don't care [about the standards]'. To their credit, they're trying to maintain standards and I understand that, but when something like this happens and I did not know… I mean I gave it to them in FrontPage, I'm expecting it to come back in FrontPage, all of a sudden it doesn't… you know.

Interviewer: "Yeah, you don't want the process to be the obstacle."

Participant: "No, but the software they used is better than FrontPage. And that's obviously why they used it. But, it wasn't standard."

Interviewer: "Who cares what software you used to develop the Web page in?"

Participant: "The concern is software cost. And that's how the company was before. If everybody went and bought their own stuff… it wasn't their fault necessarily and in some cases it was… but they would go and buy new toys just to find out what they were. They were spending a lot of money. Nothing was standard. And well…"

Interviewer: "Okay, I understand the need for controls but there's a fine line…"

Participant: "Yeah. Yeah. You have to [balance between looseness and structure]… What I think they should do, I was talking to them about this just two weeks ago when I was arguing with them over this software, I said 'Okay, fine, we have to use the standard software, the FrontPage, but I'm here to tell you this other software is better, so how do I get that information across to the people who make the decisions what is standard software?' And interestingly enough they said 'you can't.'. I said 'okay then!' So, there's a dictator over there saying 'You use this and we won't listen to any feedback'. Okay. No, I don't know if that was just the person [she was talking to about using non-standard software] but I just dropped it. I had enough anyway. I said 'okay, okay, we'll use FrontPage... fine, fine.' So."

To summarize, with respect to information culture, three sub-factors were identified as being significant in impacting the adoption and use of the enterprise portal by organizational workers: 1) the willingness of employees to share information; 2) information overload; and 3) control over portal standards.

4.3.2 Systems Development Process

In terms of the systems development process, there were various procedures for making portal enhancements. For minor modifications to portal content, a content management tool allowed the Communications group to publish news items, post pictures, and conduct surveys directly into the portal. For more extensive changes to portal content, Communications would utilize the services of a third-party systems solutions provider. This necessitated a somewhat lengthy change request procedure whereby Communications would submit a formal content change request to a customer service help desk within the organization, who in turn would issue a trouble ticket and contact the third-party systems solution provider to make the requisite content change.

One participant was concerned over the slow process by which changes to portal content occurred. This, according to the participant, was because modifications were first fed through a team in the Communications department who then informed the third-party systems solution provider to make the necessary changes. The participant explained that this third-party was often overwhelmed in terms of work to do, so changes took a long time to go into production. To emphasize her argument, she gave an example where a Vice-President of the company wanted to make simple textual changes to his biography posted on the portal. The changes took two weeks to make since the third-party company was busy at that time and the participant had to query the Communications team on what was taking so long. To exacerbate this situation, there were some minor errors in the text when it was finally posted on the portal. The VP requested these be fixed. That second round took another week and a half to implement. In total, it took three and a half weeks to implement simple textual changes on the portal. According to the participant, this was unacceptable. She pointed out that where she had worked before had a better system for making portal content changes since the portal development people sat only a couple of cubicles away from the people requesting the content changes. There, simple textual changes took only minutes to complete.

A different process was utilized for non-content portal changes. That is, suggestions for enhancements to the portal's features and functions were gathered and prioritized by the Communications group on a continuous basis. Employees could send their suggestions through a feedback option at the bottom of every portal Web page. Deemed changes were costed out by the third-party systems solution provider and brokered by the IT group. In this capacity, IT functioned as a middle man between the organization and the solution provider. As one informant from the IT group explained, it was in the company's best interest if the IT group brokered the relationship. The idea was that the IT group was familiar with technology and software development and could guarantee that the bid for work was fair, representative, and comprehensive. According to this informant, some user groups had gone to the third-party systems solution provider directly to get systems work done and the end result was a higher dollar price and questionable deliverables had IT not intervened.

There was a general desire from within the management ranks of the IT group to deliver a quick systems development process in terms of implementing changes to the portal. For instance, IT management wanted to develop a new version of the portal and release it to the user community within 60 days. However, according to one informant, this push for a timely turn-around was flawed since it was inadequate to build real change into the system within such a short timeframe. As a result, the recent new version was met with scepticism and disappointment by organizational workers who were hopeful the new redesign would better meet their needs. According to the informant, the push for a rapid installation of a new version of the portal was a compromised solution where only a few new features were added in the end, such as a classifieds section, a new search utility, and on-line news.

Other factors beyond senior management pressure influenced the design of the portal as well. Three discussed during the interview sessions were time, cost, and available man-power. For example, the portal content team in Communications consisted of only three full-time equivalents, making this a constraint towards addressing changes to the portal requested by employees in a timely fashion.

Another participant commented that the formal process of redesigning the portal or building new departmental Web sites was too expensive and slow since the policy deemed that the third-party systems solution provider was to become involved. The participant discussed how she circumvented the development process when she created her own departmental Web site, explaining the official development process was too costly and time-consuming to warrant its utilization in practice.

Interviewer: "Well you'll get there. You have to start somewhere… can't wait for everything to be perfect before rolling out a Web site."

Participant: "Yeah, but not only that. I was racing time before [the third-party systems solution provider] found out I was doing it and slapped me on the hand."

Interviewer: "Oh. They wouldn't let you do it?"

Participant: "No. I shouldn't even have done it. I should have paid them. To give you a comparison, another site was created for [another department] that we piggybacked with. But their site cost, I don't know, 40 or 60 thousand dollars or something of that nature. And it's a very nice site. It's more professionally done than mine. And I mean there's all kinds of reasons why it's a good site, but it was also expensive and it was a lot of red tape to get it. Whereas mine was just... you know, I did it in my spare time.. here, go throw it up [host it on a Web server]. So.. but [the third-party systems solution provider] is supposed to, I understand, do all.. It's supposed to become a project. And that's the problem. That's why I didn't go that route because I knew that it would take longer than we had to get it running... They're getting better though. [The third-party systems solution provider] is getting better but they're still a little bit process heavy and they're still a little bit... the pendulum hasn't swung back yet the other way where... right now they're a little too controlling of what's going on out there."

One participant gave an example of the difficulties in creating an external Web site since different policies existed on the look and feel of the site depending on whether the site was sponsored or not by an outside organization. The participant's major complaint was that she wanted freedom to design the site in the way she felt was preferable, and not to be constrained by policy.

The need to re-register departmental Web sites on the latest version of the corporate portal was met with some hostility by organizational workers who viewed the need to re-register as an impediment to the portal development process. Users were upset that links they previously depended on to get to other departmental Web sites were removed from the corporate portal without notice. Some participants did not bookmark these links and were frustrated by scrambling to locate or obtain the URL address of departmental Web sites. The following excerpt from one participant typifies user reaction to this missing functionality.

Participant: "One of the difficulties, and I understand how we got to this point, so take the comment for what it's worth, when they moved over to the new portal format, they went out to all of the people who had intranet sites and told them they had to register. Out of all of those sites, and I think there were some 200 sites, there are only 30 some that are registered. All the ones that I need aren't registered, don't fit under the portal criteria [classification category schema] that they've set out and unless I know the e-mail [URL] address, I can't get at them and neither can anyone else in any of my groups... What I think probably happened was that the form was sent out to the person who manages the site, she wasn't sure where to put it [in the portal classification scheme], and it just never got done cause everyone figured that it would be folded over and somebody [in Communications] would make that decision. So, I'm not sure where it's at. I've got somebody working on that."

A different viewpoint on the need to re-register departmental Web sites was perceived by members of the Communications group. In their opinion they wanted to acquire an updated list of active departmental Web sites. Forcing users to re-register their sites would facilitate this. They also wanted users themselves to classify their own departmental Web sites according to the portal's content categorization schema devised by Communications. It was felt that doing so would ensure greater accuracy in the classification of the content posted on those sites.

Interviewer: "Why force the individual sites to register? Why didn't you just look at the sites that were on your old list and move them to the appropriate areas?"

Informant: "We thought who better to know a certain site's customers or users than the individuals who run and operate this site. So we left it up to them to categorize themselves."

***

Informant: "We didn't port over the sites from the old portal, because in the old portal it included a lot of really outdated sites. It included sites that were not [company-related]... So, that's why we decided to start from scratch. We ported over sites that we knew existed that were strategic... And then, we provided facilities for people to register their own sites. We're also sending out an e-mail to everybody within the next couple days to the entire company saying 'hey, if you run a site, please come register your site'."

4.3.3 Information Politics

With respect to information politics, there were two broad political struggles over ownership of the enterprise portal. The first was among three internal Communications groups within the company over *the management of information content on the portal*. The three internal groups were composed of two regional communications groups (Group One and Group Two) and one company-wide group (Group Three). Group One was responsible for administering the information content on the company portal. However, since the portal serviced communications across the enterprise, the other two groups had an interest in the management of the portal content as well. In addition, both Groups One and Two serviced separate departmental Web sites (called forums) for constituents in their regions.

In general, there was much duplication of services and features across the three sites. Several participants indicated confusion over the duplication of information on these sites, which was exacerbated by hypertext links to the two forum sites directly from the portal homepage.

A key informant from one of the Communications groups discussed the political turmoil in gaining consensus among the three groups in managing the information content on the portal. Her comments below highlight the need for cooperation and shared vision within the Communications groups and elimination of duplicate information content and applications across the portal and forum sites.

> Informant: "The trouble is you've got one company... but you've got... two very strong regions which almost operate as companies unto themselves. And therefore, each wants an on-line presence to deliver regional specific information and applications. And yes, there is some duplication right now which we're working to eliminate... We're just in the process of removing that duplication... in fact, we're having a meeting later this month, in two weeks... no, next week... to discuss very seriously the relationship between the forums and the portal... how it should evolve and even if forums are needed. Should they even exist given the way the portal is evolving. I think they should... I think there's a need and a desire both at the lower levels and the executive levels... but clearly defining what the portal is and what the forums are and what they should be and reducing the duplication is a chief objective right now. It's just going to take some time because again consensus has got to be achieved. It takes time."

The meeting itself, of which the informant spoke, was illustrative of the difficulty in achieving consensus among the three groups. Though the meeting was allotted a two-hour timeframe, the meeting ended abruptly after only twenty minutes of discussion. During this time, each party voiced different visions of the forum and portal sites. Overall, there was great reluctance by representatives of these three groups to relinquish ownership of the content they currently controlled.

In terms of the second political scenario, the Communications group reported concern over *the control the IT group had in regulating portal development*. The IT group oversaw the budget for the enterprise portal and had influence over the final decision on the services and features the portal provided. The Communications group saw the portal as communications vehicle and did not agree with the technology-focus that the IT department promoted for the portal.

> Informant: "The portal is not really within Communications. It is really at the end of the day owned by the CIO, because they have the contract and engage [a third-party service provider] to maintain the servers and host the servers etc."

***

Informant: "The portal is owned by the IT organization... within the CIO's office. It's actually an adjunct of their [desktop standardization initiatives] program. So the strategies overall for the portal are still driven out of the CIO's office, and we [in Communications] are seen as one of the key stakeholders because we manage communications on the day-to-day content... They're the ones who decide the strategies. We influence them, but we don't own them."

Interviewer: "Is this a major problem? Is this a barrier?"

Informant: "Yes. In my opinion it is because they think about the site based on technology and based on its impact on e-mail. They see it as a piece of infrastructure and they treat it like a piece of infrastructure. We would prefer to treat it like a living breathing environment to the view that as the site continues to evolve and more and more people get access and the [standardization] project finishes and everybody has standardized access, this is the site where everyone should be. This is the place on-line, this is the virtual world that employees should be living and breathing and interacting in. So seen as a piece of infrastructure devalues its real purpose and treating it like a piece of infrastructure devalues its real purpose. It also tends to stagnate it because then... if you treat it like a living, breathing environment it's organic... you make changes as they're required, on an on-going basis rather than locking yourself into arbitrary development cycles... the old IT model... which is what we are locked into now... In my opinion... the way that it is done currently is problematic because in the end what the CIO says, goes. So, if he wants to turn the entire site into a rag to promote the CIO's mandates, that's exactly what will happen to it, as has happened recently, because they hold the purse strings. So we don't pay for all the stuff that happens on the portal, the CIO's office does. And that is problematic... It means that we deal with some interesting political issues."

On the other hand, the IT group felt the Communications people did not comprehend or consider technical constraints and limitations that impact portal design and enhancements to the system. According to one IT informant, Communications viewed "everything being on the portal" without any regard to the technical feasibility of doing that. This informant did concede that the IT group was the real owner of the portal since the group controlled the portal's purse-strings and acknowledged the influence the IT group had over final design decisions regarding the portal.

Two informants from Communications felt a democratic steering committee would be a more appropriate mechanism from which to manage portal development. The informants described the steering committee as a council composed of content representatives from various parts of the organization. They envisioned this committee as a mechanism by which various portal stakeholders across the company could be involved in a democratic decision-making process where modifications to the system and changes to its general strategic direction were collectively agreed upon. The informants felt that doing so would help ease tensions between portal content stakeholders.

> <u>Informant</u>: "As the portal evolves, there will be other partners that come to the table, like Purchasing or Provisioning.... Finance. When we start adding stuff like on-line expense reporting and bill consolidation etc... You know, I see the portal really as an electronic mirror, to some extent, of the company itself. There's not one group or department that owns the company. We all contribute in our various ways to its on-going management and development throughout various aspects. I think that the portal will evolve in sort of the same way. At the end of the day, there will be a council that steers it, and as the over-all owners ... the CIO will manage the vendor relationship in terms of its up-keep, maintenance, and how it's hosted... but it's becoming more of a collaborative partnership with various entities and stakeholders internally... it can't be one group, or department, or individual that's the owner [of the portal] at the end of the day. Because it has to be more collaborative team approach as a subset of the business itself... because that is how it will evolve. It just won't be a Communications tool or just an IT platform for certain on-line applications. It will be more than that. It will be an on-line community. It will be our on-line business."

***

> <u>Informant</u>: "If I were to design the portal according to my own utopian ideal, everybody should be a player... It would follow the model of a lot of the banks and large manufacturing companies are starting to follow, which is they pull together... they create a department which is literally new media or e-business and they people it with usability architects, IT people, Communications people etc. etc. And they've a dual reporting structure. So you'll report into your group but you also, you mainly report into that e-business group. And it recognizes the importance of all the business strategies, external and internal, and because you're outside of a specific business unit, it's easier to stay corporate focused and stay focused on what the whole thing is about which is creating the right e-business environments rather than trying to create a business environment based only on Communications or trying to create a business environment based on only an IT mindset to it, which is problematic because of the political aspects of it."

Though a promising idea, the actuality of establishing such a steering committee may prove difficult to achieve. This difficulty lies in reaching consensus among the various portal stakeholder members. The following excerpt from one of the Communications informants speaks to this difficulty.

Interviewer: "Are there any problems you perceive in terms of establishing policies and guidelines for portal development?"

Informant: "Achieving consensus amongst the stakeholders as to what those policies and guidelines will be."

Interviewer: "Why is that difficult?"

Informant: "Well, Communications..., for example, takes more of a user approach. What does the user want and content approach. IT looks at it more from a network and application perspective and just a general tech side.... How long does the page take to download? How stable is the server? Is it secure within the firewall? That sort of .... That's the emphasis they take. So you have different needs and desires and different mind sets coming to the table. So consensus is needed. Sometimes it's easy and sometimes it just takes a little bit of work. Sometimes politics and ego are involved. Even within Communications and the Communications groups, the IT folks... there's different opinions amongst those people too."

To recap the results of the author's case study investigation, the information environment was found to exhibit an influencing effect on portal adoption and use. As this case study illustrates, these effects can impact how employees respond and react to the introduction of a portal. Overall, the case study helps illustrate how three components of the information environment of firms, namely the information culture of the firm, the portal development process, and information politics affect portal adoption and use. The next subsection furthers this discussion by examining other works which explore information environmental concerns. From there, recommendations on the design and deployment of knowledge portal systems are made.

4.4   Towards Healthy Information Environments

4.4.1 Other Supporting Case Studies

The author's case study highlights how various components of a firm's information environment have an influencing effect on portal design, employee perceptions of the portal, and ultimately end-user adoption. Other case study investigations of organizational intranet implementations, described below, reaffirm and substantiate the effect of these components on portal use. Together, in conjunction with the author's own case study, they provide growing and mounting evidence for the need to support healthy information contexts in firms if portals are to thrive and flourish.

For example, Scheepers and Rose (2001) describe their own case study investigation of the key implementation challenges associated with the introduction of an enterprise portal in a South African telecommunications company. To collect their data, they conducted semi-structured interviews and held informal discussions with a range of organizational workers having various associations with the intranet from end user to senior executive.

The analysis of the data elicited two contradictory accounts. One was a rational description of the portal as a staged information systems project exhibiting Cooper and Zmud's (1990) defined stages of technological diffusion, namely: initiation, adoption, adaptation, acceptance, routinization, and infusion. Here, a central IT services group rolled out the intranet system in a typical systems development fashion. The other was an alternate 'version of the truth' that uncannily draws parallels to the author's own research investigation.

For instance, Scheepers and Rose found evidence of 'island intranet sites' or 'child Webs' (Bhattacherjee, 1998) identical to the 'undernets' concept mentioned in the author's case study. These internal Web site developments took place in an *ad hoc*, informal fashion, outside the auspices of the central IT services group.

Another instance was the need expressed by organizational workers to have an area in the portal where they could share ideas and thoughts in a public space without fear of reprisals and critical judgements. At the South African case study site, those workers at the lower end of the company's organizational structure liked the ability to post anonymous messages to a company-wide bulletin board coined 'The Wall'. One manager did not like its negative tone and considered it of no value. He referred to the bulletin board as 'The Wailing Wall', but the feature had become so well embedded in practice that it could not be closed down.

An intranet case study investigation by Stenmark (2002c; 2003) at Volvo Car International also substantiates the author's case study results. Volvo was similar to the author's case study site in that both organizations applied tight management controls over the development and roll-out of the portal but found that the portal had become poorly integrated into everyday work practice.

In Stenmark's study, 21 participants from managerial and non-managerial ranks in the company were interviewed on their intranet usage and perceptions. These interviews were transcribed and analysed by a small research team. Again, some parallels to the author's own investigation are apparent.

For example, at Volvo the content of the intranet was populated with mainly formal information edited and approved by intranet content staff. Thus the portal did not facilitate the sharing of informal ideas and documents. This was not a problem with workers in close proximity to one another, but was a concern for remote portal users in that they felt it difficult to share information with others and make sense of the information they did receive.

Another similar finding was that strict adherence to guidelines and policies stifled end user adoption of the technology. Such controls were found to repress the openness and malleability inherent in the use of Web technology outside of organizations. Stenmark also found evidence of the need for some control over how information was posted. For example, respondents at Volvo suggested that information be collected and organized on different organizational layers and then channelled through to a small set of intranet gatekeepers with sufficient training in corporate information policies to guarantee the quality of the posted information. This dual need for control and looseness in portal design was also evident in the author's own case study findings.

4.4.2 A Balanced Approach to Managing Knowledge Portals

Together, these case study investigations of enterprise portal use point to the social reality of gaining portal infusion in companies. The difficulties in doing so are less about technical issues or financial constraints, and more about social concerns. Though social challenges can impede any information systems implementation, this is particularly true of knowledge portals. Unlike traditional IT applications in the past, which tended to be centrally-administered and targeted to homogenous localized user communities, knowledge portals are a new breed of information system requiring healthy information environments.

First, as Web information systems, they "require people to think about them much differently than traditional systems" (Isakowitz, Bieber and Vitali, 1998, p. 79). Due to their underlying network infrastructure and common browser interface, they are defined by unique characteristics of 'superconnectivity' (Turoff and Hiltz, 1998) and ubiquitousness (Lyytinen, Rose and Welke, 1998) which enable these systems with a greater potential to change daily organizational life.

Second, they support a wider range of users. Due to their rapid proliferation, employees from any department or level of the company have access to the portal. As a result, portal users tend to be more diverse, coming from different backgrounds and having a wider range of information needs and familiarity with computers.

Third, portals have a stronger grassroots appeal than typical systems applications. This appeal leads to greater engagement and participation with these systems where users tend to be more knowledgeable of what these systems are capable of delivering and possess a heightened awareness and concern over how such systems are designed and implemented in their own organizations.

Last, in contrast to traditional IT applications, the introduction of a knowledge portal into a firm involves numerous organizational units and role players (Scheepers, 1999) and weaves together an intricate distribution of existing communication and information technologies into one rich medium (Dahlbom, 1996).

Due to these unique requirements, the typical rational approach to the management of information systems in organizations is not solely conducive to the management of enterprise portal systems. Approaching enterprise portal implementations with a traditional managerial mindset may be the reason why some of these systems do not become organizationally embedded (Scheepers and Rose, 2001). Rather, a balance between looseness and structure in the management of enterprise portals is warranted.

This philosophy is advocated by Stenmark in his case study investigation at Volvo. He argues that strict management control is a contributing factor to low intranet usage and that the common assumption that corporate intranets need to be tightly and centrally managed in order to be useful is erroneous (Stenmark, 2003). He points to the example of the World Wide Web as a Web-based system characterized by a lack of structure and control that is avidly thriving and well-utilized. In fact, he argues that the absence of control and formal hierarchies is one of the design principles underpinning the Internet and is a significant contributing factor that has propelled the popularity of this medium.

Extending this argument to 'intranet-supported knowledge creation' environments, Stenmark identifies seven enabling factors for creativity (no preconceptions, autonomy, serendipity, diverse stimuli, rich information provision, internal communication, and motivation) and concludes that intranets are most likely to contribute in this regard by providing a variety of information in dynamic and 'unmanaged' environments. According to Stenmark (2002b), to support creativity and knowledge creation in dynamic and inter-linked environments, companies may have to adopt a different approach to their intranets and abandon the traditional view more suited for stable information technologies. This necessitates a certain amount of 'letting go of control', which he acknowledges is still a rare intranet management method actively sponsored and pursued by corporate officials today.

Stenmark bases this insight on the theoretical contributions of Ciborra and Hanseth (2000) who critique the centrality of control strongly advocated within the management literature concerned with the management of IT infrastructure. Here, IT infrastructure is defined as "a set of shared, tangible, IT resources that provide a foundation to enable present and future business applications" (Duncan, 1995, pp. 39-40). It consists of IT components, human IT infrastructure such as people and skills, shared IT services, and shared applications (Weill and Broadbent, 1998). Borrowing terminology from actor network theory, Ciborra (2000a) argues that an 'under-managed' approach to IT infrastructure is warranted and that a more controlled method does not always work. Specifically, infrastructures can be understood as formative contexts where the tensions between technology inscriptions (i.e., the way technical artefacts embody patterns of use and define the roles to be played by users and infrastructure) and the process of translation (i.e., the social process of continuous negotiation between actors in order to achieve social order) cause the installed infrastructure base to drift.

Utilizing Ciborra's concept of 'infrastructure as formative context' as a theoretical lens, Stenmark (2003) finds evidence why intranets tend to drift out of control and become underutilized. He concludes that intranet management is too centred on control as the supreme management objective and calls for a decentralized vision of the management of intranets to harness the open-ended purpose for which the Web was initially designed. Stenmark's results align with Ciborra's (2000b) own case study account of an internal Web site initiative at Hoffman-La Roche which showcased how decentralized and localized methods, and not strong top-down management approaches, secured the expansion and use of Hoffman-La Roche's intranet system.

The need for a decentralized approach to the management of portals is supported by Cooper and Zmud (1990). Though these authors propose a rational technological diffusion approach to IT innovations in organizations, they acknowledge that "rational decision models may be useful in explaining information technology adoption, political and learning models may be more useful when examining infusion" (p. 123). Here, infusion is said to occur when the technological innovation is used with the organization to its fullest potential.

This argument is also supported by Scheepers and Rose (2001), who recognize the complementary rather than the contradictory nature of rational and political approaches to information systems management. Adopting a socio-technical stance, these authors draw attention to how a rational, structured, top-down approach to the management of portals in organizations as a means of securing coordination and control in the intranet implementation process may circumvent or stifle user creativity. Further, it can deter end user establishment of new departmental Web sites, leaving the portal with insufficient linkage to information content to attract further users.

> "Such an approach could deny the many local, child-level intranet initiatives, which may already be flourishing unofficially. In fact these informal efforts can actually predate the formal intranet and a heavy-handed top-down management approach may leave the pioneers of these efforts feeling alienated" (Scheepers and Rose, 2001, p. 12).

On the other hand, these authors also recognize the benefits of coordinating control in portal development and suggest that IT managers do not relinquish their responsibility and leave the enterprise portal to grow wildly. Doing so,

"can rapidly result in a proliferating mess of unrelated intranet developments, useless content, information overload and even network congestion. Such a managerial approach also hold the danger that planned intranet initiatives become diluted in the process, since the seamless nature of the technology can have a ripple effect on the perception of the whole intranet community. For example, organization-wide intranet searches that reveal outdated information or broken hyperlinks on some sites can quickly lead to a general distrust of the intranet and prompt a user to revert to alternative information sources" (Scheepers and Rose, 2001, p. 12).

Duane and Finnegan (2003) provide insight on ways to managing user empowerment and control in enterprise portal environments. Based on empirical evidence from their intranet investigation at Hewlett Packard in Ireland, these authors chart the evolution of an enterprise portal as a six-stage model and recommend the implementation of specific controls at particular stages in the evolution of a portal as a means of balancing the need to enforce control and promote user empowerment. The authors caution that not doing so may negate any attempt to independently instil controls or promote user empowerment with these systems.

4.4.3 Recommendations

So given these arguments, what can be done in organizations to create healthy information environments—ones that facilitate the utilization of enterprise portals for knowledge creation, distribution, and use?

Scheepers and Rose (2001) give three recommendations. The first is to *balance control and individual ownership*. That is, to find a balance between an organized, direct control over the management of a portal and fostering individual interest and initiatives relating to the portal that feed local developments. Too much control and individual interests die; too little control and portal chaos results. The end result in either case is portal stagnation. To address this need for balance, Scheepers and Rose call for a continual evaluation of the appropriateness and timeliness of managerial interventions.

The second is the need to *cultivate the portal as a medium* rather than managing it as a system which treats IT innovation as constant and homogenous. Scheepers and Rose warn against regarding enterprise portals as homogenous systems that can be controlled with corporate standards and policies. Rather these authors concur that the portal

"should be conceptualized and managed as a connection medium (Dahlbom, 1996) that consists of a mosaic of related components (with decentralized ownership), each evolving over time and space... [To do this] would demand a more collaborative and facilitative managerial style that acknowledges diversity and individual contributions." (Scheepers and Rose, 2001, p. 13)

The third is to *aim towards a self-sustaining portal*. This, according to Scheepers and Rose, could include incorporating 'killer applications' on the portal that induce and sustain usage and content creation, ensuring top management sponsorship and funding, providing an established network and computing infrastructure, and securing requisite technical expertise. It could also require organizational coordination and control mechanisms, such as Web councils and steering groups, that are facilitative and inclusive of representative user groups. For example, loosely-coupled departments with individual 'undernets' may better fare with a decentralized portal responsibility where decisions made about the portal are devolved to unit levels (Bhattacherjee, 1998). As well, as the portal becomes more pervasive throughout the organization, Web councils and steering groups should concern themselves with items such as information policies, content guidelines, and standards pertaining to the look and feel of Web pages (Damsgaard and Scheepers, 1999), again paying attention to the timing of such managerial interventions.

Detlor (2001) identifies certain steps an organization can undertake to foster the utilization of an enterprise portal from an information ecology perspective. First, *a democratic portal steering committee* can be established to help promote a portal design that meets the requirements of a more diverse user population and balance tensions between information content and technology perspectives. Second, *a more streamlined system development process* can be created by which modifications to a portal can be made. Third, in agreement with the above discussion, *control over portal technical standards and information content* can be loosened to encourage greater participant acceptance of these systems and help support the free flow and exchange of ideas, thoughts, and perspectives needed for the generation of new insights and ways of doing things.

It is argued that following these recommendations would lead to healthier and more supportive information environments that foster knowledge creation, distribution, and use. A healthy and supportive information environment would be one that promotes consensus and negotiation among portal information stakeholders, that tolerates a certain lack of control over portal content and design guidelines, that encourages the freedom to post and share information without fear of reprisal, and that provides a robust and sufficient staff complement of both technical and content specialists who can respond to and expedite relevant portal changes in a timely fashion.

One of the goals of this chapter is to raise awareness of the need for system designers to pay attention to such recommendations in the development and deployment of knowledge portal systems. That is, portal designers must be made aware of the situational information contexts in which knowledge portals are utilized, and to use these insights to devise ways of fostering healthy and supportive information environments that promote portal adoption and use.

Such a perspective goes a step beyond the traditional call for a strategic information management approach to the governance of knowledge resources within a company. For example, Typanski (1999) cautions that for information environments to be truly effective, an organization's resources (comprising both databases and people) need to align with the firm's goals and strategies. Though rational and logical in its approach, it fails to consider the social components inherent in any organizational information environment. Politics are at play. Stakeholder needs must be addressed. Fear of reprisals are a reality. The desire for knowledge workers to have a certain amount of independence and control in the design and management of their own information resources is a necessity to secure buy-in and acceptance of any larger corporate information management plan. Rather than trying to address problems of separated, fragmented information services that "do not have compatible objectives, goals, and structures—let alone compatible information technologies" (Typanski, 1999, p. 33), this chapter suggests that looser controls are needed and warranted to secure effective information environments.

One way for loosening controls in organizations is to create flexible and accommodating firm-wide information policies that offer employees certain guidelines pertaining to Web site development and portal content, but that do not restrict or stifle individual creativity or motivation to post new content or create new Web sites. Here, information polices are plans which guide the development of information resources, services and systems that maximize the use of information by individuals and institutions (Dosa, 1976; Montviloff, 1990) and are a key component of an organization's information environment (Bergeron, 1996; Davenport, 1997). Some organizations have specifically adapted their information policies to address Web information systems (Dufour and Bergeron, 2002). Based on the results of the case studies of enterprise portal use presented in this chapter, such policies should reflect the need for some looseness and flexibility in order to secure Web information system adoption, especially for those organizations wishing to utilize their systems for the promotion of knowledge work. Further, such policies need to be clearly articulated to organizational workers (Wild, Griggs, and Downing, 2002). Doing so can help develop organizational norms and values that support the creation and sharing of knowledge (Davenport, DeLong, and Beers, 1998).

4.5 Conclusion

This chapter focused on the information environment in which knowledge portal use is situated. The goal was to investigate and ponder the aspects or characteristics of an organization's information environment which inhibit or promote the utilization of enterprise portals for knowledge work. A detailed description was given on the theoretical components comprising organizational information environments. The author's case study results were presented to illustrate the impacts a firm's organizational culture, information system development processes, and politics have on the final adoption and use of a portal by organizational workers. Other case study investigations of intranet use in organizations substantiated the author's case study findings. From these, several recommendations were made on ways of helping organizations create healthy information environments within their own firms. Foremost was the need to balance looseness and structure in terms of the control placed over the development and design of portal functionality and content, especially if these systems are to support and foster knowledge work activities.

Having explored the user and information environment components of the Knowledge Portal Framework in detail in Chapters 2 and 3, the next chapter examines the last component comprising this framework: the portal's information design. This chapters deals with the display and presentation of information content on the knowledge portal interface. As the next chapter will illustrate, a portal's information design plays an important role in the extent to which the portal is utilized for knowledge creation, distribution, and use activities.

5. INFORMATION DESIGN AND KNOWLEDGE PORTALS

5.1 Introduction

This chapter discusses the knowledge portal interface in terms of its information design. It concentrates on the third shaping entity of the author's Knowledge Portal Framework presented in Chapter 2. To start, a definition and description of the information design construct is given. From there, results of the author's case study investigation are reported. Specifically, discussion involves the need to personalize information displayed on the portal, to deliver quality information that is sufficiently organized and intriguingly engaging, and to support collaborative tools. These results are compared and contrasted to other research findings in the literature. The objective is to give a holistic examination and discussion on the importance of information design in knowledge portal systems.

One major learning from this discussion is the need to tailor the display of information on the knowledge portal interface to support different modes of information seeking behaviour. A separate research investigation by the author in the electronic shopping domain examines user preferences for Web-based information display across browsing and searching tasks. The study's results imply the need to focus not only on goal-directed search in Web site information design, but also on non-directed browsing tasks as well.

A common thread throughout this chapter is the need to present information in ways that signal the value of information to users and that support their modes of information seeking activity. It is argued that these two points are key requisites in the design of effective knowledge portal systems. Enterprise portals which support knowledge creation, distribution, and use would be ones that are sensitive to the role human cognition plays in information processing and to the information tasks that lead users to utilize these systems in the first place. Such enterprise portals would respond with information designs that display information in ways that make information sufficiently accessible and noticeable to users, and that match or address the specific tasks for which users turn to the portal for help.

5.2 What is Information Design?

Information design is "the art and science of preparing information so that it can be used by human beings with efficiency and effectiveness" (Horn, 2000, p. 15). It is "the activity of developing representations of complex data and knowledge in ways that facilitate the analysis of information and maximize its potential value to users" (Leonidas, 2000).

According to Horn (2000), there are three primary components to information design: 1) to make information comprehensible; 2) to facilitate human interaction with the technology housing information; and 3) to support wayfinding.

Horn's *first component* deals with the importance of presenting information in ways that make information better understood. In this sense, the objective is to enhance user comprehensibility and to provide a means for translating information into effective action. Doing so, tightly aligns the purpose of information presentation with the transmission of knowledge.

Recall back in Chapter 1 where knowledge was defined as 'comprehended' or 'actionable' information. Assuming the worthiness and value of such a definition, the link between good information presentation and knowledge transfer becomes apparent. Good information design has a direct link to effective knowledge transfer in that information presentation becomes a vehicle by which information can be made actionable to users by being better understood. In terms of knowledge portals—systems which facilitate the creation, distribution, and use of knowledge throughout the enterprise—this tie becomes paramount. Information presentation no longer remains an optional nicety or something Web designers ought to do. Rather, it becomes a critical and vital means by which to signal the potential worthiness of pieces of information presented to organizational knowledge workers through the portal interface.

This viewpoint is supported by Taylor (1986) in his 'value-added approach' to information system development. Taylor, recognizing the importance of information presentation in the display of system outputs on the computer interface or 'negotiation space', suggests the merit of an information system is determined by its success in signalling the potential value of information to users (i.e., how successful it is in making users cognitively aware of the usefulness of the information displayed on the interface). Central to this position is the belief that an information message only carries the potential for value and it is the user, in his or her situated context, who has the ability to assign value to a given information message. Viewing the value of information in this way encourages the creation of value-added processes and features in system design which enhance the potential usefulness of information messages.

Thus, through his value-added approach, Taylor raises awareness of the need to be concerned with how information is presented and displayed in systems design. Such *information traits* are "the special attributes that can be used to define the ways that information can be identified and presented" (MacMullin and Taylor, 1984, p. 98). Specifically MacMullin and Taylor (pp. 99-102) identify nine information trait continuums: 1) quantitative continuum (i.e., from quantitative to qualitative); 2) data continuum (i.e., from hard to soft data); 3) temporal continuum (i.e., historical, current, forecast); 4) solution continuum (i.e., from single to multiple solutions); 5) focus continuum (i.e., from precise to diffuse information); 6) specificity of use continuum (i.e., from applied to theoretical); 7) substantive continuum (i.e., from operational to descriptive); 8) aggregation continuum (i.e., from clinical to aggregated census information); and, 9) causal/diagnostic continuum (i.e., from why to what is happening).

The author himself finds evidence of predominant information trait patterns desired by organizational users of Internet-based information systems (Detlor, 2003). His case study results suggest that certain information trait patterns are associated with specific Web-based problem situation scenarios of search, browse, and exploration activity. For instance, all three of these problem situation scenarios require hard, precise, and current information to be displayed on the Web interface. However, users in a browsing or exploratory mode are found also to need diffuse, multiple-solutioned information. These findings suggest that different situations of Web use warrant different, and perhaps unique, information trait patterns. As a result, the findings hint at the feasibility of matching the display and presentation of information to the situated contexts in which Web-based information systems are used as means of improving the utilization of these systems.

Horn's *second component* of information design concerns itself with the ease with which humans interact with the technology housing the information in question. The goal is to keep this interaction natural and pleasant as possible. This branch of information design falls under the domain of human computer interaction. Typical concerns here concentrate on the overall usability of an information system, such as its response time, its intuitiveness, and its ease-of-use.

The difficulty is figuring out how to do this. According to Cooley (2000), there are nine human-centered characteristics inherent in information systems which support good information design. The first is coherence which calls for rendering things visible, where embedded meanings are apparent and evident, not cloaked or obscure.

The second is inclusiveness where the system invites the user to be part of a community of activities with which the user is familiar and on friendly terms.

The third is malleability which is a feature of the system which allows a user to sculpt and adapt the system interface to suit his or her own situation, information needs, and aesthetic preferences.

The fourth is engagement which gives the user a sense of being invited to participate in the interaction with a system and creates a feeling that the system is empathetic towards the user's needs.

The fifth is ownership which establishes user feelings of belonging and responsibility over the creation of parts of the system.

The sixth is responsiveness where the system appears to respond to a user's requirements, needs, and ways of doing things, and makes visible the rules or underlying workings of the system and encourages the user to learn and adapt these rules at will.

The seventh is purpose where the system is capable of responding to the purpose or intent the user has in mind.

The eighth is panoramic in that the system fosters the user towards a wider set of activities or to operate within a wider context or view of the world.

The last is transcendence where the system encourages and entices the user to go beyond or transcend his or her immediate task or purpose of using the system.

Horn's *third component* of information design applies to the extent to which a system's information structure allows or enables people to find their way through it. The term 'wayfinding' is borrowed from the field of architecture and generally applies to the degree to which people can easily navigate themselves through an urban space. Wayfinding is also a term associated with the cognitive and behavioural sciences with respect to the psychological process of how people achieve space orientation, sometimes referred to as cognitive mapping (Passini, 2000). A typical example of wayfinding in an architectural sense is the use of colour-coded lines painted on hospital walls to help people orient and navigate their way through a maze of hospital wings and wards.

In Web-based environments, wayfinding refers more to the ease with which users can self-navigate through a virtual space. Passini (2000, p. 90) identifies three principal user tasks in navigating a setting or space from its main points of access to its key destination zones (areas where people perform certain functions of interest). Applying these principals to Web-based environments, an information design that supports wayfinding would be one that assists users going from main access points of a Web site such as it home page to key destination zones such as sub-pages within the site, traversing from one destination zone to another, and circulating within a specific destination zone.

Adopting Horn's view of information design as a mechanism for comprehensibility, human computer interaction, and wayfinding enables a more holistic understanding of the term. With respect to this monograph, information design is an umbrella concept representing and combining many information-related sub-fields: graphic design, technical communication, computer interface design, and information architecture.

Graphic design, a skill taught in art schools and crafted in advertising firms, is concerned with the style, fashion, novelty and impact of information on users. Technical communication, the realm of document writers, advocates clarity, precision, legibility, comprehensibility, and simplicity in the communication of information to others. Traditionally, these two fields are often at odds with each other. Computer interface design, the domain of systems engineers and usability experts, concentrates on the flow and human interaction with computerized information displays. Information architecture, a new and emerging field of study, is primarily concerned with the structure of Web sites in terms of the relationships between Web pages and the paths with which users can take among those pages (Lamar, 2001; Rosenfeld and Morville, 1998). It is an area of investigation that pertains to a systematic and primarily visual approach to the organization of and access to content on Web sites (Toms, 2002).

Treating the term information design as an umbrella concept enables a holistic understanding of this important concept. Incorporating the ideas presented above, this chapter defines *information design* as the effective and efficient presentation of information on Web spaces as a means of raising awareness of the potential usefulness or value of the information displayed to users.

In this respect, information design is a vehicle to assist users in their sense making behaviour (Dervin, 2000). It is about enabling people to interpret and re-interpret information presented to them as a means of fostering knowledge creation, distribution, and use. As such, information design is not only about the transmission of facts to users, but also about helping people interpret the meaning behind the information presented to them.

"Information design cannot treat information as a mere thing to be economically and effectively packaged for distribution. Rather... information design is, in effect, metadesign: design about design, design to assist people to make and unmake their own informations [knowledge], their own sense... this theory of information design decrees that we create an information system to assist people in designing their own information and, in particular, in sharing with each other the ways in which they have struggled individually and collectively to both create order out of chaos and create chaos out of order when order restricts or constrains them... The system would allow not only the factizing that permits regimentation as a sometimes useful way of making sense but also the myths and storytelling that permit us to tolerate and muddle through diversities and seeming incompletenesses." (Dervin, 2000. p. 43)

Adopting such an interpretive perspective, information design can be perceived as having a two-fold purpose: one of personal enlightenment or edification, and one of mutual change or commutativity (Jacobson, 2000). According to Jacobson (p. 1), "contemporary information designers seek to edify more than persuade, to exchange ideas rather than foist them on us."

In the author's opinion, this should also be the goal of information design in knowledge portals. As the results from the author's case study investigation presented below illustrate, improper information design in enterprise portal systems can fail to enlighten workers and prevent these systems from mutually affecting or changing people's perceptions of the world. Doing so can limit the extent to which portals can be utilized for knowledge work.

5.3 Knowledge Portal Case Study Results

The author's case study described in Chapter 2 highlights the importance of information design in facilitating organizational knowledge work. During the field investigation, participants were forthcoming in identifying the features and functions they preferred in the portal interface and the ones that they felt needed improvement in terms of helping them create, distribute, and use organizational knowledge.

Basically, participants gave a long list of 'likes' and 'dislikes' concerning the enterprise portal system they used. A thorough analysis of this data led to the identification of the more salient characteristics of the portal interface design that impacted the degree to which the system was utilized for knowledge work. The major categories derived from this analysis were as follows: the tailorability of the systems to specific information needs; the quality of the information presented to users with respect to its relevancy, reliability, and timeliness; the organization and access of this information in terms of an in-depth categorization schema and robust search directory; the inclusion of collaborative applications to facilitate the sharing of documents and communication among workers; and the engagement of these systems through the provision of an interactive and attractive interface to support work practice.

In terms of *tailorability*, participants identified the need to be able to personalize the information content displayed on a portal so that the information matched more closely to the personal interests and needs of individual workers. For example, one participant expressed the need to customize information presented in the enterprise portal in a manner similar to that currently available on consumer portal sites, such as *MyYahoo!*:

> Participant: "I like to see some more specific information geared towards my interests. I mean, we see [consumer] portals now... they're catering... they're tailoring information to whomever's going in. If my interests are whatever... if I'm a business analyst, why don't I get business analyst news piped to my own personal Web page? Why is the portal a static Web page? Why can't it be a customized Web page for everyone going in? It's being done by millions of people everyday on the Net."

Further, another participant indicated a desire to personalize the portal interface so that the system would present its information and applications in a manner that facilitated the participant's preferences and provide a means of accessing frequently visited sites. He specifically wanted the portal to remember his common patterns of Web navigation and to prompt him whether the system should expedite his traversal to specific sites of interest:

> Participant: "I want it to remember that I've been there and my preferences... I shouldn't have to come back every time and rearrange and jump all the way. If I frequently work my way through the menu over to, I don't know what, I should get prompted when I get in 'Is there where you want to go?'. Yep. Wham, you're over there."

With respect to *information quality*, several participants expressed the need for Web information systems to provide information that was relevant, reliable, and timely so that people could keep up-to-date in personal areas of expertise and stay abreast of current happenings. Many saw this as being critical in supporting their on-going learning in areas of personal interest, distribution of this knowledge to others in the organization, and utilization of this knowledge in their daily work practice.

For example, participants indicated a desire for the portal to provide information that was relevant to their daily work. One of the most common reasons participants gave when asked why they did not utilize the enterprise portal or departmental Web sites to a larger extent was that they found these systems did not provide the information or access to information that was needed.

A number of participants thought improvements could be made in the delivery of news information. For instance, one participant found the daily news feed on the portal to be inadequate in providing timely information that was of relevance to her. To counter this inadequacy, the participant went to a newswire site off the World Wide Web to get more current news items. She agreed that the current rate at which news was updated on the portal may satisfy a more general user, but that it did not satisfy her own personal requirements. To increase the relevancy of the news available from the portal, another participant thought that background information should accompany each news items to help readers understand the item and it implications or impact on the company. Another participant wanted more variety of news information. The strict emphasis on telecommunication happenings was too narrow in her opinion. She would prefer to see more news relating to events and activities internal to the organization:

> Interviewer: "Anything else you would like to see changed on the portal?"
>
> Participant: "I'd say more interesting stuff... and more variety. You know... again, instead of just this straight business thing like 'Sprint is doing this' or 'so and so has this new telephone' or 'so and so has these long distance rates'... more

of what's going on [inside the company] and more articles about what various departments have done."

One participant requested reliable information to be posted on the portal. In general, this user did not agree with the general tone and currency of the information posted on the portal, which led to distrust of the system:

Participant: "It's very fluffy. Very fluffy. Even if I was looking for corporate information, a lot of the time it's so politically correct, so dodging the main point that you get turned off by it... And a lot of the articles are dated. It's like old. 'Our latest this' and I'm like 'Oh, well I heard about that already... from another outside source... two weeks ago!'."

Complaints about the timeliness and reliability of information were not restricted to the enterprise portal. For instance, one participant had concerns over the timeliness of posted information on a departmental Web site. Another participant remained sceptical of the information available on external Web sites in that it may be biased or out-of-date.

In terms of the *organization and access* to information, there was a general consensus among participants to have better mechanisms for finding information and navigating to frequently utilized Web pages on the enterprise portal. Typical statements made by participants were as follows:

Interviewer: "What changes would you like to see made to the corporate portal?"

Participant: "Easier access to it. Like easier... like there's too many screens. Like the HR [Human Resources] Web site, to get in to it... I'm sure you could set your bookmarks and that, but it seems like there's so many screens you have to go through before you reach the one that you need. Or if you could type in a word so that it could bring you straight to that section."

***

Participant: "I think all those frequently accessed Web sites should be somewhere in the collection of everyday activities or at least frequently accessed Web sites should be a button or something or a very easy way to get all of them together... I would suggest that these things be put together in a collection somewhere of most frequently accessed Web sites in an easy accessed place."

One participant lamented the problem of tracking down information posted on a departmental Web site that had been changed:

Participant: "As a matter of fact, there was one episode like that. I had sometime previously got to a place where I saw a valuable perspective and complete perspective of the company. And they ended up changing it... the Web site got changed. So that perspective which I found valuable ended up sort of disappearing. Then it was browse around trying to find it. Not good though, right? It shouldn't be happening. Either you should get a better perspective, or somebody else didn't think that was valuable or who knows what... I don't know. It went from being able to locate it... where it had been before... to down in the woodwork indirectly through this site map."

Another participant had concerns on the difficulty in navigating across various departmental Web sites in that many did not have a mechanism to return easily to the enterprise portal home page.

Some users thought that more meaningful icon labels and improved positioning of the icons on the portal interface would facilitate better navigation. For example, the following quotation is from a participant who was frustrated by the placement of the e-mail icon to a sub-level with the portal and not on the portal homepage:

> Participant: "And the link to the e-mail Web page. I mean e-mail's so important to the organization now. It's difficult to find that [the e-mail icon]... where do I get into the e-mail homepage off of the portal? It's almost impossible to find."

> Interviewer: "Really?"

> Participant: "Oh yeah. Right now it's 3 or 4 layers down. You have to go into Help, blah blah blah. Earlier, on the last version of the portal, it was simply click on the icon [on the portal homepage]. I understood that real estate on that homepage is valuable but so is e-mail!"

Another user thought navigation could be improved if newly-posted information were highlighted or flagged on the link to this information from the portal. Her complaint was based on the fact that she found that she had to peruse the entire portal and various departmental Web sites to discover what had recently been added or updated.

Many navigation problems stemmed from the implementation of a new version of the enterprise portal. Several users were frustrated since the redesign caused them difficulty in tracking down information in a way that they previously had been familiar with or that links to departmental Web sites were removed on the new version of the portal:

> Participant: "I mean I had the same problem that most people have... to learn where to find everything quickly. You know, we develop that point and shoot mentality.. you know, it's up in the top left hand corner... they change it! And often when they change these things, it's radical. Completely new. I don't think any of us mind adding features or throwing in a new icon, but up it comes 3 months later and it's a brand new page. Everything's changed."

***

> Participant: "I mean I've talked to several people in my office who have been in technology for awhile and they've had to relearn... they couldn't find the

directory... one guy couldn't find the directory for 20 minutes. He's a very well-paid contractor... that's 20 minutes of his time and kind of indicative of what end-users could run into there!"

To facilitate improved information access, most participants stated a need for a more robust directory within the enterprise portal. For instance, the company's old mainframe application system was perceived as being a more robust and usable tool for directory searching since it supported search queries by functional group as opposed to exact name matches.

Interviewer: "You mentioned the directory could be better?"

Participant: "It's very slow, first of all. It's slow in two regards. It's slow to bring the information back. It's slow to complete it's search. But also it's cumbersome to go through what you have to go through to get someone's... to bring someone up... I still use [the company's old] organizational directory instead for the very reason I can search by employee number, I can search by telephone number... because sometimes you get a voice-message and someone says it's "mumble, mumble, mumble" and my number is. So you can search by number, if I don't know who it was. You can search by department. You can search by a whole bunch of things.. by title! I find it very ironic that our [old] system does a better job at that than our portal does."

Many participants commented on the difficulty in utilizing the portal search engine in terms of helping them find the information they need. Their frustration centered on the inability to search across all information sources and the return of long lists of 'hits' from search queries, many of which were felt to be irrelevant and inappropriate to participant needs. Some users pondered ways to ameliorate the problems associated with portal searching. For instance, the following participant thought that searching could be improved if a descriptor were added to the hit items returned from a portal search to help differentiate the content returned. Her idea was to label the hit items with the classification categories used to organize the departmental Web sites off the portal main page:

Interviewer: "What features would you like added to the portal to increase your motivation for using it?"

Participant: "In terms of the portal, a better search engine. I find that many of the things if you search on certain words, it will find them in articles files on the intranet. But you can't tell enough from the title that it brings up of what it really is. It would be nice if it said where it located the information. Now you can sort of tell that from the URL in some cases, but it would be nice, if it just... I noticed that they had a general layout of all the departments [the classification list of sites on the company homepage]. Now if they could add that piece [of information] of which department it came from... since they laid out the site that way I assume you can."

Other participants thought a site map on the portal would help users find the information they were looking for. A few participants thought information searching could be improved on the portal if it contained hot links to frequently accessed sites. Others mentioned that a more elaborate and extensive categorization of information on the home portal page would help people wade through the vast information available and offer an alternate means of finding information other than performing a search query. For example, one participant expressed a desire for proper categorization of information content on the portal by subject category as a means of helping her navigate the site. Another user felt being able to access an index of information categories on the portal would help her locate the information she needs.

In frustration, some participants gave up on utilizing Web search tools to track down specific pieces of information and relied on contacting people to retrieve specific Web addresses. An interesting response by several participants to deal with the above mentioned navigation problems was to create bookmarks to sites containing relevant information. Many users extensively used the bookmark feature available in Netscape Communicator to maintain lists of useful and frequently visited sites—in a way, creating their own personalized portals to access the information they desired.

With respect to the inclusion of *collaborative applications*, these were considered necessary by several participants in helping them connect and share ideas and documents with other co-workers. For example, one employee thought that the enterprise portal should support an environment where people could create their own project areas to facilitate the sharing of documents, ideas, and Netscape bookmarks with other team members. Another participant suggested that the company create a shared document space to upload documents for others to view. This type of solution could solve the problem voiced by many participants of e-mail bottlenecks where different versions of a single document were routed throughout the company as e-mail attachments, causing network degradation and the overrun of e-mail inboxes across the organization.

Several participants suggested that the enterprise portal could better support collaboration if the system offered a means of helping users find other experts in the organization. This could be done through the provision of: 1) more robust organizational charts based on expertise lines rather than from a department hierarchical perspective; 2) learnings about other initiatives and projects underway throughout various parts of the company; and 3) special interest group forums that facilitate the connection and sharing of ideas among experts within the firm.

Participant: "That's the other thing, that's bizarre in here [the portal]. There's not even an org chart per se; there is a directory but an org chart of what... that's something else that could be on there... they have org charts in terms of, you know, vice-presidents and general managers... the mega ones, but if you were to go through and do a search on 'is there another documentation group somewhere?'. I haven't been able to find anything.

Interviewer "So the organization charts are fairly high level?"

Participant: "They're high level and again very business-oriented rather than expertise-oriented. They're like the business divisions. This is this project... this is that project... this person looks after this. But it doesn't really say... if you were to look at... say, find someone else who was an expert in databases, that you wanted to talk to... I haven't been able to find the capability on there that you could actually find a group of people who specialized in databases. So it's hard to find people who have the same expertise or the same interests that you have, unless you just happen to come across them."

***

Participant: "It's hard to know where the resources are in [the company] because it's such a huge company. Who does what?... Who's the expert? Who should I be dealing with? ?"

***

Participant: "I would like an overall view or an overall information on what's happening within the entire organization. Because I find that we're kind of silos... I think it would be nice if we could get a combined view of what everybody is doing... I think it would be great if all of us knew what was happening through the entire organization. You know, big successes, big wins, what are the drawbacks, where we can do better... that kind of thing."

***

Participant: "They keep saying that it's not set up yet but they're planning on it... various groups of common interests. For example, if there's a large group of technical writers... to have a mailing list or an interest group that you could get involved with... but to my knowledge they aren't real interest groups set up, unless they have individually and privately been set up... but it would be nice to have a documentation group or whatever... general interest groups. It's key. Again, I'm getting that 'one man band' feeling... it's nice to know that you're not alone."

In terms of providing an *engaging interface* through which to support organizational work practice, a sizeable portion of participants thought the portal should be more interactive, support dynamic screen updates, and support online information queries:

> Participant: "What I'm trying to say is this. The corporate portal is very read-only. It's not interactive."

***

> Participant: "What I found here is that this [portal] is just a bunch of Web pages... I want a Web page that is defined by what's in a database. So if I add more, then my page changes... my pages change... There are many examples out there of other Web sites where things dynamically change as you go along."

***

> Participant: "It would be nice if the client... our clients... that look at these results could go in and fill in a query window or menu, and then we'd have the engine in the backend pulling exactly the data they asked for. As opposed to... these are canned reports we're showing them now."

***

> Interviewer: "What type of features would you like seen added to the portal?"
>
> P11: That get people involved! Not just sit there and give you an interface. 'Here's the results that give you 10,000 items, go and find it if you like!'.

Moreover, to be an attractive and heavily-utilized application, a couple of participants and key informants thought that the portal should move beyond its current role as an information publishing or corporate communications medium and towards the facilitation of everyday work tasks and applications. For example, one participant commented as follows:

> Participant: "Why do I go here [to the portal]? Because I want to do things, but what can you do? Frankly, I don't want to search all the time... It's not a matter of searching. Searching is only a research activity. All the other things you do in your daily job, that's really where I sort of see it [the portal] going... What I believe the goal should be is all the tasks employees want to do, they do it through the portal... It [should] allow you to do all tasks you've got to do in your job. I would like it to provide a much more clear context and interface to the activities you have to perform and the information you have to use that is available there. Basically, you can't do any of your tasks with it [with the current version of the portal] because it's not designed to allow you to do tasks. It doesn't give you access to the applications that might be used in the tasks you might do."

In summary, the above case study results provide insights into the types of features and functions an enterprise portal should possess to foster knowledge creation, distribution, and use. Overall, participants from the case study investigation identified the more salient characteristics of the portal's information design that impacted the degree to which these systems can support knowledge work. These characteristics consisted of the tailorability of the portal system to specific information needs, the quality of the information presented, the organization and access of this information, the inclusion of collaborative applications, and the engagement of the portal interface in supporting work practice.

In terms of tailorability, participants at the case study site identified the need to be able to personalize the information content displayed on the portal so that the information matched more closely to user interests and needs. With respect to information quality, participants identified the need for the portal to provide information that was relevant, reliable, and timely so they could stay abreast of current happenings, keep up-to-date in personal areas of expertise, distribute their ideas and learnings to others, and utilize this information and knowledge in daily practice. In terms of organization and access, there was consensus among participants to have better mechanisms of finding and navigating information, specifically through inclusion of an in-depth categorization schema and robust search directory. With respect to collaborative applications, these were found to be desirable by participants in helping them connect with others and share ideas and documents. A need for mechanisms that helped participants find other experts in the organization was indicated, such as the provision of organizational charts based on expertise lines, information on various company initiatives and projects underway, and special interest group forums. In terms of an engaging interface, participants indicated a need for interactivity, the dynamic display of information, and the provision of applications that supported work-based tasks.

5.4 Leveraging Information Design

Based on these case study results, certain implications can be drawn on ways to improve the development and use of enterprise portals in organizations for knowledge work. In terms of information design, Web information systems can contain certain features and functions that improve the utilization of these systems for knowledge creation, distribution, and use. For instance, Web information systems can contain:

- *a robust search engine and company directory* to help employees locate information and other experts in the company;
- *a personalization mechanism* to modify the portal interface to accommodate individual information needs, uses, and preferences;
- *an extensive classification schema* of information categories to facilitate improved organization and access to information;
- *collaborative applications* such as a shareable document space and a

communication area for shared discussions; and

▪ *links to a wide variety of external information sources* on competitors, vendors, and external issues and *internal information sources* on company products and services.

Other research results presented below offer additional insights on the information design of knowledge portals.

5.4.1 Displaying Search Engine Results

There are a variety of ways in which a portal's information design can be improved to facilitate human information seeking. A common complaint identified in the author's case study was the dissatisfaction of participants with the quality of returned hits from the portal's search engine. In general, there are two means by which improvements can be made to the robustness of items retrieved by a search engine: returning higher-quality hits via better index coverage and ranking algorithms; and through the provision of information that helps users evaluate returned hit list results more quickly and accurately (Woodruff et al., 2002).

Woodruff et al. concentrate on the second approach and attempt to find a method to ameliorate the standard practice in this area of providing textual summaries of retrieved hit list items. In response, these authors purport that improvements in the information design of retrieved items displayed in a hit list may be achieved through the presentation of thumbnail images (i.e., graphical summaries of retrieved documents and/or Web pages).

These authors identify several advantages and disadvantages to each method of display. Text summaries are terse, require little storage space, download quickly, and provide valuable information about each retrieved document or Web page, such as its URL, title, size, and a few phrases or sentences that summarize the document or highlight search keywords. However, text summaries do not show images contained in the retrieved item or Web page, nor provide much information about its layout, and are tiring to read through and process. On the other hand, thumbnail images typically require more storage space, download more slowly, and are not as convenient in terms of summarizing information content. Despite these misgivings, thumbnails do provide information about the genre, layout, and style of the retrieved item, can help users recognize the item or classify it, and most importantly, since humans can process graphical information much more quickly than information that is textually-based, do all this at greatly enhanced speeds.

Related work in the Information Studies field offers evidence of the differences in the effectiveness of various document representations. Historically, several studies conclude that document representations do affect a user's judgement of the relevance of a document to his or her information needs (Kent et al., 1967; Saracevic, 1969; 1971; Marcus, Kugel, and Benenfeld, 1978; Janes, 1991). In particular, these studies suggest that lengthier document representations better enable users to predict the relevance of documents, most likely because these representations contain more information about the document.

Work in this area by Barry (1998) extends this hypothesis by suggesting that in addition to sheer lengthwise characteristics, document representations may, in themselves, provide varying cues which allow users to determine the presence or absence of traits and qualities that signal the relevance of a particular document to a user's situation. To investigate this possibility, Barry examined the effectiveness of four different document representation types in terms of their suitability to the personal research areas of 18 test subjects.

The first method of document representation was that of showing only descriptive cataloguing information pertaining to a particular document, such as the document's title, author(s), author and editor affiliations, the name of the journal, conference proceedings, or book in which the document was published, publication date, and publisher. The second was displaying notes that pertained to particular documents, such as: the presence of tables, graphs, illustrations, or photographs; the presence of references, footnotes, or a bibliography; the primary sources on which the document was based; the document type; and the target audience. The third was providing test subjects with the abstracts of retrieved documents. The fourth was displaying the index terms used to classify individual documents.

Each of the 18 test subjects discussed the reasons for pursuing or not pursuing documents based on the information contained within the four different types of representations for those documents. Based on the analysis of subjects' responses, Barry concluded that document representations do differ in their effectiveness as indicators of potential relevance because different types of document representations vary in their ability to present cues for specific traits and qualities.

For example, Barry's (1998, p. 1301) results indicate that "titles and abstracts may perform more effectively than indexing terms as predictors of relevance, not simply because they are longer than indexing terms... but because they present information about this *specific* document that allows users to determine the presence or absence of a greater number of quality categories." Such findings have bearing on our discussion here on utilizing different methods of display for returned search hit items in that specific methods of display may better represent and showcase a retrieved document's content.

To test their hypothesis that the display of thumbnail images in a search engine's retrieved hits list items would significantly increase the efficiency by which end-users process search engine results, Woodruff et al. (2002) conducted a study in which participants used three different types of summaries displayed in a list of returned hit items (enhanced thumbnails, plain thumbnails, and text summaries) to search Web pages to find different types of information. Enhanced thumbnails were plain thumbnails augmented with readable textual elements.

In terms of performance, enhanced thumbnails exhibited the most consistent performance overall. It appears that this type of information display offers the efficiency benefits of both text summaries and plain thumbnails, which is in accordance with Paivio's (1971) theory of dual coding which suggests that the representation of information in multiple formats, such as verbal and visual representations, can lead to better cognitive retention and retrieval.

An interesting aspect of their study was the application of information foraging theory (Pirolli and Card, 1999) to explain how the concept of *information scent* can be used to explicate the strong overall performance of enhanced thumbnail displays in the presentation of search engine results. Information scent refers to the strength of local cues, such as text labels, in providing an indication of the utility or relevance of a navigational path leading to some distal information. Here, participants can behave or react to an information display on a high-scent or low-scent strategy.

In Woodruff et al.'s study, a high scent strategy would be one where participants utilize the cues provided by individual returned hit items to identify a hit that would likely lead to the correct answer the user was looking for. A low scent strategy would be one where cues provided by individual returned hit items were inadequate or insufficient for a user to decide what is worthwhile so the user ends up choosing hit items on a fairly arbitrary basis.

In these two scenarios, Woodruff et al. suggest a high-scent strategy is preferable. These authors find evidence in their study's results that enhanced thumbnail displays consistently support high scent strategies in that this particular information design format led to short visits to the summary page of retrieved hit items, medium-length visits to an item's content page, fewer overall visits to content pages in general, and a low number of visits to irrelevant content pages.

Woodruff et al. conclude that high-scent summary pages of retrieved hit items, as offered by the enhanced thumbnail displays, have the benefit of reducing the overall amount of time spent on a search task. As such, the study offers initial evidence for portals to adopt information designs of a search engine's returned hit list items that foster high scent strategies, such as that supported through the use of enhanced thumbnail displays.

Another interesting aspect of the Woodruff et al. study was that the best presentation method (enhanced thumbnail, plain thumbnail, or text summaries) was dependent on the type of question which led users to conduct a search. For example, for some search questions, text summaries outperformed plain thumbnails, while for other questions, plain thumbnails outperformed text summaries. Based on this finding, it appears that a 'one size fits all' solution does not apply in terms of the information design of returned hit items. Rather, it appears that the best presentation of information display is dependent on the context in which the user is situated. In this scenario, the context is shaped by the given search question. So, though enhanced thumbnail displays offered the best performance overall, even greater performance could be obtained if the display of retrieved hit items could be adapted to the context in which the user were situated. This need to tailor the presentation and display of information items depending upon a user's information seeking task is elaborated upon in section 5.5.

5.4.2 Displaying Multimedia Information

The results of Woodruff et al.'s study touch upon the broader utilization of multimedia information formats in Web page design over that of textual representations. The Cognitive and Technology Group at Vanderbilt (1993, p. 118) defines multimedia as the "linkage of text, sound, video, graphics, and the computer in such a way that the user's access to these media becomes nonlinear and virtually instantaneous." Typical formats of multimedia displays include combinations of text, graphics, audio, video, and animations. A series of three experiments investigating text versus multimedia information displays in organizational Web-based systems are described below. A major motivation for this work was the need to improve enterprise intranet design and to respond to the new challenge of deriving "a set of guidelines on how and when to use this rich array of tools (text, graphics, audio, video, and animations) so that organizational members can make better sense out of the information" displayed on the interfaces to these systems (Lim and Benbasat, 2000, p. 464). Together the three-related studies extend our comprehension of the conditions under which multimedia would be beneficial to the information design of organizational Web-based systems, such as knowledge portals.

The first study, by Lim, Benbasat and Ward (2000), examines the advantages of multimedia over text-based information presentation with respect to *first impression bias*. This cognitive construct, similar to the primacy effect, refers to a specific limitation of human information processing in which people are strongly influenced by the first piece of information they are exposed to, and that they are biased in evaluating subsequent information in the direction of this initial influence (Asch, 1946). It is generally acknowledged that "issues of cognition and human information processing are still widely neglected and barely influence hypermedia design" (Thuring, Hannemann and Haake, 1995, p. 57), so Lim et al.'s first study is an important contribution in this area. Of relevance is the study's experimental results which suggest that multimedia presentation formats, but not text-based ones, reduce the influence of first impression bias. Extending this to the information design of knowledge portals, incorporating multimedia formats may help minimize potential bias that may result from the order in which organizational participants browse and retrieve information from these systems.

The second study, by Lim and Benbasat (2000), investigates the effects of multimedia representation on the perceived ambiguity and the usefulness of information displayed on a Web interface. The purpose of the study was to investigate ways of capturing and presenting information in a variety of representation formats, such as text, graphics, audio, video, and animations, so that organizational workers can make better sense out of the information available. Moreover, the study examined whether or not rich information representations, such as multimedia, were better suited to specific types of tasks, than lean information representations, such as text.

The theoretical framework underpinning this research was task-technology fit theory (Goodhue and Thompson, 1995; Goodhue 1998) which stipulates that in order for an information system to have a positive impact on performance, then it must be designed and utilized in a way that fits or matches the tasks it supports. For this study, performance was measured by the extent to which a Web system reduced information equivocality in analyzable versus less-analyzable tasks. Information equivocality refers to "the multiplicity of meaning conveyed by information about organizational activities" (Daft and Lengel, 1986, p. 211) or rather, the ambiguousness of the information displayed. Analyzable tasks are ones in which "predetermined responses to potential problems, and well-known procedures, are available and useful" (Rice, 1992). In contrast, less-analyzable tasks are ones where there is a lack of predefined responses, procedure, or knowledge of what is required to solve the problem or perform the task (Daft and Macintosh, 1981).

The study's results support the task-technology fit model. For analyzable tasks, both text-based and multimedia representations were found to be equally effective in reducing perceived information equivocality in users. However, for less-analyzable tasks, only multimedia representations were found to be instrumental in reducing perceived information equivocality levels in users. These findings have implications on the information design of knowledge portals in that the presentation of information on portal interfaces need to fit or match the task for which users turn to the portal in the first place. For example, users in a browsing situation (a less analyzable task) may need to be shown more multimedia formatted information than those users performing a goal-directed search (a more analyzable task). More discussion on tailoring portal information design to match browsing versus searching modes can be found in section 5.5.

The third study, by Lim and Benbasat (2002), focuses on measuring the impact of different media on an individual's ability to make inferences beyond the actual information provided. Acknowledging that comprehending text-based information requires intensive cognitive processing effort on the part of readers, the study examined the extent to which multimedia information display could improve the comprehensibility of organizational information presented on an intranet site. The idea underlying this proposition was that multimedia formats present complementary cues which highlight or raise awareness of the potential value of the information displayed.

The study's findings showed that multimedia representations of the same information content as displayed in textual formats facilitated the retention and subsequent recall of explanative information, but not of descriptive information. *Explanative information* refers to organized facts connected by underlying functional relationships. *Descriptive information* consists of isolated facts without an explanation of the relationships between these facts.

Extending these results to the information design of knowledge portals, the study's findings suggest that the utilization of multimedia formats in portal systems could potentially help organizational workers retain and recall explanative information. This, in turn, could lead to a greater ability by knowledge portal users to make correct inferences about new organizational situations.

5.4.3 Information Presentation

In terms of the presentation of information in hypermedia documents, Thuring, Hannemann and Haake (1995) suggest that such documents need to be designed in ways that enhance human comprehension of the document's text and structure. In cognitive science, comprehension is often characterized by the construction of mental models which represent objects and semantic relations described in a text (van Dijk and Kintsch, 1983). Thuring et al. identify two factors in particular which are crucial in assisting users in the construction of mental models: strengthening coherence and reducing cognitive overload. A hyperdocument is said to be *coherent* if a reader is able to construct a mental model from it that corresponds to known facts and relations (Johnson-Laird, 1989). *Cognitive overhead*, on the other hand, refers to "the additional effort and concentration necessary to maintain several tasks or trails at one time" (Conklin, 1987, p. 40) and assumes a limited capacity of the human mind to conduct information processing tasks (Kahneman, 1973).

To help users comprehend and make sense out of the hyperdocuments they read, Thuring et al. suggest users require insight about the overall structure of the documents and ways to keep track of their moves through individual document structures. One way of doing this is through the provision of graphical presentation formats in hyperdocument designs that offer visual impressions of the document's information space as a means of giving users some orientation to the document's structure. There is a strong correlation between comprehension and memory of spatial information or location (Dillon, McKnight and Richardson, 1994). One interpretation of this correlation is that

> "memory for content and memory for spatial information are different aspects of the same mental representation, i.e., the reader's mental model. Hence, all factors that facilitate the construction of such a model by reducing mental effort or increase a model's quality by improving its completeness and consistency can be expected to affect both comprehension and orientation" (Thuring et al., 1995, p. 60).

To leverage this relationship, Thuring et al. propose that the readability of hyperdocuments can be improved via support of mental models that: 1) increase document coherence in terms of facilitating the construction of semantic relations between information units; and 2) reduce cognitive overhead by freeing a user's information processing capacities which otherwise may be over-taxed in terms of focusing user attention to orientation, navigation, and user-interface adjustments.

To do this, Thuring et al. offer eight cognitive design principles for designers of hypermedia applications to follow. These principles aim to increase local coherence of information displayed on a Web page, increase global coherence of information displayed across an entire Web site, improve user orientation of a Web site's overall structure to help users find their way, and facilitate navigation within a Web site to help users actually make their way to specific destination areas. These eight principles are:

1) using typed hyperlink labels to represent semantic relations between information units;
2) indicating equivalencies between information units, such as that which may occur when different windows appear simultaneously on the computer interface referencing the same information items;
3) preserving the context of information units by showing neighbouring nodes in the document or Web site structure and their relationships;
4) using higher order information units that aggregate information from lower-level, more detailed information units;
5) visualizing the structure of the overall document or Web site;
6) incorporating cues into the visualization of the structure of the document or Web site which show a user's current position, the way that led to this position, and navigational options for moving on;
7) providing a set of complementary navigation facilities which cover

aspects of the direction to a destination area and the distance involved in getting there; and

8) using a stable screen layout with windows having fixed positions and default sizes.

These eight principles can help guide the design of knowledge portals in terms of the presentation of information on the portal interface. Doing so addresses concerns of increasing coherence of the information displayed on a portal both within individual Web pages and across the entire site, as well as helping users orient themselves within the portal and navigate themselves to areas of potential interest.

As such, these eight principles of design can be considered high-level guidelines for formatting and presentation preferences applied to all pages and sites within a portal. As suggested by Bell DeTienne and Jensen (2001), such guidelines are not meant to determine portal content but rather to provide consistency in the organization and layout of portal pages so that users utilizing the portal can more easily navigate through its pages (Cronin, 1999).

Smart, Rice and Wood (2000), though recognizing that a single set of universal Web design standards cannot apply to all situations, utilize a semiotic approach to understanding Web conventions to elicit six categories of information design. These may be appropriate to the design of Web-based portals.

The first dimension is that of *typography* or *appearance* which refers to the art of utilizing typefaces, page layouts, and colour to convey the meaning of text. When presenting information on a Web site, designers need to ask questions about these variables. Is the typeface appropriate or legible for online display? Does the typeface cause confusion or elicit sufficient contrast between the text and the background colour? Is there an appropriate usage of white space? Are related items chunked together? Is the page size appropriate for online display? Are appropriate colours, hues, and density utilized?

The second dimension concerns *site structure* which refers to how information is organized on a site with respect to its navigation, information architecture, and cognitive design. Various questions can be posed to test the worthiness of a Web site's overall structure. How well does the site support navigation? Would additional types of navigational structures, such as navigation bars, indexes, menus, intelligent agents, pop-up windows, pull-down menus, be of benefit? Is the structure and order of the site appropriate, intuitive, and clear? Are signs and symbols displayed on the site used consistently? Does the site provide sufficient user control? Is the site disorienting or does it distract users from their goals? Are the site's metaphors and mental models ill-fitting or paradoxical?

The third dimension is that of *medium use* which refers to the appropriate utilization of unique Web features, such as scrolling, hypertext, multimedia in ways that enhance the overall user experience and that respects the constraints and limitations of these features. Designers should question how well a Web site utilizes the medium of the Web. Does it make appropriate use of features and respect constraints such as graphics download time, different browser versions, hardware platforms and connectivity speeds?

The fourth dimension is the *message* of the Web site in terms of the actual content the site provides and the comprehensiveness of this information. Various questions can be asked of this dimension. Is the content useful and sufficient? Is it relevant, timely, and up-to-date? Is the narrative style too rich or too lean? Is the modality of the communication (e.g., verbal, non-verbal, graphical) appropriate for the site's intended audience? Is the message appropriate? Does the target audience possess the requisite skills to make sense of the material presented on the site in terms of the message's vocabulary, grammar, and tone?

The fifth dimension is the Web site *appeal* which refers to the degree to which the site is aesthetically pleasing and the extent to which users find the site desirable, inviting and satisfying. There are a variety of questions to ask with respect to this dimension. Does the site attract user attention? Is the site engaging? Is the site challenging enough to encourage exploration and rewarding enough to elicit and promote users to return to the site at future points in time?

The sixth and last dimension is the *accessibility* of the Web site which refers to characteristics that can encourage or discourage users to approach and utilize the Web site at all. Accessibility factors include cultural differences that may exist between users and designers, such as language, gestures, social conventions, that prevent usage, as well as special access needs of potential users, such as those with physical challenges (e.g., hearing-impaired, colour blindness, motor control) and mental challenges (e.g., dyslexia, spatial organization disorders). Designers need to ask questions concerning the degree to which the site reflects and is sensitive to its target audience's cultural background and any special access needs impaired populations may have.

Altogether, the six information design dimensions purported by Smart et al. (2000) offer a good set of suggestions on things to look for and consider when designing Web-based information displays. An interesting and burgeoning area reflecting the application of these dimensions in Web-based design is the development of virtual reality environments. The purpose of virtual reality environments is not only to display and present information, but also to create engaging, interactive worlds by which to elicit the attention and awareness of users.

With recent advances in computer graphics, a sizeable number of innovative approaches to information visualization in virtual reality environments have been developed (Card, Robertson and Mackinlay, 1991). Navigation in such systems becomes a matter of moving through imaginary worlds where spatial proximity between items in the environment indicates context and relatedness. For example, information retrieval in virtual worlds can be fully three dimensional, or a series of two-dimensional birds-eye snapshots that can be traversed as if users were utilizing operations such as panning and zooming interactively (Modjeska and Chignell, 2003). "Ultimately it may turn out that virtual reality provides the most 'natural' medium for hypertext" (Dieberger and Bolter, 1995, p. 98). As such, it is expected that more and more portal and Web-based designs will leverage virtual reality in the future as a means of presenting information in engaging ways.

Adaptations of virtual reality environments in the design of knowledge portals may be a worthy avenue for organizations to consider. Such systems would attempt to counter criticisms concerning the lack of attention currently paid to the presentation and display of information in knowledge management systems. For example, according to Thomas, Kellogg and Erickson (2001), the majority of KM systems developed for business environments today "seem to focus on the content of systems while ignoring the method of presentation." In response, these authors lament that "beyond considerations of cost, there sometimes seems to be almost a puritanical business-culture ethic toward avoiding presentations that stimulate the senses and utilize the complete human brain" (Thomas et al., 2001, p. 866). Focusing attention on the display and presentation of information in knowledge portals would address this concern.

5.4.4 Evaluating Information Design

The above accounts offer preliminary suggestions on possible portal information design scenarios. Though valid and insightful, there is not an absolute discrete set of information design guidelines for portal developers to follow, as suitable information designs can vary from context to context. Given this, any preliminary portal information design needs to evaluated in terms of its usability before its true effectiveness can be determined. In general, there are four basic ways to evaluating user interfaces: 1) automatically, where usability measures are computed by running a user interface specification through some computer program; 2) empirically, where usability is assessed by testing the interface with real users; 3) formally, where exact models and formulas are utilized to calculate usability measures; and 4) informally, where rules of thumb and the general skill and experience of trained usability experts or evaluators are employed (Nielsen and Mack, 1994).

Empirical methods are the predominant way of evaluating user interfaces, though in reality, it is often difficult to recruit users in sufficient numbers for lengthy periods of time to test all aspects of an interface's information design. To compensate for these drawbacks, Nielsen and Mack (1994) advocate the use of inspection methods, such as: *heuristic evaluation*, an informal method where usability specialists judge whether an interface's dialogue elements follow established usability principles; *cognitive walkthroughs*, a formal method where a usability specialist simulates a potential user's problem solving process through each interaction with the computer interface, checking if the user's goals and memory content can be assumed to lead to the next correct action; *feature inspection*, a usability expert inspects sequences of interface features utilized by users to accomplish typical tasks, checking if sequences are too long, cumbersome, awkward, or require an inordinate amount of prior knowledge or extensive experience, and *pluralistic walkthroughs*, where groups of usability specialists, users, and system developers step through a typical scenario of interaction with the computer interface together discussing each dialogue element as they go along. Several studies have shown that inspection methods can complement empirical testing performed by users in that both methods can identify usability problems overlooked by the other (Desurvire, Kondziela and Atwood, 1992; Karat, Campbell and Fiegel, 1992; Desurvire, 1994).

Garzotto, Mainetti and Paolini (1995) identify several dimensions for analyzing and evaluating hypermedia applications which give users "direct access to the content and interconnections with an information domain" and include functions such as navigation, annotation, and information overviews (Bieber and Isakowitz, 1995, p. 28). These dimensions incorporate content, structure, presentation, dynamics and interaction—dimensions which mimic and closely align with the identification of information design concerns from the author's case study investigation in section 5.3. *Content* refers to the actual pieces of information contained in a hypermedia application. This can consist of static, passive media such as formatted data, text strings, images and graphics, or more active, dynamic media such as video clips, sound tracks and animations. *Structure* pertains to the organization of the hypermedia application's content. *Presentation* refers to how application content and functions are shown to users. *Dynamics* and *interaction* pertain to how users interact with individual granules of information and move among them, such as how users control the playing of active media.

In response, Garzotto et al. propose a design-oriented evaluation method for the analysis of hypermedia applications. Their method differs with more commonly accepted user-oriented approaches to the evaluation of computer application interfaces in that their method evaluates the internal strength of the design underlying a hypermedia application rather than the application's fit with user profile concerns or specific user tasks. Garzotto et al. propose that evaluators first need to express the internal structure of any hypermedia application under scrutiny into a formal design model. The model serves as a facility by which evaluators can perform a systematic and rigorous analysis of a hypermedia application's structures and their dynamic properties. That is, the resulting systematic description of a hypermedia application helps detect potential problem areas within that application.

According to Garzotto et al., the problem areas that the design model will help showcase include concerns over the hypermedia application's richness, ease, consistency, self-evidence, predictability, readability, and reuse. *Richness* refers to the abundance of information items presented in the hypermedia application and ways to reach them. *Ease* refers to how accessible the information is and how easy it is for potential users to grasp what the operations are. *Consistency* refers to the extent to which the hypermedia application treats conceptually similar elements in a similar fashion and conceptually different elements differently. *Self-evidence* refers to how well the application allows potential users to guess at the meaning and purpose of whatever is being presented to them, be it an information content item or navigational element or whatever. *Predictability* refers to the extent to which potential users can anticipate an operation's outcome. *Readability* refers to the overall feeling about an application's validity. Last, *reuse* refers to how well the application is useful in utilizing objects and performing operations in different contexts and for different purposes.

Regardless of what actual method of evaluation is employed, the message here is the necessity of knowledge portal designers to evaluate the potential usability and worthiness of their developed applications prior to actual deployment and implementation of portals in real-life settings. Doing so, it is argued, will help improve the overall information design of the developed applications, and more importantly, lead to increased satisfaction and use with the developed systems.

End-user satisfaction with computer application systems has been both theoretically and empirically linked to five information design components of information content, accuracy, format, ease-of-use, and timeliness (Doll and Torkzadeh, 1988). Further, Web site success has been significantly associated with Web site download delay (e.g., speed of access, and the display rate within the Web site), navigation (e.g., organization, arrangement, layout, and sequencing), content (e.g., the amount and variety of information presented), interactivity (e.g., customization and engagement), and responsiveness (e.g., feedback options and FAQs). As such, it is suggested that systems designers focus on these information design components and Web site success factors when evaluating their knowledge portal solutions.

5.5   Supporting Browse and Search

One of the major lessons from this chapter is the call for knowledge portal information designs to reflect and support different tasks for which users turn to the portal for help. Recall back in Figure 1-3 which showcased the situated use of knowledge portals in organizational information environments where knowledge workers operate in an information needs-seeking-use cycle of interaction with the knowledge portal interface. Knowledge work consists of a set of information-laden processes and, as a result, users are continually engaged in direct information seeking activity with the portal.

Information seeking is a broad behavioural endeavour. It is "a process in which humans engage to purposefully change their state of knowledge" (Marchionini and Komlodi, 1998, p. 97). In this sense, information seeking is not a restrictive, narrow activity but rather a dynamic process comprising a wide array of tasks ranging from wayward browsing and exploration to specific, goal-directed search. This process is

> "inherently interactive as information seekers direct attention, accept and adapt to stimuli, reflect on progress, and evaluate the efficacy of continuing. Information seeking is thus a cybernetic process in which knowledge state is changed through inputs, purposive outputs, and feedback" (Marchionini and Komlodi, 1998, p. 97).

Most electronic information systems that support information seeking focus on the information retrieval aspects within the larger information seeking process. In response, interfaces to these systems are needed which support the broader information seeking processes of problem definition, source selection, problem articulation, examination of results, and information extraction (Marchionini, 1992; 1995).

There have been many attempts over the years to classify and study the various phases or components comprising user information seeking behaviour. For example, Marchionini (1995, p. 106) in his review of the research of browsing observed that "there seems to be agreement on three general types of browsing that may be differentiated by the object of search (the information needed) and by the systematicity of tactics used." First, directed browsing occurs when browsing is systematic, focused, and directed by a precise object or target. Second, semidirected browsing occurs when browsing is predictive or generally purposeful (i.e., the target is less definite and browsing is less systematic). Third, undirected browsing occurs when there is no real goal and very little focus.

In a similar fashion, Wilson (1997; 1999) describes a comparable typology of information seeking scenarios ranging from wayward browsing to structured searching consisting of four distinct types: passive attention, passive search, active search, and on-going search. As described in section 1.3.4, Wilson favours Ellis' (1989a; 1993) six moves of information seeking behaviour: *starting, chaining, browsing, differentiating, monitoring,* and *extracting*.

Choo, Detlor and Turnbull (1999; 2000a; 2000b) empirically validate a model of how knowledge workers seek information on the Web that relates these six moves to distinct modes of organizational scanning (Aguilar, 1967; Weick and Daft, 1983; Daft and Lengel, 1984). The model portrays information seeking on the Web as a spectrum of browsing and search behaviour where knowledge workers are engaged in four complementary modes of information seeking. Two of these modes pertain to browsing (e.g., *undirected browsing* and *conditioned browsing*); the other two pertain to search (e.g., *informal search* and *formal search*).

Of relevance is Choo et al.'s discovery that specific Web browser-based actions (i.e., page forward, page back, print, stop, selecting a hypertext link, using a local search engine etc.) that align with Ellis' six moves of activity are associated with specific Web modes. Table 5-1 outlines the association of Web moves, Web browser-based actions, and Web modes by organizational knowledge workers.

Recent work by the author extends Choo et al.'s model of Web information seeking by organizational knowledge workers to the electronic shopping domain. Choo et al.'s model suggests that Web users do operate in distinct ways that can be categorized along browse and search task contexts, at least in terms of the way these users utilize their Web browser interfaces. It follows, or at least suggests, that perhaps the information design of Web shopping sites needs to follow suit. That is, there may be a requirement for Web sites to display information in different ways to online consumers depending upon their browsing and searching modes of information seeking behaviour.

Detlor, Sproule and Gupta (2003) explore work in this area which indirectly has relevance on the information design of Web-based information seeking systems, such as knowledge portals. Specifically their research investigation asks what kinds or types of information online consumers prefer or favour in browsing and searching modes. Further, they question how users prefer to have such information displayed and presented to them in each of these modes.

In their investigation, 31 participants performed two online shopping tasks (one searching and one browsing in nature) on predetermined e-tailing sites and were asked to evaluate the display of product information on these sites in helping them carry out these tasks. The browse task instructed participants to find a gift for a friend. The search task required that participants search for a particular product, namely a digital camera, as a gift.

Table 5-1: Web modes and moves (adapted from Choo et al., 1999; 2000a; 2000b)

WEB MODES	WEB MOVES AND ASSOCIATED WEB BROWSER ACTIONS
Undirected Browsing occurs when people use the Web to scan broadly	Many instances of **starting** and **chaining** activity where participants start at portal or news-related sites and follow links they find interesting on those pages.
Conditioned Browsing occurs when users focus on pre-selected sources	Many instances of **browsing** (scanning top level pages and site maps), **differentiating** (selecting useful pages, bookmarking/adding to favorites and printing), and **monitoring** (receiving site updates or revisiting sites of interest).
Informal Search occurs when users conduct a query with relatively limited and unstructured effort to deepen their knowledge and understanding of a specific issue	Many instances of **differentiating, monitoring**, and **extracting** activity. Typically this involves going to a known site and using a local search engine on the site to find information.
Formal Search occurs when users conduct more systematic, rigorous searches	Many instances of **extracting** activity with some complementary **monitoring**. Typically this involves utilizing search engines that scan numerous Web pages comprehensively.

Prior to each task, participants filled out a questionnaire that asked them to identify and rank the types of information they expected to access on the Web site to help them carry out their tasks. To prevent the possibility of influencing participant response with suggested information items, no information items were listed on the questionnaire. Rather, participants had to self-identify particular information items they felt were important. After each task, participants completed another questionnaire, which required participants to identify and rank information they found useful during their tasks. Again, no prompts for potential information items were suggested.

Results suggest three things: 1) information such as pricing, product description, retailer selection, retailer advice, and a good interface design are required in both tasks; 2) searching requires more detailed product information; and 3) browsing places greater emphasis on information about the retailer. Based on these findings, the study's results imply the need to focus not only on goal-directed search in the information design of online shopping sites, but also on non-directed browsing tasks as well.

Currently work in this area is being extended (Harold and Detlor, 2003). An experiment is being run which tests various potential layouts of information and features on electronic shopping sites across scenarios of browse and search activity in order to determine the best information design layouts for online shopping and the more salient mediating variables affecting user satisfaction with such designs. The experiment deductively tests a theoretical model based on constructs derived from the consumer behaviour and information technology literatures. The model depicts how certain information attributes (e.g., information presentation, information focus) mediate online pre-purchase browsing and search behaviour to the outcomes of perceived ease of use, perceived usefulness, satisfaction, efficiency, and effectiveness. The study measures these outcomes within a simulated Web shopping environment that utilizes Amazon's Associates Web Services program to retrieve and display product information.

Studies, such as the above, have bearing on the information design of knowledge portals in that they suggest the need or significance of tailoring the display and presentation of information in Web-based environments. Choo et al.'s study shows that online knowledge workers operate in at least two broad information contexts of browse and search. The author's recent research endeavours in the electronic shopping domain offers preliminary suggestions on how best to tailor the information design of Web sites to reflect the unique requirements necessitated by the specific information seeking tasks for which users turn to utilize these systems in the first place. Possible manipulation items consist not only of the types or kinds of information to display, but also the way or method by which this information is presented on the computer interface.

5.6   Conclusion

The purpose of this chapter was to discuss and analyze the knowledge portal interface in terms of its information design. First, a detailed definition and description of the information design construct was given. A working definition was put forth where information design was considered to be an umbrella concept. Specifically, information design was defined as the effective and efficient presentation of information on Web spaces as a means of raising awareness of the potential usefulness or value of the information displayed to users. Doing so, it was argued, would increase the comprehensibility of information presented on the portal interface thus better enabling knowledge workers to translate this information into effective action.

Findings from the author's case study investigation supported the need for information designs in knowledge portals that enlightened workers and promoted the use of information presented in the portal to mutually affect and change users' perceptions of the world. Five tangible characteristics to improve the information design of knowledge portals were derived from the case study. They were: 1) the ability of the system to support *tailorability* or personalization of the information content displayed and the applications available for use; 2) the *quality of the information* displayed—users generally expect information on the portal to be relevant to their work practice, reliable in terms of its validity and trustworthiness, and timely in that the information is refreshed frequently and is as up-to-date as possible; 3) the *organization of the information* in that there are methods by which to navigate and access information quickly in terms of a robust search engine and an elaborate classification schema of intranet sites; 4) the presence of *collaborative tools* which support collaboration, communication, and the sharing of documents between organizational workers; 5) and *engagement* of these systems in providing an interactive and attractive environment for conducting work-related tasks.

From there, related findings in the literature were presented. Specifically, attention turned to ways of better displaying search engine results, deploying multimedia applications, presenting information on the Web interface, and evaluating the goodness of a basic Web site design. In each of these areas, findings were applied to ways of utilizing such insights in the information design of knowledge portals.

Last, discussion turned to the need to tailor the display of information on the knowledge portal interface to support different modes of information seeking behaviour. A separate research investigation by the author in the electronic shopping domain highlighted the existence of user preferences for Web-based information display across browsing and searching tasks. The study's results imply the need to focus not only on goal-directed search in Web site information design, but also on non-directed browsing tasks as well.

Overall, the chapter presented two major ideas for supporting good information designs in knowledge portal interfaces. The first was the need to present information in ways that signal the value of information to users. Effective information design would be respectful and sensitive to the role human cognition plays in information processing and present information in ways that enable the ease with which information can be readily understood.

The second was the need for the portal to support users' browse and search modes of information seeking activity. Information seeking is an integral part of how organizational employees, situated in the information environments of their firms, go about utilizing a portal for knowledge work. Thus enterprise portal designs need to support the various modes of information seeking behaviour under which the portal is utilized.

It is argued that these two points are key requisites in the design of effective knowledge portal systems. Enterprise portals that support knowledge creation, distribution, and use would be ones that respond with information designs that display information in ways that make information sufficiently accessible and noticeable to users, and that match or address the specific tasks for which users turn to the portal for help.

This chapter ends the detailed investigation of portals under the lens of the Knowledge Portal Framework presented in Chapter 2. The next chapter delves into an emerging area of importance in terms of the design of knowledge portal systems in organizations. The chapter launches into a futuristic, yet plausible, discussion on how recent advances in artificial intelligence, Web technologies, and Internet standards have raised the possibility of enabling and deploying intelligent agents in knowledge portal designs in ways that can improve an organizational knowledge worker's information seeking behaviour.

6. INTELLIGENT AGENTS AND KNOWLEDGE PORTALS

6.1 Introduction

This chapter discusses the future role of intelligent agents in terms of their ability to transform enterprise portals into richer and broader mediums for organizational knowledge work. Though the artificial intelligence community has been making good progress in the development and application of intelligent software for several decades now, it has only been in recent years that a new set of technologies and standards has come to fruition which promises the real development of agent-based applications in portals which facilitate the creation, distribution, and use of knowledge across the firm. The beauty behind these new technologies and standards is that they facilitate the formation of intelligent agents in knowledge portal designs which can access the meaning behind the information stored in Web-based content, and moreover, utilize and capitalize on that meaning in ways that have never been done before.

To start the discussion, the chapter commences with a definition and description of intelligent agents, along with their benefits and challenges. Next, the Semantic Web is discussed and its potential to provide an agent-based infrastructure for organizational knowledge work. The underlying technologies deployed in the Semantic Web are documented. More importantly, the strong role ontologies play in knowledge portal design are described. From there, the need for robust agent development toolkits in organizational settings is discussed.

Next, the potential application of intelligent agents in knowledge portals is described. It is shown that agents can be deployed in many ways within each component of the information needs-seeking-use cycle of individuals described in Chapter 1. As such, intelligent agents give much promise in helping knowledge portal users go about their information-laden creation, distribution, and use tasks. Last, the chapter presents a preliminary, high-level architecture of intelligent agents that knowledge portals designers can potentially utilize to map out the functionality of and relationships between various intelligent agents deployed within the knowledge portal.

6.2 Intelligent Agents

There are wide variations in the literature of a formal definition of agents ranging from "adaptable information filters" to "autonomous programs that work in conjunction with, or on behalf of, a human user" (Adam and Yesha,

1996, p. 821). Shoham (1997) defines agents to be software entities that perform specific tasks continuously and autonomously in a particular environment often inhabited by other agents and processes. Serenko and Detlor (2002; 2003b), borrowing a definition supplied by Reticular Systems in its user guide for the AgentBuilder toolkit, describe agents as a newer class of software that acts on behalf of users to find and filter information, negotiate for services, automate complex tasks, and collaborate with other agents to solve complex problems. As such, agents can be viewed as software entities that perform functions continuously and autonomously in particular environments. The degree to which an agent performs its tasks continually has implications on the extent to which an agent can learn from its experience. Likewise, how independently an agent performs its tasks has implications on its ability to carry out activities in a flexible and intelligent manner and respond to changes in the environment (Bradshaw, 1997).

So what are the defining characteristics of an intelligent agent? First and foremost, intelligent agents are software programs. This does not obfuscate the fact that humans can be agents too. For instance, agents are people who act on someone else's behalf such as real estate agents, travel agents, and publicity agents. However the term 'intelligent agent' refers strictly to the software sort-of-variety and bears no relevance on the degree of intelligence of their human counterparts. Secondly, these programs possess certain key characteristics that distinguish them from other software systems or applications: autonomy (i.e., independence) and persistence (i.e., long-livedness) (Shoham, 1997). Thirdly, agents communicate and collaborate with other agents and humans. Last, agents monitor and react to the environment around them.

By assuming the viability and authority of such defining attributes, we can describe two general types of agents. The first are *interface agents*, whose primary role is to assist users. This type of agent knows user preferences and interests, is concerned with helping users perform their tasks, and largely deals with the display of information presented to users on the computer interface. Interface agents are identified by characteristics of autonomy and learning (Nwana and Ndumu, 1999) and are championed as fulfilling the role of personal assistants (Maes, 1994). Examples include information filters and personal news-editors. The second type are *information service agents*. These predominantly perform information-laden background tasks. Typically, they find, analyze, and retrieve large amounts of information and mitigate information overload (Nwana and Ndumu, 1999). Examples include Web indexing spiders and crawlers.

Not all agents are created equal. Some agents are in fact more intelligent than others. More intelligent agents may possess one of more of the following characteristics: the ability to learn, mobility, and the capacity to make decisions. As such, agents are neither smart nor stupid but have intellectual capabilities that exist along a continuum. Greater capabilities implies greater intelligence. In certain scenarios, agents with limited or restricted capabilities may be all that is required for intelligent processing.

So why do we want or need intelligent agents? Maes (1997) offers several suggestions. First, more everyday tasks are becoming computer-based. As computer technology becomes pervasive and ubiquitous, the feasibility of deploying software agents to facilitate those tasks becomes more likely. Secondly, the sheer volume of dynamic, unstructured information available on Web-based platforms necessitates the need for some automated solution to help people wade through this information. People alone do not possess sufficient resources to digest and sort through the vast amounts of information available on the Web. Thirdly, more and more novice users, who lack the skill and knowledge to carry out computer-based tasks in an efficient and effective manner, are utilizing the Web. Help is needed.

According to Maes, agents are also beneficial in that they facilitate an indirect management metaphor to human-computer interaction. Rather than assuming a direct management metaphor which positions users in control of all actions with a computer, an indirect management metaphor recognizes a perhaps more realistic perspective of the information environment in which we live. Information resources are not closed, static, small and structured; rather they are open, dynamic, vast, and unstructured. As such, people need assistance to navigate and operate in this new information environment. Agents can help in this regard. Users can delegate certain actions to agents who 'know' the user's interests, habits, and preferences, who can make suggestions or act on behalf of the user, and who can continue to work even when the user is not actively engaged with the computer interface. Further, agents can hide the complexity of difficult tasks, train or teach the user how to interact and utilize a computer application, bring different users together for collaboration purposes, and monitor events on a continual basis.

Despite these benefits, there are several challenges confronting the adoption and use of agents today. Maes (1994) identifies competence and trust as two significant challenges. In terms of competence, how do agents go about acquiring the knowledge they need to decide when to help the user, what to help the user with, and how to help the user? With respect to trust, how can we ensure that users feel comfortable delegating tasks to agents? According to Maes, two past approaches to agent building fall short of addressing these challenges. The first is the 'making the user program the interface' approach where the agent is viewed as a collection of user-programmed rules for processing information related to a particular task. This approach does not address the competence challenge well since it requires too much insight, understanding, and effort on behalf of the user. It also does not do much for the trust challenge in that it requires users to have trust in their own programming abilities.

The second is the 'knowledge-based' approach in which a third party knowledge engineer creates an agent, endowing it with extensive domain knowledge concerning the application and the user. This approach falls short on both competence and trust issues too. In terms of competence, it requires a significant amount of work (and domain knowledge) on behalf of the knowledge engineer, and creates static agents in that the knowledge becomes fixed once and for all. With respect to trust, it delegates the control of tasks directly to the agent from its initial conception, and fails to give the user a good mental model of the agent's design and limitations since the agent was developed by a third party.

In response, Maes recommends a 'personal assistant' approach to the development and design of agents to overcome the challenges of competency and trust. This approach is based on machine learning techniques and assumes an agent can program itself. Upon creation, the agent is enabled with minimal background knowledge and, over time, learns the appropriate behaviour to exhibit from the user and from other agents. In this way, the agent learns the preferences and habits of its user and adjusts its operations to satisfy and better address the user's needs. In this respect, the agent becomes more competent in that it is trained to work in ways that the user prefers and expects. There are a variety of ways in which agents can acquire such competency: continuously watching for patterns in the user's behaviour over time and offering ways to automate these actions; by acting only in ways that the user acknowledges is appropriate and changing course of actions when suggestions by the agent are neglected or rejected by the user; learning from explicit examples given by the user; and by asking for advice from other agents that assist other users with the same task. In terms of the trust challenge, the approach provides the user with sufficient time to understand how the agent works and to have faith in its actions. For example, the agent can give explanations on its behaviour as a means of building trust with its user. Another advantage with the 'personal agent' approach is that it requires much less work from the user and agent developers than the two other approaches since the agent is programmed to learn and adapt its own behaviour on a continual basis rather than relying on the user or a third party to do this.

Nwana and Ndumu (1999) provide a critical assessment of the challenges confronting agent technologies. They offer six primary areas of concern affecting the design and deployment of multi-agent systems. The first pertains to *information discovery* in terms of the difficulty of helping agents find appropriate information resources to scour and retrieve information. Potential solutions to this problem include building a yellow-pages type of service for agents to utilize for locating resources by category or a white-pages type of service for discovering information sources by name. The difficulty in creating such directory structures is that they tend to be static or manually maintained. An infrastructure is needed to enable agents to find and discover new and relevant information resources on their own behalf on a on-going and dynamic basis.

The second involves *communication* with respect to devising ways of facilitating information exchange between agents and between agents and other information source systems. Though work is underway in developing standardized agent communication languages, such as the Knowledge Query Manipulation Language (KQML) and the Foundation of Intelligent Physical Agent's Agent Control Language (FIPA ACL), no language yet has become the de facto standard. A standardized agent communication language would allow agents to interact with one another while hiding the intricate details of their internal workings; such an approach would result in agent communities that can tackle problems no individual agent could (Labrou, Finin and Pong, 1999). According to Finin, Labrou and Mayfield (1997) a good agent communication language would possess the following characteristics: good form (i.e., syntactically simple, easy to parse and generate); layering between language primitives and content of the message; clear semantics, sound implementation (i.e., offers efficiency in speed, bandwidth, and easy-to-use interface); compatibility with network technology; interoperability with other systems and agents; and reliability in supporting secure and private communications. Work is needed in these areas.

The third pertains to the development of shared *ontologies*. Common vocabularies are required to enable meaningful communication and clear understanding between multiple agents working together, or even for a single agent for that fact, to do intricate tasks with information discovered on a Web site. It is difficult to obtain agreement on standard terms and meanings a priori to agent design. The current reality is the use of domain-specific ontologies and converter applications to translate terms between them. Often, general purpose ontologies run the risk of being far too complex for most purposes and too vague to handle domain-specific intricacies.

The fourth involves enabling agents to interact with existing *legacy software* systems. Historically, systems built on older technologies have great difficulty in terms of interacting with other systems, especially newer ones like agents. Potential solutions are to: 1) rewrite the software of these older systems (this is a costly proposal); 2) use a transducer (i.e., interpreter software between the agent and the legacy system); or 3) utilize a wrapper (i.e., a legacy system augmented with code to communicate in the agent's language).

The fifth pertains to *reasoning and coordination*. To facilitate the robust and purposeful actions of agents, these software applications need to possess a certain level of reasoning, planning and constraints satisfaction capabilities. Though work is underway in this area by artificial intelligence researchers, more work is needed.

The last involves *monitoring*. Agents must monitor external events in order to fulfill tasks successfully and react appropriately. How to enable agents to do this is a difficult problem, with again, more work required.

6.3   The Semantic Web

The significance of the Semantic Web is that it provides a solution to many of the challenges confronting agent development and their deployment outlined above. The Semantic Web is an extension of the current Web in which information is given well-defined meaning, better enabling computers and people to work together in cooperation (Berners-Lee, Hendler and Lassila, 2001). Doing so, it is argued, will facilitate better use of current Web environments in terms of the provision and automation of more effective information discovery, integration, and reuse across various applications (Cherry, 2002).

This is good news for those of us interested in designing software agents to facilitate knowledge work. The Semantic Web provides an underlying infrastructure that allows software programs to search, filter, and prepare information in new and robust ways. As such, the Semantic Web offers promise in providing an environment where intelligent agents can better support the information laden tasks that organizational knowledge workers typically carry out (Port, 2002).

Full deployment and utilization of the Semantic Web is a few years away. Till then, agent solutions are limited in their capacity to help us devise more robust knowledge portal designs. The problem lies inherently within the current Web infrastructure in that it provides little means for software applications to deduce and understand the meaning behind information posted on the Web. Though deciphering the semantics of Web-based content may be an easy task for humans to do, it is in fact a very difficult feat for software. Consider, for instance, the problems typically encountered in Web information retrieval today where a search for a query term returns hits on documents that bear little relevance to one another. For instance, a search on the term 'agent' would likely generate an answer set pertaining to various types of agents, such as intelligent agents, real-estate agents, travel agents etc. The problem is that such Web-based searches rely strictly on syntactical dimensions of a search term, and not on any underlying semantics.

Another challenge facing software applications in the current Web environment is in deducing the relationship between various information items posted on the Web and knowing what operations can be performed on them. For example, it would be a fairly simple task for a human to figure out that a zip code posted on a U.S. Web site references a physical location or address, is a number on which you would never perform arithmetic operations, and is roughly analogous in function to what one could do with a postal code referenced on a Canadian Web site. However, it would be difficult, if not an impossible situation, for a computer program to handle since the current Web environment provides no facility by which to deduce relationships between one information item and another, nor infer anything about the rules of logic that govern them.

The promise of the Semantic Web is that it will help overcome these challenges in two fundamental ways (Miller and Swick, 2003). First, it will separate the identification of semantic meaning underlying an information item posted on a Web site from the presentation or formatting of that particular item. Second, it will provide a means for humans to generate descriptions of how different information items relate to one another and operations that can performed on or with them. For example, a person's name posted on a Web site can be tagged behind the scenes in such a way that informs or tells any software application, such as an agent or search engine, that this person has relations to other pieces of information (e.g., 'is an author of', 'is a parent of' or 'is an employee of').

To generate such descriptions, Web sites will reference ontologies which provide a conceptual mapping of an area of domain. What are ontologies? Most often, an *ontology* is defined as a formal conceptualization of a particular problem domain shared by a group of people (Gruber, 1993). Based on this definition, an ontology in the environment of the Semantic Web can be thought of as a partial, simplified conceptualization of a given knowledge domain shared by a community of users created for the explicit purpose of sharing semantic information across automated systems and defined in a formal, machine-processable language (Jacob, 2003).

An example given by Berners-Lee et al. to help describe the concept of ontologies is the ontology of cooking. Such an ontology would not only include things such as ingredients, and how to stir and combine them, but also the difference between simmering and deep-frying, and the expectation that the prepared item will be consumed, that oil used for cooking will not be used for lubrication etc. In this respect, an ontology consists of a set of objects or classes, the semantic interconnections among them, and simple rules of inference and logic which explain what actions can be done on or performed with these objects.

As such, ontologies provide a formal description of a domain area in terms of: 1) classes, their properties, and values; 2) the relationships between classes, between properties, and between classes and properties; 3) constraints on properties; and 4) inference rules. The extent and definition of classes, properties and their relationships are utterly limitless. Moreover, modifications to existing ontologies or the creation of brand new ones can be conducted at any time.

When generating ontological descriptions of information items posted on a Web page in the new Semantic Web environment, most Web sites will not create their own ontologies, but rather point to or reference existing ontologies stored in files on one or more Web servers. In this way, ontologies can be shared by a community of users. However, a Web site is not regulated to utilizing only one ontology in the mark-up or tagging of information items. Rather, multiple ontologies can be referenced. This is one of the benefits of the Semantic Web. Rather than proposing the development of 'agreed-upon' ontologies that are standardized to specific industries, groups or applications, the Semantic Web advocates a method by which to share and combine multiple ontologies together. The reasoning for taking such an approach is that it is too hard to predict in advance all possible pre-defined terms and relationships into a single ontology and that it would be better and more realistic to provide a means by which Web sites can readily share, combine, and re-use existing ontologies on an ad hoc basis and create new ontologies for others to use as well.

In this capacity, it is easy to understand why ontologies will play a pivotal role in the workings of the Semantic Web, and why it is an area of research and development where considerable activity is taking place these days. In fact, in term of Berners-Lee et al.'s layered architectural approach to the Semantic Web, ontologies serve as this environment's central component.

In Berners-Lee et al.'s architecture, ontologies in the Semantic Web will utilize Resource Description Framework (RDF) description statements to define classes and properties and the relations between them. The ontologies will also specify logical rules for reasoning about classes and their properties. Developed by the WWW Consortium (W3C), RDF is a general purpose knowledge representation tool for describing ontologies. It defines a vocabulary of domain classes in an 'is a' hierarchy that supports inheritance of defining features, properties, and constraints. Of importance is that it incorporates the use of other W3C-compliant standards, such as XML (eXtensible Markup Language) and URIs (Universal Resource Identifiers), which are already heavily adopted and fundamental components of the current Web. XML is a mark-up language that lets individuals define and use their own tags. Its key role lies in its provision of a syntax for describing tags. The most commonly utilized URIs are URLs (Uniform Resource Locators) which are the familiar codes used to represent a physical location of a Web site. There are other types of resources though, such as part of a Web page, devices, and people. Of importance is that URIs provide the ability to identify unique resources of all types, as well as relationships among resources.

Simplistically-speaking, an ontology in the Semantic Web environment can be thought of conceptually as a file that contains a collection of statements written in RDF plus inference rules. The importance of RDF is that it provides a mechanism for representing knowledge in a uniform way that facilitates machine understandability. RDF statements are expressed as triples having a subject, predicate, and object. The triples can be written using XML tags and URIs. The predicate typically takes the form of an 'is a' statement, which defines the relationship between two terms (e.g., 'is an author of', 'is a parent of' or 'is an employee of'). Again, these files can be stored anywhere, perhaps on centrally-located Web servers, and are referenced by Web pages that wish to utilize these ontological descriptions in the mark-up of their information items.

Work is underway to create standard development languages for defining structured, Web-based ontologies that extend the capabilities of RDF. Two initiatives in this area include OWL (i.e., the Web Ontology Language; see http://www.w3.org/TR/owl-features), as well as DAML+OIL (i.e., the DARPA Agent Metadata Language/Ontology Inference Layer; refer to http://www.w3.org/TR/daml+oil-reference). These initiatives facilitate greater machine readability of Web content than that supported by RDF statements alone through the provision of additional vocabulary along with formal semantics. For example, OWL adds more vocabulary for describing properties and classes, such as the relationship between classes (e.g., disjointedness), cardinality (e.g., 'exactly one'), equality, richer typing of properties, characteristics of properties (e.g., symmetry), and enumerated classes. Similarly, DAML+OIL builds on RDF and RDF Schema standards by extending these languages with richer modelling primitives.

Such ontology-defining languages are an important facet of leveraging the Semantic Web for knowledge work. It is purported that ontologies can be used by automated tools "to power advanced services such as more accurate Web search, intelligent software agents, and knowledge management" (Miller and Swick, 2003, p. 9). Moreover, the W3C identifies several use scenarios of ontologies, such as Web portals and intelligent agents, that showcase the potential ways ontologies can improve existing Web-based applications (see http://www.w3.org/TR/webont-req).

For instance, one example given by the W3C at the above mentioned URL is the use scenario of Web-based portals. The situation pertains to knowledge workers posting documents on a portal for others in the organization to utilize. This may involve a knowledge worker assigning an index term to the document which he or she believes best represents the document's content. Typically, this involves assigning a metadata tag from a list of pre-defined terms from a taxonomy created and maintained by one or more information specialists in the firm. If the term were assigned from an ontology (rather than a taxonomy), additional meta information could also be associated with the document. For instance, the ontology might include terminology such as 'journal paper', 'publication', 'person, and 'author'. This ontology may define relationships that state things such as 'the author of a publication is a 'person' or 'all journal papers are publications.' From these relationships, certain inferences could be made; such inferences could be utilized to facilitate better information retrieval results from the portal that may be impossible to obtain otherwise. For example, the SEmantic portAL (SEAL) is built on a rich ontology which allows the developed portal to give integrated answers to queries and enables personalization of portal content to match the specific needs of its users (Staab et al., 2000; Maedche et al., 2003).

The assumption and pivotal point in the above use scenario is that knowledge workers must have a viable and easy means by which to annotate or mark up the information they post to the portal with terms from one or more of the organization's pre-defined ontologies. If such annotation tools do not exist, it is unlikely that any improvements in knowledge portal use could be made, no matter how robust and thorough an organization's ontologies were. According to Greenburg, Sutton and Campbell (2003, p. 18), "the glories of the Semantic Web will ultimately depend on tools that will enable authors to create with very little effort RDF annotations and other useful semantic metadata on their Web pages." Painless annotations depend on the existence of predefined ontologies that spare knowledge workers of creating their own terms and relationships, as well as easy-to-use, user-friendly interfaces that permit knowledge workers to create mark-up intuitively.

A variety of annotation tools are available at the Semantic Web Authoring and Annotation Web site (http://annotation.semanticweb.org/tools). These tools include: Annotation System; Annotator; Annotea; Annozilla; COHSE Annotator; MnM; Shoe Knowledge; SMORE; Trellis Web; OntoMat Annotizer; OntoAnnotate; and Yawas. Of interest is that the mark-up tags created with annotator tools will not change the presentation of information posted on the Web. The reason is that all this work (i.e., the tagging of information items to one or more shared ontologies) is done behind the scenes, so that to the naked human eye, a Web site posted in today's Web environment would look little different than a Web site posted in tomorrow's Semantic Web.

Ideally such annotator tools need to be freely available as a means of encouraging a sufficient quorum of people utilizing and sharing ontologies with one another. Moreover, directory services that maintain master catalogues of ontologies would need to be created as a means of: facilitating re-use and propagation of existing ontologies; the extension, modification, and combination of ontological definitions; and the creation of new ontologies posted back to shared directories for others to utilize.

Once organizations have the ability to create and reuse ontological definitions and can give their employees an easy means of annotating the information they create and share, knowledge portals will be primed for the use of intelligent agents. This is one of the true strength and benefits of the Semantic Web. It creates an underlying infrastructure that enables intelligent agents to perform more robust tasks since agents now have the capability of understanding and integrating information from diverse sources. Software agents, acting on behalf of knowledge workers, will be able to reason about this information, ask for and validate proofs of the credibility of this information, and negotiate as to whom will have access to what information and ensure that the personal wishes of knowledge workers about privacy will be met (Berners-Lee, 2003).

To do such things will require that the higher-level layers of Berners-Lee et al.'s (2001) architectural structure of the Semantic Web are working. These layers operate conceptually above the ontology layer. Namely these layers are the logic and proof layers. The logic layer handles more complex logic, thus enabling software agents to infer things, choose courses of action, and answer questions. The proof layer provides explanations about the answers given by automated agents, and is a key mechanism for fostering user trust with intelligent agent software.

In an ideal world, two agents operating over a knowledge portal would utilize the same ontology, preferably an ontology pre-defined for use by the organization, so that any transactions that occur between these two agents would utilize terms consistently with the usage mandated by that ontology. However, it is more likely that two agents would utilize ontologies that were only partially or imperfectly matched. This necessitates the ability of these agents to perform 'on the fly' translation of ontologies and agree on this translation. Another option would be for the organization to create ontologies that infer the mapping of terms utilized in other ontologies.

Further, agents would need ontologies that contain and represent the entities involved in planning and doing, such as: activities, tasks, plans, agent capabilities, and so on. Work is underway towards the creation of a common ontology that contains representations for plans, processes, and other information related to activity (Tate et al., 2003). The provision of such ontologies would facilitate the creation of intelligent agents in knowledge portals that better carry out tasks and generate plans.

6.4   Agent Toolkits

To encourage the deployment of agents in knowledge portal design, agent toolkits are needed to promote the rapid creation and diffusion of robust intelligent agents. An agent toolkit is any software package, application or development environment that provides agent developers with a sufficient level of abstraction to design and implement intelligent agents with desired attributes, features and rules (Serenko and Detlor, 2003a). Some toolkits may offer only a simple environment for creating basic agent systems, whereas others may provide a complicated platform for agent development with features for visual programming.

Throughout the intelligent agent literature, the need for robust agent toolkits has been well-documented (Jennings, Sycara and Wooldridge, 1998; Sloman, 1998; Eiter and Mascardi, 2001; Wooldridge and Ciancarini, 2001). First, toolkits offer run-time simulation, monitoring, analyzing, testing and debugging environments (Luck, Griffiths and d'Inverno, 1997; Wooldridge and Jennings, 1998). Specifically, they allow programmers to reuse classes of previous designs so that new developers do not have to start from scratch every time. This is essential given that creating intelligent agent software currently requires significant training and skills (Winikoff, Padgham and Harland, 2001). Secondly, toolkits provide a certain level of abstraction and encapsulation in which programmers can develop their objects. Last, toolkits incorporate some features of visual programming, which saves time and makes development easier, more attractive and enjoyable. This is critical given the increasing complexity of software and the skyrocketing costs of development and deployment of agent software systems.

Many of the reasons why agent developers use agent toolkits are similar to the reasons why software developers who deal with object-oriented programming (OOP) prefer to use special development environments like Java VisualAge or MS Visual Basic. However, such OOP development platforms and compilers do not support all facets of agent development such as agent interaction rules, communication languages and common knowledge bases. This is why agent toolkits have emerged on the software market in the last few years—to provide a development environment that fully supports agent creation, analysis, testing, debugging and reuse.

Serenko and Detlor (2002; 2003b), in their assessment of available toolkits on the market, identify four major categories of agent toolkits: mobile agent toolkits, multi-agent toolkits, general-purpose toolkits and Internet agent toolkits.

Mobile agent toolkits are toolkits primarily dedicated to the creation of mobile agents. A mobile agent is an executing program that can migrate, at times of its own choosing, from machine to machine in a heterogeneous network. On each machine, the agent interacts with stationary service agents and other resources to accomplish its tasks (Gray et al., 2000). In other words, it is an object that can move from one computer or host machine to another performing a set of tasks that are specified by a user. A remote super computer that becomes a 'place of agent meeting' for information exchange may act as a broker linking together agents performing similar tasks.

Multi-agent toolkits are toolkits primarily concerned with the development of a multi-agent system (MAS). A MAS is usually composed of several interacting agents. This interaction involves the coordination of actions between agents, and the adaptation of agent behaviour in response to the environment. MAS is an emerging area of research in the field of distributed artificial intelligence. Often, an agent cannot solve a complex problem alone and needs cooperation with other agents to exchange data and information or delegate tasks. Over the last five years, there has been rapid development and deployment of MAS. Many conferences, workshops and seminars have been organized around this topic. There are also several Web sites (e.g., www.multiagent.com) that are entirely devoted to MAS. DeLoach (2001) identifies numerous challenges confronting the building of successful MAS. These include: decomposing problems and allocating tasks to individual agents; coordinating agent control and communications; making multiple agents act in a coherent manner; reasoning about other agents and the state of coordination; reconciling conflicting goals between the agents; and engineering practical multi-agent systems.

General purpose agent toolkits are agent development environments that do not concentrate on one specific area of agent development, like the toolkits discussed above. Instead, they allow users to create different kinds of agents for different purposes. Toolkits in this category are also identified by vendors as being agent development environments, agent development tools, agent frameworks, or agent architectures.

Internet agent toolkits are toolkits dedicated to the creation of Internet agents. These agents are dedicated to searching and retrieving information off the Internet and/or improving the interface with which users themselves search the Web. Various functions may be performed by Internet agents. They may search the Web while a user is not surfing. They may automate routine and time-consuming tasks (e.g., sorting the results that come back from search engines). They may find products a user needs or make the surfing experience more interesting and pleasant. Internet agents are usually interactive and emphasize personalization of retrieved search results.

As part of their investigation, Serenko and Detlor downloaded and tested 20 agent toolkits. Specifically, they examined how each toolkit supported the development of agents that exhibited the following characteristics: agency (i.e., the degree of independency of an agent; intelligence (i.e., the amount of learning an agent can achieve); mobility (i.e., the ability of an agent to travel from one place to another); and personalization (the amount of personalized service an agent can perform for an individual user or group of users). These characteristics were used to measure and determine the level of robustness of the agents developed by the various toolkits. For our purposes, this assessment may also hint at the ability of toolkits to generate intelligent agents that can support and foster knowledge creation, distribution, and use.

In terms of how well agent toolkits on the market currently supported these characteristics, results from Serenko and Detlor's investigation indicate that there is not yet a 'perfect' toolkit available. None of the 20 toolkits assessed by the authors supported all four agent features to a large extent. Rather, each toolkit had certain strengths in supporting a certain subset of these characteristics. For instance, mobile agent toolkits were strong in generating agents that were highly mobile. Internet agent toolkits supported the creation of agents that could personalize and tailor Web-based information display to personal or group user needs. Of the four categories, multi-agent toolkits exhibited the strongest intelligence capability. Agent toolkits in this category were required to generate agents that could think independently, and communicate and coordinate actions with other agents—tasks which require a high degree of intelligence. The most well-rounded category of toolkits were general purpose toolkits in that they tended to allow the creation of agents that possessed all four agent characteristics. The other toolkit categories tended to support agents that were restricted to one or two characteristics; however these characteristics were supported to a greater extent than those possessed by agents generated by the general purpose toolkits.

It should be noted that agent toolkits are in the early stages of agent development. Though most agent development toolkits do not yet support all of the four agent characteristics described above, such as personalization and basic intelligence features (e.g., common knowledge bases), the pace of adoption and development of agent toolkits has been constantly increasing. Serenko and Detlor suggest that agent toolkits are likely to move closer to supporting all four agent characteristics in the near future. Once this is done, it will be easier for organizations to generate robust agents that can help organizational knowledge workers better utilize their enterprise portal systems for knowledge creation, distribution, and use activities.

6.5   Applications of Agents in Knowledge Portals

Having given background on the nature of agents and their potential to leverage the power of semantic information posted on the Web, attention turns now to the application and deployment of agents in enterprise portals in ways that can promote knowledge creation, distribution, and use across the firm.

Recall back in Figure 1-3, the on-going information needs-seeking-use cycle in which knowledge workers are engaged as they interact with the company's knowledge portal. In the information needs stage, users are confronted with discrete problem situations typically faced in their work settings. The social roles of users, as well as their cognitive and affective make-up, influence how people perceive and react to these problem situations. In the information seeking stage, users turn to the knowledge portal to obtain the requisite information required to help resolve their problems. In the information use stage, the knowledge worker utilizes the information and knowledge obtained from the portal, which in turn, modifies the problem situation that initiated the cycle in the first place, potentially spawning new cycles of needs-seeking-use activity with the portal.

This chapter suggests that intelligent agents can be deployed in each of these three stages and that doing so can provide a sufficient and ample means of fostering knowledge work across the enterprise. Figure 6-1 illustrates how agents can uniquely serve in each stage of the information needs-seeking-use cycle that knowledge workers undergo.

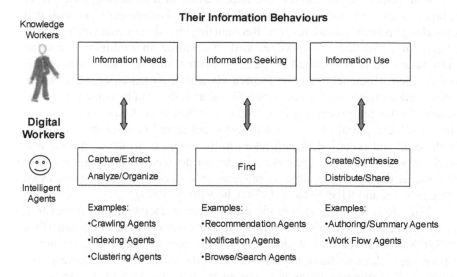

Figure 6-1: The application of agents in knowledge portals

Here, both knowledge workers and intelligent agents function as *digital workers*. The diagram depicts human participants engaged in three primary information behaviours with knowledge portals: information needs, seeking, and use. The diagram also shows how intelligent agents can respond and ameliorate these behaviours with their own set of actions. These actions are derived from the five key information processes identified by Mack, Ravin and Byrd (2001) that knowledge portals should support, initially described in section 2.4: capturing and extracting, analyzing and organizing, finding, creating and synthesizing, and distributing and sharing. Figure 6-1 also depicts some examples of specific types of agents that can be developed to service these particular processes. As such, the figure attempts to map out various types of agents to be deployed in knowledge portal designs that can service and support employees in their knowledge work tasks. Details on the functionality of such agents are described in the following sub-sections.

6.5.1 Information Needs

The information needs stage depicted in Figure 6-1 represents the state where individuals become aware of gaps in their knowledge and their ability to make sense of a problem situation. In this stage, agents can be used to gather information of relevance to users, and to prepare this information in advance that facilitates quick and timely retrieval when the information is actually required.

With respect to the capture and organization of information, Mack et al. (2001) identify several activities involved in this knowledge work task that knowledge portals should support. Recognizing that documents created in the course of performing knowledge work are stored in multiple places, an automatic means is required to gather, register, manage, and analyze this information. Documents can be located via a process called crawling where relevant documents are located. Once found, an index can be constructed. The reason for this pre-processing is to prepare a robust collection of documents in the knowledge portal of relevance to users and stored in ways that facilitates high recall and precision. *Recall* refers to the extent to which an information retrieval system is able to retrieve all relevant documents; *precision* refers to the extent the system is able to retrieve only documents that are relevant (Baeza-Yates and Ribeiro-Neto, 1999; Chowdhury, 1999).

Indexing is a critical step in the preparation of documents for retrieval. It is the process of assigning identifiers to the contents of a document (Pao, 1989; Sparck Jones and Willet, 1997). This can be done on a document surrogate, such as a title or an abstract, or on the full text of a document. The purpose of creating an index is to permit the easy location of documents by topic at a later point in time, to define topic areas housed in the portal's collection of documents, and to predict (again, at a later point in time) the relevance of any given document to a user's query (Keen, 1977; Salton and McGill, 1983). Automating this task results in an index structure having better consistency and less bias than if the process were done manually; this in turn improves retrieval performance. Further, with the large volumes of documents posted on portals, the task is too large for humans alone to do in an efficient and cost-effective manner.

All attempts at automatic indexing depend in some way on the text of the original document or document surrogates. Typically, the words occurring in each document are listed and certain statistical measures are made, such as absolute or relative term frequencies. From there, key words in a document are identified that can be used to index or represent the document. Usually, the more frequent the occurrence of a word in a given document, the more significant is the term in denoting the document's subject content.

Automatic indexing, in general, involves two distinct steps: 1) determining the index terms to represent the document; and 2) assigning weights or values to those index terms which best reflect the document's content. With respect to the first step, the most obvious place to look for terms that represent a document is to look at the words contained in the document itself. A common way to do this is to calculate the frequency of words contained in a document and to pick terms that fall within a threshold range. Words that appear too frequently or are too unique often make poor index terms. Frequent words appear so often that almost all documents contain them. Unique words are so rare that they generally have no relation to the ideas contained within the text. Prior to calculating word frequencies, usually common words are eliminated through use of a stop list (e.g., words like 'a', 'an', 'the' etc.), sometimes called a 'negative dictionary', and word stems are prepared through suffix stripping (i.e., stemming). Stems make better index terms since a single stem can represent many related words (e.g., the stem 'comput' can represent words like 'compute', 'computing', 'computation', 'computable' et cetera). Several stemming algorithms for suffix stripping exist for the English language; three fully described in the information retrieval literature are the Lovins stemmer (Lovins, 1968), the Porter stemmer (Porter, 1980), and the Paice/Husk stemmer (Paice, 1990).

The second step involves assigning weights to the chosen terms from the first step as a means of identifying those terms which best represent the contents of a document. The best index terms are ones that appear frequently in a few documents, but not in all documents in the collection. Therefore the typical calculations used for assigning weights to index terms involve taking into account the frequency with which a term occurs in a document with respect to the frequency with which that term occurs across the collection. The most common method used is the inverse document frequency (idf) calculation (Sparck Jones, 1972). With idf, to determine the weight of a term in a document, the term's word count frequency is multiplied by a factor that depends logarithmically on the proportion of the documents in the collection that contain that term. Alternative weight calculations include computing the signal-noise ratio or the discrimination value of terms (Salton and McGill, 1983).

After this second step, a set of index terms is selected to represent the contents of each document in the collection. As such, each document in the collection can be represented by a vector of index terms. By comparing the vectors of documents with one another, similar documents can be gathered together into smaller groupings. This process is known as *clustering* (Chowdhury, 1999; Salton, 1989; Mack et al., 2001). Algorithms exist which determine when two vectors are similar enough to warrant allocating the documents represented by those vectors into the same cluster. More robust algorithms are capable of building hierarchical structures of clusters and sub-clusters. Once the clusters are created, they must be named. *Cluster labelling* is the process of inspecting cluster contents and choosing the best term to represent or name each cluster (Mack et al., 2001). Cluster names must be easily understood by humans and readily distinguish the content of clusters from neighbouring ones. Once this step is done, it is relatively simple to generate a hierarchically organized mapping of clusters. This is called a *taxonomy*, with each labelled cluster referred to as a *node*. Typically, a human expert familiar with classification schemas and the cataloguing of information is required to refine the generated taxonomy to ensure it is easily understandable and matches the terminology utilized by users when describing their subject and topic areas of interest. Fortunately, most clustering processes produce a rank associated with each document's assignment to a particular cluster. This rank reflects the degree of confidence a user should have in the assignment of a document to a category (Mack et al., 2001).

It is argued that agents could help in all the above tasks. Software agents could work in the background to perform the above mentioned operations of crawling, indexing, and clustering on a continual basis. It is likely that each of these tasks could be allocated to different, independent functioning agents, such as *crawler agents*, *indexing agents*, and *clustering agents*. In this way, agents can facilitate knowledge portal use by capturing and organizing information on the portal in ways that facilitate future retrieval. Such background tasks prep the portal to respond more effectively and efficiently to the information needs of its user base by providing a comprehensive and organized infrastructure that contains indexes and taxonomies which users can utilize to access information of direct interest to them.

6.5.2 Information Seeking

The information seeking stage in Figure 6-1 represents the state where the information needs of individuals are articulated as questions or topics that guide the identification of, and interaction with, information sources available through the knowledge portal. In this stage, agents can be used to inform people of information items of potential interest and relevance, ameliorate the display and presentation of information retrieval results, and to help users navigate their way to particular items.

With respect to making users aware of information on the portal of potential relevance and interest, two types of agents could be deployed: recommendation agents and notification agents (Maes, 1999; 2001). *Recommendation agents* make suggestions on potential information items of interest that best suits a user's needs and preferences. This could be done on a just-in-time basis or continually over regular intervals of time. To do this, an agent would look for patterns in a knowledge worker's information behaviour and make recommendations on related documents or Web sites of interest. If user profiling databases are maintained, the information preferences and behaviours of users with similar profiles could be aggregated and analyzed to deduce potential information items. This process is better known as collaborative filtering (Goldberg et al., 1992; Resnick and Varian, 1997). Further, a user could explicitly give a recommendation agent a set of topic areas or identify specific titles of documents that the user finds interesting and instruct the agent to find related information. Ideally the user could specify additional parameters and constraints, such as a timeframe by which to return the results by, or information pertaining to a specific genre of documents, such as journal articles appearing in top-tier, double-blind, peer-reviewed publications.

Notification agents announce or notify users of events that they were instructed to monitor. For example, a user could instruct an agent to monitor the posting of new information items in the portal pertaining to certain subject areas. The agent would watch for such events and notify the user when these events occur. The possible scenarios of things to monitor are endless. For example, an agent could be instructed to notify the user when other people read any document authored by that person. Or the agent could be asked to let the user know when a certain report eagerly awaited becomes available for public viewing.

In terms of ameliorating the display and presentation of information retrieval results, agents could also help in this regard. They could highlight information items or rank the display of retrieved documents in ways that raise awareness or signal the potential value of relevant information to users. This can be done by emphasizing key words (e.g., bolding, italicizing) in the list of retrieved document summaries, or ordering the retrieved documents so that priority is placed on documents that align with user subject interests or the extent to which other users with similar profiles find such documents relevant and useful.

Several types of agents that tailor the display of retrieved document sets are suggested by researchers at the Massachusetts Institute of Technology's Media Laboratory. Three (of the many) agent prototypes developed there are Letizia (Lieberman, 1995; 1997), Lets Browse (Lieberman, Van Dyke and Vivacqua, 1999), and PowerScout (Lieberman, Fry and Weitzman, 2001).

Letizia is an autonomous interface agent that, through its own monitoring of a user's online browsing activity and its own internal algorithm, adapts a portion of the interface with a list of recommendations of potential documents to consider based on the set of documents the user is currently browsing. In this way, the agent customizes the interface 'in context' of a user's current browsing state. Letizia compensates for the typical depth-first search pattern of exploration behaviour associated with Web search engine information retrieval. It does this by doing a controlled breadth-first search on documents or pages selected by the user. For each document or page selected, an idf calculation is performed to determine the subject areas the user is currently exploring. From these, Letizia uses this information to find recommended or similar pages among the answer set of URLs in the user's current session. Letizia then displays its results in an independent window on the interface for the user to see.

Letizia offers certain advantages over traditional Web search engines. It does not break or alter the user's normal flow of activity. That is, the user does not have to direct Letizia in any way. Rather, Letizia gets its input indirectly from the user by watching his or her browsing activity. Further, Letizia can continue working while the user is inactive—better refining its breadth-first seeking strategy over time.

Lets Browse is a different sort of interface agent than Letizia also used to tailor the display of retrieved document hits. Rather than monitoring the browsing activity of a single user, Lets Browse facilitates collaborative or group browsing. Here, the agent utilizes stored user profiles of people engaged in a group-browse session to tailor the direction and selection of information items. For each user in the group, a neighbourhood of Web pages is selected. For example, this neighbourhood could be generated beforehand by performing an idf calculation on each user's home page or by maintaining an up-to-date user profile database for group members. As users join or leave a group's browsing session, the Lets Browse agent makes recommendations on sites which are good candidate matches to the current group of users' collective set of neighbourhood pages.

PowerScout is an agent similar to Letizia in that it monitors a user's current set of retrieved document sets and comes up with its own set of recommended documents and displays these in a separate window. Unlike Letizia which restricts its recommended items based the answer set of URLs the user is currently viewing, PowerScout issues a separate search query over the Web via a conventional search engine. This search query is generated by extracting keywords from the current page or document the user is browsing combined with concepts obtained from the user's profile database.

These three agents concentrate on the browse side of the information seeking spectrum. Recall the Choo, Detlor and Turnbull (1999; 2000a; 2000b) study described earlier in section 5.5 which identified four discrete types of information seeking activity by users of Web-based browsers: two browsing related (e.g., undirected browsing, conditioned browsing); and two search related (e.g., informal search, formal search). One could speculate that *browse/search agents* could be designed to support each of these modes across the entire spectrum of Web-seeking behaviour.

Moreover, one could also leverage Choo et al.'s findings which identify certain Web-based browser actions or moves (e.g., page forward, back, print, stop, selecting a hyperlink) as being associated to each of these four Web seeking modes. Namely, these findings suggest the feasibility of designing an agent which monitors a user's Web actions and then deduces the particular Web seeking mode in which the user is engaged. Once known, the agent could react and offer help or assistance to the user in ways that were reflective of the user's Web seeking mode. For example, if the user were engaged in undirected browsing, the agent could navigate the user to potential sites of interest. If the user were exhibiting conditioned browsing behaviour, the agent could quickly navigate the user to his or her preferred Web sites or showcase what was newly added to those sites that may be of interest. If the user were engaged in informal search, the agent could offer pre-packaged search strategies, or display pre-selected sources and search engines to facilitate quick searches. If the user were exhibiting formal search behaviour, the agent could direct the user to meta-search engines or multiple information sources, advise the user when to use different information services, or train the user on advanced search techniques.

In these ways, agents could be deployed in knowledge portal systems that help users better navigate their way to information items of interest since these agents are cognisant and reactive to a variety of user information seeking modes ranging from browse to search.

6.5.3 Information Use

The information use stage depicted in Figure 6-1 represents the state where individuals select and process information obtained from the knowledge portal. This final stage is often overlooked by designers of Web-based retrieval systems, but it is arguably the most critical stage of the three in terms of knowledge work. The information needs stage concentrates on the types of information to capture, extract, analyze, and organize to facilitate quick and relevant information retrieval. The information seeking stage pertains to the finding of information content in ways that raises awareness or highlights the potential value of information items retrieved and deemed relevant to a user's request. The information use stage involved helping the user create and synthesize the information selected by the user to be of value and to distribute and share that information with other people. In this way, the information use stage is where knowledge creation, distribution, and use actively occur. It is the stage of activity that bears fruit from the underlying work done in the previous two stages.

Mack et al. (2001) recognize the limitation of current enterprise portal implementations in providing facilities which promote information use and posit that knowledge portals in the near future will leverage advancements in intelligent technologies, such as agents, to support an expanding knowledge workplace. Specifically, in Mack et al.'s view:

> "the digital knowledge workplace of the future will be driven by a more intelligent and task-oriented infrastructure than the one enabled by current KM technology. This emerging knowledge workplace will support targeted knowledge work tasks more directly and integrally, with reference to specific project roles and responsibilities in a collaborative work environment. This workplace will emerge as the KW's [knowledge worker's] software environment expands and becomes more distributed and varied" (Mack et al., 2001, p. 948).

Mack et al. identify two processes that knowledge portals should support to promote information use: the authoring and summary of information; and the distribution and sharing of information. It is argued that agents could help in both regards.

Authoring/summary agents are agents that help knowledge workers analyze and synthesize the information they select to use from the portal. A variety of standard work tools currently exist, such as word processing software, presentation graphics tools, spreadsheets, and project management software. Agents could be employed within these work tools available on a knowledge portal to help users analyze and process information. For example, such agents could suggest document templates (perhaps those used elsewhere in the company), provide helpful instruction on how to utilize those tools, or recommend exemplar documents, reports, plans etc. on which to model the information currently being massaged. In contrast to these single-authoring agents, collaborative authoring agents could be made available in the background to help groups of users create and synthesize information together; for example, helping project team members collaborate on the authoring of project documents. Such agents would be responsible for managing version controls, ensuring that no one project member 'checks out' a collaborative document for editing for too long a period of time, or perhaps merging multiple edits together.

Work flow agents are agents that help knowledge workers distribute and share information with one another in order to meet a work task goal. This type of agent working in the background would be key in helping to coordinate the actions between project team members and ensuring that project deadlines, milestones, and deliverables were met. One critical function of such an agent would be to ensure that final-versioned project documents are posted back in the knowledge portal for others to use.

Firestone (2003) identifies ten areas of work flow process control where agents (i.e., avatars) can be successfully applied:

1) facilitating specification of routing and distribution;
2) supporting rapid and easy change in the routing structure, the distribution process, and the business rules governing the work flow;
3) providing the capability of either storing the product of a work flow task or pushing it to the next step in the work flow;
4) providing the capability to distribute the work flow process across multiple computers;
5) providing the capability to gather knowledge resources to support the work flow;
6) supporting collaborative transactions among work flow participants;
7) supporting subject matter integration into the portal user interface;
8) providing the capability to model and present individual, personalized work flows in the portal interface;
9) providing the capability to simulate collaborative work flow; and,
10) providing the capability to customize work flows by integrating custom, legacy, or external data and applications.

6.6 An Agent Architecture for Knowledge Portals

The above depiction in Figure 6-1 of the application of agents in knowledge portals illustrates how various sorts of intelligent agents can be used to foster the information needs-seeking-use cycle in firms that knowledge workers undergo. Attention now turns to the development of an agent-based architecture for knowledge portals that organizations can potentially implement. This architecture maps out a possible means of deploying a knowledge portal system in a way that is structured in terms of a network of cooperating agents. Various multi-agent architectures have been proposed for intelligent information retrieval (Tu and Hsiang, 2000), financial risk monitoring systems (Wang, Mylopoulos and Liao, 2002); electronic business (Papazoglou, 2001); virtual enterprises (Ram, 2001), and intranet document management (Ginsburg, 1999).

Of relevance to our discussion on knowledge portals is a generic agent-based model of information seeking and retrieval developed by Detlor and Arsenault (2002). Though that particular model was applied to library contexts, it can serve as a basis for an underlying agent-based architecture for knowledge portals. The suggested model is shown in Figure 6-2. The figure utilizes four types of agents: interface agents; information agents; server agents; and directory agents. These types of agents correspond with the agent types described earlier in this chapter: interface agents and information service agents. Interface agents are the same. Their primary role is to assist users; they know user preferences and subject interests and typically concern themselves with the display of information on the computer interface. Information agents, server agents, and directory agents are a further decomposition of the formerly described information service agent. All function as background agents. Information agents are middleman agents— coordinating action and activity among interface agents, server agents, directory agents, and even other information agents. Server agents maintain access to and manage data and document collections housed on one or more Web servers in the portal. Directory agents maintain directories or indexes of agents available for cooperative action to alleviate the need for information agents themselves to maintain lists of data and document collections available in the portal and other knowledge workers and their information agents available for possible collaboration.

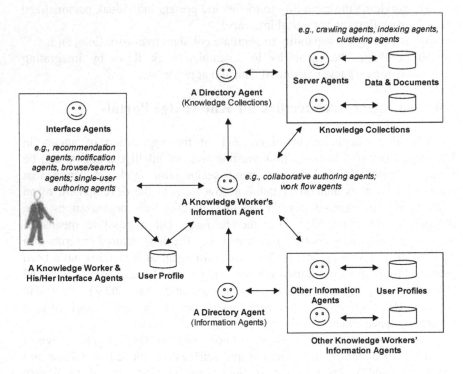

Figure 6-2: An agent-based architecture for knowledge portals

Figure 6-2 illustrates how all these agents would work cooperatively together in a knowledge portal. The figure also shows how specific examples of intelligent agents depicted in Figure 6-1 map to the proposed architectural design.

The model portrays individual knowledge workers each having one or multiple personal *interface agents*. Upon signing into the knowledge portal with a username and password, an interface agent would utilize user profile information to help tailor the display of information on the computer interface. Examples of such agents would be recommendation agents, notification agents, browse/search agents, and single-user authoring agents. The user profile database would contain personal information about the user such as subject areas of interest, favourite document resources, a history of previous information requests, and perhaps feedback information from the user on the relevance of material retrieved from past information seeking activity. The profile would also contain outstanding and on-going information requests. Outstanding requests refer to information queries not yet deemed complete by the user. On-going requests would be general topics the user has expressed an interest in gathering more information about or being told of new additions to the knowledge portal that pertain to interest areas outlined in his or her profile.

A key purpose of the interface agent would be to communicate and coordinate activities with the user's *information agent*. One possible role of an information agent would be to function as an information intermediary on behalf of the user. This entails scouring various data and document collections to fulfill information browsing and searching requests, as well as monitoring the information landscape for new information items that may be of interest to the user. Another possible role would involve coordinating action and activity among groups of users, such as those participating in projects. This is where collaborative authoring agents come into play. To perform these roles, an information agent would coordinate its actions with directory agents, server agents, and other knowledge workers' information agents.

As mentioned above, information agents would engage in dialogue with *directory agents* to secure lists of document collections for possible access and lists of other employee's information agents for possible collaboration and coordination activity. For instance, an information agent may need to know all data and document collections within the portal and on the Web pertaining to certain subject areas or the project members currently participating in a particular project or corporate venture. Rather than burdening each individual information agent with these tasks, such vital lists could be housed and administered by directory agents who facilitate the management and update of such pertinent information.

Server agents would service requests to collections in the portal from multiple information agents. It would be the role of the server agent to verify the authority of an information agent to utilize resources in the collection. For example, a document collection pertaining to a particular project may only be available for project team members. It would also be the role of the server agent to retrieve relevant information items from the collection that satisfy an information agent's seeking and retrieval requests. Another key duty of the server agent would be to prepare the document collection in advance for quick and efficient information retrieval. This is where crawling agents, indexing agents, and clustering agents come into play—organizing the data or document collection in advance by preparing indexes, document clusters, and taxonomies.

It would be up to the information agent to decide which server agents to poll for information (perhaps through the assistance of a directory agent) as well as the frequency of this polling. For instance, specific information queries may be performed once to satisfy a one-time information request on behalf of a user wanting immediate feedback in real-time. Meanwhile, other information queries may be made on a continual basis to fulfill a user's outstanding information requests.

Other knowledge workers' information agents would be polled regularly as well to determine information items of relevance from users with similar profiles. Each information agent would know its own user's interest areas, preferences for certain collections, and ratings of the relevance of information items retrieved from past requests, all via access to the user's profile database. By coordinating and sharing this information among information agents servicing the needs of like-minded individuals, information agents could facilitate collaborative filtering with the goal of identifying retrieval items of higher relevance to users. Another function of interacting with other knowledge workers' information agents would be to coordinate and carry out collaborative tasks, such as that required in the multiple-authoring of documents and the management of work flow activities.

There are subtle differences between how the interface and information agents would operate. Interface agents would be in direct communication with knowledge workers and active only during user sessions. On start-up of a portal user session, interface agents would need to 'talk' with the user's information agent to retrieve possible results from outstanding and on-going information requests and the status of events in any coordinated group work activity. In contrast, information agents would not engage in dialogue directly with users and would operate continuously, even when users terminated their sessions with the knowledge portal. When users are disengaged from the portal, an information agent would be in constant communication with directory agents, server agents and other information agents as a means of coordinating group work and satisfying any information requests on behalf of its knowledge portal user.

Overall, the model presented above depicts a feasible, agent-based architectural design organizations can adopt to foster knowledge work in their portals. The model highlights various different types of agents that must work cooperatively together. Doing so, it is argued, would provide an infrastructure that is amenable to supporting and fostering the information needs-seeking-use cycle of knowledge portal users.

6.7   Conclusion

The purpose of this chapter was to discuss the future role of intelligent agents in facilitating knowledge work in enterprise portals. A definition and description of intelligent agents, along with their benefits and challenges were first described. This was followed by a detailed description of the Semantic Web, in particular its potential to provide an agent-based infrastructure for organizational knowledge work. The need for robust agent development toolkits in organizational settings was then discussed.

All this led to a description of how intelligent agents could be deployed in knowledge portals in ways that matched and fostered the information needs-seeking-use cycle of organizational knowledge workers. Specifically, distinct sets of agents were described that supported each phase of the information needs-seeking-use cycle, initially described in Chapter 1. Agents that captured and extracted information, as well analysed and organized it, were purported to facilitate user information needs. Agents that found information were described as supporting individuals in their information seeking behaviour. Agents that created and synthesized information, as well as distributed and shared it among organizational workers, were posited to promote organizational information use.

From there, the chapter presented a robust, high-level architecture of intelligent agents that was reflective of this information needs-seeking-use cycle. Various sorts of agents, such as interface agents, information agents, directory agents, and server agents were described and shown to work cooperatively together in ways that fostered knowledge work. It is hoped that the architecture will provide guidance to knowledge portals designers in mapping out the requisite functionality of enterprise portal agents and their interactions with one another that promote knowledge creation, distribution, and use throughout the firm.

7. KNOWLEDGE PORTALS AND DIGITAL WORKERS

The purpose of this monograph was to provide an in-depth description and account of how enterprise portals can promote firm-wide knowledge creation, distribution, and use. To facilitate this discussion, knowledge portals were examined from an information perspective. As such, the proceeding chapters covered a variety of topics pertaining to portal adoption and use that explored "human issues" as well as the utilization of "intelligent agents" as a means of fostering the design of portal systems to support knowledge-based tasks.

In this way, the monograph was crafted to explore, investigate, and postulate ideas concerning the role of knowledge portals in relation to the digital worker. Here, the digital worker was perceived as both the "human" organizational knowledge worker as well as the automated software agent or digital assistant who works on behalf of a user or group of users in support of their knowledge work activities.

The task now is to recap and summarize the many ideas and concepts detailed in this text into a more compact synthesis. Recognizing the complexity of the ideas put forth in the preceding chapters, the hope is to better communicate and emphasize the major themes explicated and threaded throughout prior pages.

To accomplish this goal, the predominant and important lessons from each chapter are first summarized. From there, a meta-analysis is done with discussion centred on ways to leverage the role of enterprise portals to facilitate knowledge work. The description centres on the design and roll out of knowledge portals in ways that are respectful and sensitive to the information needs-seeking-use cycle of organizational participants. It is argued that such information behaviours, which occur in context of a firm's information environment, are pivotal in shaping the extent to which portal systems are eventually utilized for knowledge work. As such, this chapter calls for an approach to portal design and its technology that is responsive to the human element. The output of this meta-analysis is the presentation of a model of enterprise portal use for knowledge work. This is followed by some ideas on research directions and a few final words.

7.1 Summary of Chapters

At the heart of this monograph is the notion that enterprise portals are potentially more than mere information retrieval systems in that they ultimately can become vehicles which promote and leverage organizational knowledge creation, distribution, and use. In this sense, enterprise portals are viewed as being situated in "the larger mosaic of knowledge management – their purpose in this broader context being to help organizations and individuals adapt to the changing environment of the workplace and the organization" (Firestone, 2003, pp. xvii-xviii).

This viewpoint was purported in Chapter 1. Such a perspective led to the introduction and definition of the term *knowledge portal* as being a specific breed of enterprise portal which supported the three main facets of information content storage and retrieval, organizational communication, and group collaboration. By functioning as a shared information work space, it was argued that these systems could truly support *knowledge work*, defined as a set of three core processes comprising knowledge creation, distribution, and use. These processes were shown to be information-laden activities where human participants drew upon both tacit and explicit types of knowledge in the production and reproduction of information, often yielding information outputs. Knowledge portals were portrayed as instruments which could support such activity, namely through the provision of information content, communication, and coordination spaces.

Based on an overview of various key models of information behaviour from the Information Studies field, several common ideas were elicited which gave indication how organizational workers go about identifying their information needs, search for information to satisfy those needs, and use or transfer that information into action. Such *information behaviours* were viewed as being critical in the knowledge work activities of organizational participants. The common ideas emanating from this review of information behaviour models included the cognitive and affective characteristics of users, problem-based tasks or goals which invoke user needs, the cyclic nature of information needs-seeking-use behaviour, and the situated environmental context in which this behaviour occurs. As such, Chapter 1 culminated in Figure 1-3 which illustrated how knowledge portals were situated within the information environment of the firm, and moreover, were engaged within the on-going information needs-seeking-use cycle of knowledge workers as they go about interacting with the portal as a means of resolving their problem situations.

In the *information needs stage*, users are confronted with discrete problem situations typically faced in their work contexts. What problem situations are viewed by workers as being important and worth resolving depends on people's social roles and cognitive and affective compositions. In this phase, knowledge workers become aware of one or more gaps in their *knowledge* (defined as actionable, comprehended information) to resolve the problem situations they face.

In the *information seeking stage*, users turn to the knowledge portal to obtain the requisite knowledge and information to help resolve their problem situations. Here, several intervening variables can promote or inhibit the act of information seeking. These include psychological, demographic, role-related, environmental, and information source specific factors. Further, users can exhibit a wide spectrum of information seeking behaviour ranging from wayward browsing to goal-directed searching. These may be one-time retrieval requests or on-going information seeking tasks.

In the *information use stage*, users complete their scan of a knowledge portal's resources and actively utilize the information and knowledge obtained. As a result of this action, the original problem situation which evoked participants to utilize the portal in the first place is modified in some way. Either the situation becomes resolved, altered, or generates a new set of problem situations. If not resolved, the information needs-seeking-use cycle repeats, thus reflecting the dynamic nature of knowledge portal use in firms.

Having defined knowledge portals, described their potential, and showcased a model of their utilization, Chapter 2 extended the discussion on knowledge portals in terms of their implementations in organizational settings. The chapter acknowledged that barriers to knowledge distribution and use are really not technical, and that the culture of a company and its user behaviours play a more critical part in determining the extent to which any knowledge system is adopted and avidly used. From there, attention turned to various knowledge portal implementation scenarios in terms of the general characteristics, features, and processes enterprise portals typically support. Ideas on the strategic factors to increase the likelihood of portal adoption and use were also described. These included aligning the portal's mandate with the organization's mission and vision, establishing clear metrics on which to evaluate the portal's return on investment, promoting the benefits of portal usage across the enterprise, and assigning clear roles and sufficient budgets to manage portal development and update portal content.

A look at the Behavioural/Ecological Framework by Choo, Detlor, and Turnbull identified the need to incorporate both top-down and bottom-up approaches to Web information system design and roll-out. In essence, the framework called for the need for designers of such systems to look beyond technical constraints that inhibit adoption and use of these systems and to consider the social, cultural, and behavioural factors that also play an active role in determining user system acceptance and utilization of the system for knowledge work activity.

Based on this overview, a *Knowledge Portal Framework* was proposed. The framework acknowledged the integral role information plays in organizational knowledge creation, distribution and use and called for portal developers to construct features within these systems that promote a supportive information environment and which address the information needs and uses of organizational participants. The framework suggested that this could be facilitated by presenting information on the portal interface in ways that highlight the potential value of information to users and which support specific information seeking tasks. In this way, the Knowledge Portal Framework posited that three key shaping entities determine or influence the utilization of an enterprise portal for knowledge work, namely: users, the information environment, and a portal's information design.

From there, the details of the author's methodology for an in-depth case study investigation of knowledge portal usage were explained. The investigation utilized both qualitative and quantitative research methods to hone its interpretation and analysis of the collected data. Each of the three successive chapters of this monograph presented findings from the author's research investigation. These were complemented with additional opinions, anecdotes, and theory from related works yielding a rich account and description of the factors which inhibit or promote knowledge portal use in organizations from each of the three shaping factors of the Knowledge Portal Framework. Chapter 3 reported on the user entity of the Knowledge Portal Framework. Chapter 4 delved into a detailed discussion on information environments and their effect on knowledge portal adoption and use. Chapter 5 discussed the knowledge portal in terms of interface design issues.

In terms of the *user* entity, the author's case study investigation showcased many factors affecting portal adoption and use. First, user roles played a critical part in how portals were utilized and the types of activities performed on them. Secondly, certain user characteristics played an important part in shaping the extent of use of the portal for knowledge creation, distribution, and use. Key Web information system knowledge workers were shown to exhibit an avid interest in portal technology, a positive perception of the portal as a viable tool for knowledge work, and self motivation in learning and keeping up-to-date in personal areas of expertise, all more so than non-key WIS users. From these results, certain recommendations were made on ways to promote the development and use of knowledge portals in firms. These included placing greater emphasis on marketing the portal to organizational workers and training them on its strategic advantage. It was suggested that following such recommendations could help showcase the functionality of the portal, facilitate a more accurate perception of the features and functions available for use, instil a greater interest or passion in this technology, and increase the potential to utilize the portal to maintain currency in personal areas of expertise.

Of related interest to the user entity was the application of the Technology Acceptance Model and its antecedents to the adoption and use of knowledge portals. TAM provided a well-demonstrated and validated rationale for the flow of causality from external variables concerning knowledge portal design characteristics and development processes through user-based perceptions to attitude and finally to knowledge portal use. TAM suggests that building user friendly interfaces is in itself insufficient to warrant extensive user buy-in. Equally important is the need for users to be made aware of the functionality portals provide and the ease with which the portal facilitates those tasks. Further, social constructs such as subjective norm, voluntariness, and image, as well as cognitive variables such as job relevance, output quality, and result demonstrability, were shown to influence attitudes towards the portal and strengthening the chances of the portal actually being used. In this respect, both cognitive factors, in terms of user perceptions towards a portal's usefulness and ease of use, and social factors, in terms of the degree to which users believe those with social currency or power in the organization adopt and utilize the portal, have large influencing effects on knowledge portal usage in the firm.

With respect to the *information environment*, that construct was shown to comprise several variables including a firm's information culture, information systems development processes, and information politics. *Information culture* was defined as the degree to which information in an organization is readily shared, valued, and filtered across the company. *Information systems development processes* were defined to be procedures in place in a firm which dictate how information systems, such as knowledge portals, are developed and maintained. *Information politics* was defined to be the human struggle over the management of information in a firm, in this particular case, the management of enterprise portal content and applications. Results from the author's case study investigation indicated that these environmental components constrained and enhanced how well organizational participants utilized the portal for knowledge work tasks. Specifically, a lack of information sharing, too much information overload, and controls placed over the composition and presentation of information available in the portal, all deterred or hampered use of the portal for knowledge work.

Of importance were related findings in other case studies of knowledge portal implementations which substantiated the author's own case study investigation. Together, these case studies raised awareness of the environmental factors that can challenge the successful implementation of knowledge portal systems in any organization. Due to the very nature of knowledge portals as systems characterized by superconnectivity, ubiquitousness, a broad range of users, a strong grassroots appeal, and a wide expanse across all branches of an enterprise, the typical rational approach to the management of information systems was shown to be a flawed mechanism by which to govern the development and promotion of these systems. Instead, a balance between looseness and structure in the management of enterprise portals was shown to be warranted, especially if these systems were to support and foster knowledge work activity.

Given these arguments, certain recommendations were outlined to foster information environments in organizations that were more conducive to the utilization of enterprise portals for knowledge work. These recommendations included the need to balance control and individual ownership, to cultivate the portal as a medium rather than as a system, and to aim toward a self-sustaining portal. Other recommendations included the need to establish a democratic portal governing structure composed of various representatives of major stakeholders, to create a streamlined systems development process, and to create flexible and accommodating firm-wide information policies.

In terms of *information design,* the need to present information in ways that highlight the potential value of information to users was shown to be a critical aspect affecting knowledge portal adoption and use. In this sense, good information presentation was no longer portrayed as something portal designers ought to do, but rather something that was a critical and vital piece by which to signal the potential worthiness of pieces of information displayed to organizational workers on the portal interface. Five characteristics to improve the information design of knowledge portals were derived from the author's case study investigation. These were the ability of the portal to support tailorability, to display information of high quality, to organize information in ways that facilitated quick access and navigation, to include collaborative tools, and to provide engaging interactions.

Another key discussion point of the chapter was to tailor the display of information on the knowledge portal interface in ways that support the range of information seeking modes in which knowledge workers engage. This includes supporting users in both browse and search modes of activity. Doing so, it was suggested, would better match or address the specific tasks for which users turn to the portal for help.

In all, information design was described as having three primary components: 1) to make information comprehensible; 2) to facilitate human interaction with the technology housing the information; and 3) to support wayfinding. A review of related findings in the literature offered suggestions of how portal designers could go about improving knowledge portal interface designs. These suggestions included ways of better displaying search engine results, deploying multimedia applications, presenting information on the Web interface, and evaluating the goodness of a basic Web site design.

Chapter 6 investigated how intelligent agents could be deployed in knowledge portals in ways that fostered knowledge creation, distribution, and use. Of importance was the application of agents in knowledge portals depicted in Figure 6-1. Categories of agents were described that matched the information needs-seeking-use cycle of knowledge workers. Specifically, agents that captured, extracted, analyzed, and organized information were shown to support the information needs of knowledge workers. Examples of agents in this genre were crawling agents, indexing agents, and clustering agents. Other agents that concentrated on finding information were purported to facilitate the information seeking behaviour of knowledge workers. Examples of agents in this particular category included recommendation agents, notification agents, and browse/search agents. Finally, agents that created, synthesized, distributed, and shared information were proposed to ameliorate information use. Examples of agents here included authoring and summary agents, as well as work flow agents.

To showcase how such agents could potentially help organizational participants in their knowledge work tasks, an agent architecture was proposed that was reflective of the information needs-seeking-use cycle that organizational knowledge workers undergo. Though actual implementation of such an integrated and robust agent architecture may be a few years off, its importance should not be undermined. With the advent of the Semantic Web, the feasibility and likelihood of agents in facilitating the knowledge work processes of organizational employees is a viable means by which to leverage and enhance knowledge portal adoption and use.

7.2   Meta-Analysis

So what have we learned from all this? Hopefully, many things. Foremost is the recognition of the importance and viability of enterprise portals to support and foster organizational knowledge work. This concept is key and should not be overlooked.

Another pertinent insight made throughout these pages was the need to design and implement these systems in ways that are reflective and responsive to the human participant and, in particular, how he or she goes about daily organizational knowledge work. This largely pertains to situating knowledge portals within the information needs-seeking-use cycle of organizational participants.

By recognizing this need, designers and managers of enterprise portal systems can begin thinking of means to improve the functionality and interface of these systems in ways that help employees successfully and easily go through their on-going cycles of knowledge work activity. As such, mechanisms are required in portal designs which help users become aware of gaps in their knowledge, and moreover, help users bridge these gaps. These mechanisms need to respect and react to the cognitive and affective make-up of individual workers as well as their social roles and relationships across the firm.

Further, the interface design of the portal should concentrate on highlighting information of importance and relevance to individual knowledge workers and in addressing the full spectrum of information seeking activity from browse to search. As well, the information environment of the firm needs to be monitored and enhanced on a continual basis to ensure that the firm's information context is conducive to portal adoption and use and encourages the creation and sharing of information among colleagues.

Such a viewpoint is an extension of the typical recommendations postulated by information systems consultants or found inside most management information systems books today. Though these sources do give practical advice on ideas for promoting enterprise portal use and offer a rational approach to portal design and implementation, it is suggested that these mechanisms fall short in helping organizations fully leverage their portal systems for knowledge work activity.

Typical recommendations lauded by such sources include items like the need to secure top-management buy-in and support, to offer rewards or incentives for portal use, or to build an easy-to-use interface. Agreed such tactics are useful and will undoubtedly lead to moderate increases in portal adoption. In fact, these suggestions are included within this book's own pages. However, these ideas are not rich or powerful enough on their own to provide a catalyst which truly instils high levels of knowledge work activity.

What is required, and what this book advocates *in addition to* such typical recommendations, is the need to place continual emphasis and understanding on the human element in enterprise portal design and roll-out. That is, to understand what knowledge work is—a set of information-laden activities comprising knowledge creation, distribution, and use—and the potential of enterprise portals to support these processes by fostering healthy information environments and building functionality in portals which match and support the on-going information needs-seeking-use cycle in which knowledge workers engage.

How can such systems be built? From a user perspective, several solutions have been suggested. For instance, communities of practices can be formed which meet virtually through the portal as a place to discuss and exchange both tacit and explicit types of information. A participatory design approach to portal design can be followed which ensures the active engagement of end user representatives and which adheres to the good principles of fair representation, meaningful participation, fun in design, meaningful projects, and cooperative action between designers and the user community.

From an information environment perspective, democratic and representative portal steering committees can be struck, and a loosening of the controls dictating portal content and its look and feel can be advocated.

From an information design perspective, the personalization of information content on the portal in ways that highlight the importance and relevance of information to individual users can be provided. Full portal support for both wayward browsing and goal-directed search can be built into the functionality of the system. This might entail the provision of robust search engines, meaningful category schemas and taxonomies, and the automatic indexing of any document or information content item posted on the portal by individual knowledge workers.

From a technology perspective, a network of cooperating intelligent agents can be deployed. These agents can consist of interface agents which interact with knowledge workers, provide guidance, format the presentation of information displayed, and maintain a history of previous information requests and lists of information subject areas of interest. Other types of agents include those that work diligently in the background, such as information agents, directory agents, and server agents. Information agents would function as middle-man agents and handle the on-going coordination of tasks. Directory agents would maintain current lists of available server agents and other information agents. Server agents would manage individual document collections, guarding access and providing pre-retrieval processing such as indexing, crawling, and clustering to ensure fast and expedient information retrieval at the time of request. The underlying concept here is that such an architecture of agents would employ agents which align with knowledge workers' on-going information needs-seeking-use cycles of activity. For example, these agents would work in ways that support how organizational participants go about conducting their knowledge work tasks with the portal.

Figure 7-1 below summarizes the key elements or categories that should be considered when designing knowledge portal systems. One element is not more important than another; all play a predominant role in the design of robust enterprise portal solutions in terms of the degree to which the portal fosters and supports knowledge creation, distribution, and use activity across the firm.

Central to the diagram are the three key processes of knowledge work: knowledge creation, knowledge distribution, and knowledge use. These are represented in the diagram by a shining light; how brightly that light shines is meant to portray the various magnitudes of knowledge work activity that can be supported by the portal.

In essence, five factors can impact this intensity. Two are digital workers: both human user and intelligent agent. *Users* are the organizational workers who utilize the portal to conduct their knowledge work activities. *Agents* are the software applications that operate within the portal to facilitate such knowledge work. Both types of digital workers are process-driven in that they are active in an *information needs-seeking-use cycle* of activity. Humans are engaged in this cycle as they go about addressing their problem situations and turn to the knowledge portal for help. Intelligent agents offer functionality which support unique aspects of each of these three process areas. A portal's *information design* reflects the degree to which the portal interface highlights the potential value of information to users and supports users in their information seeking tasks. Last, the *information environment* refers to the organizational context from an information perspective and reflects situational variables that promote or inhibit the use of the portal for knowledge work.

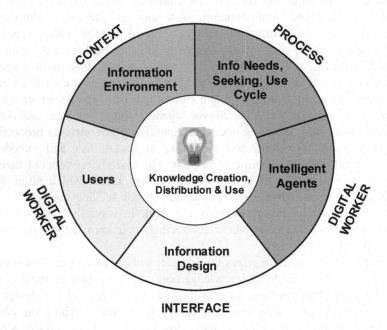

Figure 7-1: Key elements involved in the adoption and use of enterprise portals for knowledge work

What is hoped now is that the diagram can serve a vehicle by which to remind and emphasize knowledge portal stakeholders of the critical elements that influence the ability of a portal to support knowledge work and encourage consideration of these elements when building portal systems. As such, the diagram attempts to provide a holistic approach to knowledge portal design in a way that raises awareness of the need to consider contextual, process, and interface factors, as well as the characteristics of digital workers when developing and implementing portal solutions in organizations.

7.3 Research Directions and Final Words

This monograph is not meant to be the final synthesis on portal development and use for knowledge work, but rather a mere starting point for more discussion and research on this topic. Hopefully, this book has provided some new insights and directions for the reader to ponder—ones based on theory and sound empirical research rather than wishful thinking.

One of the catalysts of this book project was the author's own grappling with the reasons why so many companies have trouble building and encouraging their employees to adopt and utilize their organization's enterprise portal in meaningful and strategic ways. It is not too difficult to find people in all levels of an organization who see the potential of this technology to help make their company work smarter and be more productive. It is in fact another story (and a very difficult challenge) to identify and pinpoint the exact causes for such lack of use.

So many factors come into play why people do and do not use these new systems. They range from the cognitive to the social, from the technical to the political, and from the contextual to the functional. It appears there are a variety of factors which come to bear upon the success of a portal in terms of fostering knowledge creation, distribution, and use. These stem from the information needs of knowledge workers, how they go about seeking and using information off the portal, the information environment in which this activity occurs, and the information design of the portal interface. These factors are also influenced by the cognitive, affective, and social characteristics of knowledge workers and the extent to which intelligent technologies, such as agents, support knowledge workers in terms of their information needs-seeking-use activity.

All these factors, though immense, suggest many avenues of future research. One pertinent area is the need for more case study investigations of portal use in organizational settings. Another is the need for experiments to be run which test the effectiveness of various information designs. The development of different types of agents and the testing of alternate scenarios of agent architectures is one more burgeoning area of investigation. An additional avenue of research is the design and testing of various portal system design methodologies that organizations can utilize to increase the likelihood of the development and installation of portals used for knowledge work.

If anything, it is hoped that the ideas contained within this monograph have raised awareness and the interest of the reader in considering the role of an enterprise portal. These systems can do so much more than merely retrieve information items via a Web interface. These systems can function as shared information work spaces. Places where people can be inspired, learn, discuss, and effectively and efficiently create new knowledge, share it with others, and use it in daily work practice. With the advent of the Semantic Web, intelligent agents can soon be deployed in ways that truly can help organizational employees access relevant content, search and browse pertinent information, and utilize such content in day-to-day work tasks and projects.

As such, knowledge portals can help realize the dream of Vannevar Bush's Memex machine. They can do this by turning an employee's Web-based browser into a convenient, single-point gateway system that provides access to a relevant and personalized knowledge base—turning information into action and thus helping to create new knowledge and leverage existing organizational know-how. Doing so, it is suggested, will encourage use of these systems for knowledge work.

REFERENCES

Ackoff, R. L. (1974). *Redesigning the future: A system approach to societal programs*. New York: John Wiley.

Adam, N., and Yesha, Y. (1996). Strategic directions in electronic commerce and digital libraries: Towards a digital agora. *ACM Computing Surveys, 28*(4), 818-835.

Adams, E. C. (2000). Communities of practice: Bridging technology and knowledge assessment. *Journal of Knowledge Management, 4*(1), 38-44.

Agnew, N. M., Ford, K. M., and Hayes, P. J. (1997). Expertise in context: Personally constructed, socially selected and reality relevant? In P. J. Feltovich, K. M. Ford, and R. R. Hoffman (Eds.), *Expertise in context: Human and machine* (pp. 219-244). Cambridge, Massachusetts: AAAI Press / The MIT Press.

Aguilar, F. J. (1967). *Scanning the business environment*. New York: Macmillan.

Alavi, M., and Leidner, D. (1999). Knowledge management systems: Issues, challenges, benefits. *Communication of AIS, 1*(7), 2-41.

Alavi, M., and Tiwana, A. (2002). Knowledge integration in virtual teams: The potential role of KMS. *Journal of the American Society for Information Science and Technology, 53*(12), 1029-1037.

Al-Hawamdeh, S. (2002). Knowledge management: Rethinking information management and facing the challenge of managing tacit knowledge. *Information Research, 8*(1). Retrieved July 14, 2003, from http://InformationR.net/ir/8-1/paper143.html.

Aneja, A., Brooksby, B., and Rowan, C. (2000). Corporate portal framework for transforming content chaos on intranets. *Intel Technology Journal, 11*(March), 21-28.

Asch, S. E. (1946). Forming impressions of personality. *Journal of Abnormal Social Psychology, 41*, 1230-1240.

Baeza-Yates, R., and Ribeiro-Neto, B. (1999). *Modern Information Retrieval*. Harlow, England: Addison-Wesley.

Bannon, L. J., and Schmidt, K. (1991). CSCW: Four characters in search of a context. In J. M. Bowers and S. D. Benford (Eds.), *Studies in computer supported cooperative work: Theory, practice, and design. Proceedings of the First European Conference on Computer Supported Cooperative Work, 1989* (pp. 3-16). New York: North-Holland.

Barry, C. (1998). Document representations and clues to document relevance. *Journal of the American Society for Information Science, 49*(14), 1293-1303.

Bell DeTienne, K., and Jensen, R. J. (2001). Intranets and business model innovation: Managing knowledge in the virtual organization. In Y. Malhotra (Ed.), *Knowledge Management and Business Model Innovation* (pp. 198-215). Hershey, PA: Idea Group.

Benbasat, I., Goldstein, D. K., and Mead, M. (1987). The case research strategy in studies of information systems. *MIS Quarterly, 11*(3), 369-386.

Berg, B. L. (1998). *Qualitative research methods for the social sciences.* (3rd ed.). Needham Heights, MA: Allyn and Bacon.

Bergeron, P. (1996). Information resources management. In M. E. Williams (Ed.), *Annual Review of Information Science and Technology* (Vol. 31, pp. 263-300). White Plains, New York: Knowledge Industry Publications.

Berners-Lee, T. (2003). Foreword. In D. Fensel, J. Hendler, H. Lieberman, and W. Wahlster (Eds.), *Spinning the semantic web: Bringing the world wide web to its full potential* (pp. xi-xxiii). Cambridge, Massachusetts: MIT Press.

Berners-Lee, T., Cailliau, R., Luotonen, A., Nielsen, H. F., and Secret, A. (1994). The world wide web. *Communications of the ACM, 37*(8), 76-82.

Berners-Lee, T., Hendler, J., and Lassila, O. (2001). The semantic web. *Scientific American, 284*(5), 34-43.

Bhatt, G. D. (2002). Management strategies for individual knowledge and organizational knowledge. *Journal of Knowledge Management, 6*(1), 31-39.

Bhattacherjee, A. (1998). Management of emerging technologies: Experiences and lessons learned at US West. *Information and Management, 33*(5), 263-272.

Bieber, M., and Isakowitz, T. (1995). Designing hypermedia applications. *Communications of the ACM, 38*(8), 26-29.

Blackler, F. (1993). Knowledge and the theory of organizations: Organizations as activity systems and the reframing of management. *Journal of Management Studies, 30*(6), 863-884.

Blair, D. C. (2002). Knowledge management: Hype, hope, or help? *Journal of the American Society for Information Science and Technology, 53*(12), 1019-1028.

Blomberg, J., and Trigg, R. (2002, October 31). *Participatory design in non-profit and commercial settings.* Paper presented at the Knowledge Media Design Institute Public Lecture Series at the University of Toronto, Toronto, Ontario, Canada.

Boland, R. J., and Tenkasi, R. V. (1995). Perspective making, perspective taking in communities of knowing. *Organization Science, 6*(4), 350-372.

Boland, R. J., Tenkasi, R. V., and Te'eni, D. (1994). Designing information technology to support distributed cognition. *Organization Science, 5*(3), 456-475.

Bonoma, T. V. (1983). *A case study in case research: Marketing implementation* (Working Paper 9-585-142). Boston, Massachusetts: Harvard University Graduate School of Business Administration.

Botkin, J. (1999). *Smart business: How knowledge communities can revolutionize your company.* New York: The Free Press.

Bouthillier, F., and Shearer, K. (2002). Understanding knowledge management and information management: The need for an empirical perspective. *Information Research, 8*(1). Retrieved July 16, 2003, from http://InformationR.net/ir/8-1/paper141.html.

Bowers, J. (1994). The work to make a network work: Studying CSCW in action. In R. Furuta and C. Neuwirth (Eds.), *Proceedings of CSCW '94* (pp. 287-298). Chapel Hill, NC: ACM Press.

Bradshaw, J. M. (Ed.). (1997). *Software agents.* Menlo Park, California: American Association for Artificial Intelligence.

Buchwald, C. C. (1999). *Canada's coalition for public information: A case study of a public interest group in the information highway policy-making process.* Unpublished Ph.D. Dissertation, University of Toronto, Ontario, Canada.

Burke, C. (1994). *Information and secrecy: Vannevar Bush, Ultra, and the other Memex.* Lanham, Maryland: Scarecrow Press.

Bush, V. (1945). As we may think. *Atlantic Monthly, 176*(1), 101-108.

Card, S. K., Robertson, G. G., and Mackinlay, J. D. (1991). The information visualizer: An information workspace. In S. P. Robertson, G. M. Olson, and J. S. Olson (Eds.), *Proceedings of the Conference on Human Factors in Computing Systems* (pp. 181-188). New York, NY: ACM Press.

Catledge, L. D., and Pitkow, J. E. (1995). Characterizing browsing strategies in the World Wide Web. *Computer Networks and ISDN Systems, 27*, 1065-1073.

Chamot, D. (1987). Electronic work and the white-collar employee. In R. E. Kraut (Ed.), *Technology and the transformation of white-collar work* (pp. 23-33). Hillsdale, NJ: Lawrence Erlbaum Associates.

Checkland, P. (1995). Soft systems methodology and its relevance to the development of information systems. In F. Stowell (Ed.), *Information systems provision: The contribution of soft systems methodology* (pp. 1-17). Berkshire, England: McGraw-Hill.

Cherry, S. M. (2002). Weaving the web of ideas. *IEEE Spectrum, 39*(9), 65-69.

Choo, C. W. (1998). *The knowing organization.* New York: Oxford University Press.

Choo, C. W., Detlor, B., and Turnbull, D. (1999). Information seeking on the Web: An integrated model of browsing and searching. In L. Woods (Ed.), *Proceedings of the 62nd Annual Meeting of the American Society for Information Science.* Washington, D.C., October 31 - November 4 (pp. 3-16). Medford, NJ: Information Today.

Choo, C. W., Detlor, B., and Turnbull, D. (2000a). *Web work: Information seeking and knowledge work on the World Wide Web.* Dordrecht, The Netherlands: Kluwer Academic Publishers.

Choo, C. W., Detlor, B., and Turnbull, D. (2000b). Working the Web: An empirical model of Web use. In R. H. Sprague (Ed.), *Proceedings of the 33rd Annual Hawaii International Conference on System Science (HICSS-33).* Maui, Hawaii, January 4-7 (pp. 2794-2802). Los Alamitos, CA: IEEE.

Chowdhury, G. G. (1999). *Introduction to modern information retrieval.* London, UK: Library Association.

Ciborra, C. U. (2000a). A critical review of the literature on the management of corporate information infrastructure. In C. U. Ciborra et al. (Ed.), *From Control to Drift* (pp. 15-40). Oxford: Oxford University Press.

Ciborra, C. U. (2000b). From alignment to loose coupling: From MedNet to www.roche.com. In C. U. Ciborra et al. (Ed.), *From Control to Drift* (pp. 193-211). Oxford: Oxford University Press.

Ciborra, C. U., and Hanseth, O. (2000). Introduction: From control to drift. In C. U. Ciborra et al. (Ed.), *From Control to Drift* (pp. 1-11). Oxford: Oxford University Press.

Cognitive_and_Technology_Group_at_Vanderbilt. (1993). Examining the cognitive challenges and pedagogical opportunities of integrated media systems: Toward a research agenda. *Journal of Special Education Technology, 12*, 118-124.

Cohen, D. (1998). Toward a knowledge context: Report on the first annual U.C. Berkeley forum on knowledge and the firm. *California Management Review, 40*(3), 22-39.

Cole, R. E. (1998). Introduction. *California Management Review, 40*(3), 15-21.

Collins, H. (2002). *Enterprise knowledge portals*. New York: AMACOM.

Conklin, J. (1987). Hypertext: An introduction and survey. *IEEE Computer, 20*(9), 17-20; 32-41.

Conklin, J. E. (1992). Capturing organizational memory. In D. Coleman (Ed.), *Proceedings of Groupware '92* (pp. 133-137). San Mateo, CA: Morgan Kaufmann.

Cooley, M. (2000). Human-centered design. In R. Jacobson (Ed.), *Information Design* (pp. 59-81). Cambridge, Massachusetts: MIT Press.

Cooper, R. B., and Zmud, R. W. (1990). Information technology implementation research: A technological diffusion approach. *Management Science, 36*(2), 123-139.

Creswell, J. W. (1994). *Research design: Qualitative and quantitative approaches*. Thousand Oaks, CA: Sage.

Cronin, M. J. (1999). The corporate intranet Ford Motor. *Fortune, 139*(10), 112, 114-116, 121-125.

Daft, R. L., and Lengel, R. H. (1984). Information richness: A new approach to manager information processing and organizational design. In B. Staw and L. L. Cummings (Eds.), *Research in Organizational Behavior* (Vol. 6, pp. 191-233). Greenwich, CT: JAI Press.

Daft, R. L., and Lengel, R. H. (1986). Organizational information requirements, media richness and structural design. *Management Science, 32*(5), 554-571.

Daft, R. L., and Macintosh, N. B. (1981). A tentative exploration into the amount and equivocality of information processing in organizational work units. *Administrative Science Quarterly, 26*, 207-224.

Dahlbom, B. (1996). The new informatics. *Scandinavian Journal of Information Systems, 8*(2), 29-48.

Damsgaard, J., and Scheepers, R. (1999). Power, influence and intranet implementation: A safari of South African organizations. *Information, Technology and People, 12*(4), 333-358.

Davenport, E. (2001a). Knowledge management issues for online organisations: 'Communities of practice' as an exploratory framework. *Journal of Documentation, 57*(1), 61-75.

Davenport, E. (2001b). New knowledge and micro-level online organization: 'Communities of practice' as a development framework. In R. H. Sprague (Ed.), *Proceedings of the 34th Annual Hawaii International Conference on System Sciences (HICSS-34)*. Maui, Hawaii, January 3-6 (pp. 1297-1306). Los Alamitos, CA: IEEE.

Davenport, T. H. (1997). *Information ecology: Mastering the information and knowledge environment*. New York: Oxford University Press.

Davenport, T. H., DeLong, D. W., and Beers, M. C. (1998). Successful knowledge management projects. *Sloan Management Review, 39*(2), 43-57.

Davenport, T. H., Eccles, R. G., and Prusak, L. (1992). Information politics. *Sloan Management Review, Fall*, 53-65.

Davenport, T. H., Jarvenpaa, S. L., and Beers, M. C. (1996). Improving knowledge work processes. *Sloan Management Review, 37*(4), 53-65.

Davenport, T. H., and Prusak, L. (1998). *Working knowledge: How organizations manage what they know*. Boston, Massachusetts: Harvard Business School Press.

Davis, B. (2002). Doorway to data. *Professional Engineering, 15*(3), 59-60.

Davis, F. (1989). Perceived usefulness, perceived ease of use, and user acceptance of information technology. *MIS Quarterly, 13*, 319-339.

Davis, F. (1993). User acceptance of information technology: system characteristics, user perceptions and behavioral impacts. *International Journal of Man-Machine Studies, 38*, 475-487.

Davis, G. (1991). *Conceptual model for research on knowledge work* (MISRC working paper MISRC-WP-91-10). Minneapolis: University of Minnesota.

DeLoach, S. (2001). Analysis and design using MaSE and agentTool. In F. W. Moore (Ed.), *Proceedings of the 12th Midwest Artificial Intelligence and Cognitive Science Conference (MAICS 2001)*. Miami University. Oxford, Ohio, March 31-April 1 (pp. 1-7). Oxford, OH: Miami University Press.

Denzin, N. K. (1978). *The research act*. New York: McGraw-Hill.

Dervin, B. (1992). From the mind's eye of the user: The sense-making qualitative-quantitative methodology. In J. D. Glazier and R. R. Powell (Eds.), *Qualitative Research in Information Management* (pp. 61-84). Englewood Cliffs, CO: Libraries Unlimited.

Dervin, B. (2000). Chaos, order, and sense-making: A proposed theory for information design. In R. Jacobson (Ed.), *Information Design* (pp. 35-57). Cambridge, Massachusetts: MIT Press.

Dervin, B., and Nilan, M. (1986). Information needs and uses. In M. E. Williams (Ed.), *Annual Review of Information Science and Technology (ARIST)* (Vol. 21, pp. 3-33). White Plains, New York: Knowledge Industry Publications.

Desurvire, H. W. (1994). Faster, cheaper!! Are usability inspection methods as effective as empirical testing? In J. Nielsen and R. L. Mack (Eds.), *Usability Inspection Methods* (pp. 173-202). New York: John Wiley and Sons.

Desurvire, H. W., Kondziela, J. M., and Atwood, M. E. (1992). What is gained and lost when using evaluation methods other than empirical testing. In A. Monk, D. Diaper, and M. D. Harrison (Eds.), *People and Computers VII* (pp. 89-102). Cambridge, U.K.: Cambridge University Press.

Detlor, B. (2000a). The corporate portal as information infrastructure: Towards a framework for portal design. *International Journal of Information Management, 20*(2), 91-101.

Detlor, B. (2000b). *Facilitating organizational knowledge work through Web information systems: An investigation of the information ecology and information behaviours of users in a telecommunications company.* Unpublished Ph.D. dissertation, University of Toronto, Ontario, Canada.

Detlor, B. (2001). The influence of information ecology on E-commerce initiatives. *Internet Research, 11*(4), 286-295.

Detlor, B. (2002). An informational perspective towards knowledge work: Implications for knowledge management systems. In D. White (Ed.), *Knowledge Mapping and Management* (pp. 195-205). Hershey, Pennsylvania: Idea Group.

Detlor, B. (2003). Internet-based information systems use in organizations: An information studies perspective. *Information Systems Journal, 13*(2), 113-132.

Detlor, B., and Arsenault, C. (2002). Web information seeking and retrieval in library contexts: Towards an intelligent agent solution. *Online Information Review, 26*(6), 404-412.

Detlor, B., and Finn, K. (2002). Towards a framework for government portal design: The government, citizen, and portal perspectives. In A. Gronlund (Ed.), *Electronic government: Design, applications, and management* (pp. 99-119). Hershey, Pennsylvania: Idea Group.

Detlor, B., Sproule, S., and Gupta, C. (2003). Pre-purchase online information seeking: Search versus browse. *Journal of Electronic Consumer Research, 4*(2), 72-84.

Dias, C. (2001). Corporate portals: A literature review of a new concept in information management. *International Journal of Information Management, 21*, 269-287.

Dieberger, A., and Bolter, J. D. (1995). On the design of hyper "spaces". *Communications of the ACM, 38*(8), 98.

Dillon, A., McKnight, C., and Richardson, J. (1994). J. Space: The final chapter or why physical representations are not semantic intentions. In C. McKnight, A. Dillon, and J. Richardson (Eds.), *Hypertext: A psychological perspective* (pp. 169-191). New York: Ellis-Horwood.

Doll, W. J., and Torkzadeh, G. (1988). The measurement of end-user computing satisfaction. *MIS Quarterly, 12*(2), 259-274.

Dosa, M. L. (1976). Design and development of an information policy seminar. In S. K. Martin (Ed.), *Proceedings of the American Society for Information Science (ASIS) Annual Meeting*. Washington, D.C.: ASIS.

Dourish, P. (2001). *Where the action is: The foundations of embodied interaction*. Cambridge, MA: Cambridge University Press.

Drucker, P. F. (1988). The coming of the new organization. *Harvard Business Review, 66*(1), 45-53.

Drucker, P. F. (1993). *Post-capitalist society*. Oxford: Butterworth Heinemann.

Duane, A., and Finnegan, P. (2003). Managing empowerment and control in an intranet environment. *Information Systems Journal, 13*(2), 133-158.

Dufour, C., and Bergeron, P. (2002). The impact of the introduction of Web information systems (WIS) on information policies: An analysis of the Canadian federal government policies related to WIS. In E. G. Toms (Ed.), *Proceedings of the American Society for Information Science and Technology*. Philadelphia, PA, November 18-21, (Vol. 39, pp. 107-114). Medford, New Jersey: Information Today.

Duncan, N. (1995). Capturing flexibility of information technology infrastructure: A study of resource characteristics and their measure. *Journal of Management Information Systems, 12*(2), 37-57.

Eckel, R. (2000). A road map to identify the portal for your company. *DM Direct Journal, 14*, 11-15.

Eckerson, W. W. (1999). *Business portals: Drivers, definitions, and rules* (White Paper). Boston, MA: Patricia Seybold Group. Retrieved October 2001 from http://www.viador.com/pdfs/seyboldwhitepaper.pdf.

Ehn, P., and Sjogren, D. (1991). From system descriptions to scripts for action. In J. Greenbaum and M. Kyng (Eds.), *Design at work: Cooperative design of computer systems* (pp. 241-268). Hillsdale, New Jersey: Lawrence Erlbaum Associates.

Eisenhardt, K. M. (1989). Building theories from case study research. *Academy of Management Review, 14*(4), 532-550.

Eiter, T., and Mascardi, V. (2001). *Comparing environments for developing software agents* (INFSYS Research Report 1843-01-02): Knowledge-Based Systems Group.

Ellis, D. (1989a). A behavioural approach to information retrieval design. *Journal of Documentation, 45*(3), 171-212.

Ellis, D. (1989b). A behavioural model for information retrieval system design. *Journal of Information Science, 15*(4/5), 237-247.

Ellis, D., Cox, D., and Hall, K. (1993). A comparison of the information seeking patterns of researchers in the physical and social sciences. *Journal of Documentation, 49*(4), 356-369.

Erickson, T., and Kellogg, W. A. (2000). Social translucence: An approach to designing systems that support social processes. *ACM Transactions on Computer-Human Interaction, 7*(1), 59-83.

Erickson, T., and Kellogg, W. A. (2002). Knowledge communities: Online environments for supporting knowledge management in its social context. In M. Ackerman, V. Pipek, and V. Wulf (Eds.), *Sharing expertise: Beyond knowledge management* (pp. 299-326). Cambridge: MIT Press.

Erlandson, D. A., Harris, E. L., Skipper, B. L., and Allen, S. D. (1993). *Doing naturalistic inquiry: A guide to methods.* Newbury Park, CA: Sage.

Feltovich, P. J., Ford, K. M., and Hoffman, R. R. (Eds.). (1997). *Expertise in context: Human and machine.* Cambridge, Massachusetts: AAAI Press / The MIT Press.

Fidel, R. (1993). Qualitative methods in information retrieval research. *Library and Information Science Research, 15*, 219-247.

Finin, T., Labrou, Y., and Mayfield, J. (1997). KQML as an agent communication language. In J. M. Bradshaw (Ed.), *Software agents* (pp. 291-316). Menlo Park, California: American Association for Artificial Intelligence.

Finn, K., and Detlor, B. (2002a). Youth and electronic government: Towards a model of civic participation. *Quarterly Journal of Electronic Commerce, 3*(3), 191-209.

Finn, K., and Detlor, B. (2002b). Youth, civic participation and electronic government. In M. Head and C. Bart (Eds.), *Proceedings of the 3rd World Congress on the Management of Electronic Commerce.* Hamilton, Ontario, Canada. January 16-18. Hamilton, Ontario: McMaster University.

Firestone, J. M. (2000). *The enterprise knowledge portal revisited* (White Paper 15). Wilmington, DE: Executive Information Systems Inc.

Firestone, J. M. (2001). Enterprise knowledge portals, knowledge processing, and knowledge management. In R. Barquin, A. Bennet, and S. Remex (Eds.), *Building Knowledge Management Environments for Electronic Government.* Vienna, VA: Management Concepts.

Firestone, J. M. (2003). *Enterprise information portals and knowledge management.* Burlington, MA: Butterworth-Heinemann.

Gallivan, M. J. (2000). Examining workgroup influence on technology usage: A community of practice perspective, *Proceedings of the ACM SIGCPR Conference on Computer Personnel Research* (pp. 54-66). New York: ACM Press.

Garzotto, F., Mainetti, L., and Paolini, P. (1995). Hypermedia design, analysis, and evaluation issues. *Communications of the ACM, 38*(8), 74-86.

Ginsburg, M. (1999). An agent framework for intranet document management. *Autonomous Agents and Multi-Agent Systems, 2,* 271-286.

Goldberg, D., Nichols, D., Oki, B. M., and Terry, D. (1992). Using collaborative filtering to weave an information tapestry. *Communications of the ACM, 35*(12), 61-70.

Goodhue, D. L. (1998). Development and measurement validity of a task-technology fit instrument for user evaluations of information systems. *Decision Sciences, 29*(1), 105-138.

Goodhue, D. L., and Thompson, R. L. (1995). Task-technology fit and individual performance. *MIS Quarterly, 19*(2), 213-236.

Gottschalk, P. (2000). Knowledge management in the professions: The case of IT support in law firms. In R. H. Sprague (Ed.), *Proceedings of the 33rd Annual Hawaii International Conference on System Sciences (HICSS-33)*. Maui, Hawaii, January 4-7 (pp. 945-954). Los Alamitos: IEEE.

Grammer, J. (2000). The enterprise knowledge portal [Electronic version]. *DM Review, 10*(3), 20+. Retrieved July 9, 2003, from http://www.dmreview.com/master_sponsor.cfm?NavID=193&EdID=1940.

Gray, R. S., Cybenko, G., Kotz, D., and Rus, D. (2000). *Mobile agents: Motivations and state of the art* (Technical Report TR2000-365). Hanover, New Hampshire, USA: Department of Computer Science, Dartmouth College.

Greenbaum, J., and Kyng, M. (Eds.). (1991). *Design at work: Cooperative design of computer systems*. Hillsdale, NJ: Lawrence Erlbaum Associates.

Greenberg, J., Sutton, S., and Campbell, D. G. (2003). Metadata: A fundamental component of the semantic web. *Bulletin of the American Society for Information Science, 29*(4), 16-18.

Gruber, T. H. (1993). A translation approach to portable ontology specifications. *Knowledge Acquisition, 6*(2), 199-221.

Grudin, J. (1990). Groupware and cooperative work: Problems and prospects. In B. Laurel (Ed.), *The art of human computer interface design.*: Addison-Wesley.

Grudin, J. (1994). Groupware and social dynamics: Eight challenges for developers. *Communications of the ACM, 37*(1), 92-105.

Hackbarth, G., and Grover, V. (1999). The knowledge repository: Organizational memory information systems. *Information Systems Management, 16*(3), 21-30.

Hagedorn, K. (2000). *The information architecture glossary.* Ann Arbor, Michigan: Argus Center for Information Architecture (Argus Associates).

Hahn, J., and Subramani, M. R. (2000). A framework of knowledge management systems: Issues and challenges for theory and practice. In W. J. Orlikowski, S. Ang, P. Weill, H. C. Krcmar, and J. I. DeGross (Eds.), *Proceedings of the International Conference on Information Systems.* Brisbane, Australia, December 10-13 (pp. 302-312). Atlanta, GA: Association for Information Systems (AIS).

Harold, A., and Detlor, B. (2003, Oct 10). *Tailoring the design of web shopping sites for both product browsing and product searching.* Paper presented at the Working Paper Session of the Association of Consumer Research (ACR) Conference, Toronto, Ontario, Canada.

Harper, R. (1992). Looking at ourselves: An examination of the social organization of two research laboratories. In J. Turner and R. Kraut (Eds.), *Proceedings of the 1992 ACM Conference on Computer Supported Cooperative Work (CSCW '92).* Toronto, Ontario, Canada, October 31 - November 4 (pp. 330-337). New York: ACM.

Hayman, A., and Elliman, T. (2000). Human elements in information systems design for knowledge workers. *International Journal of Information Management, 20,* 297-309.

Hildreth, P. M., and Kimble, C. (2002). The duality of knowledge. *Information Research, 8*(1). Retrieved June 22, 2003, from http://InformationR.net/ir/8-1/paper142.html.

Hildreth, P. M., Wright, P., and Kimble, C. (1999). Knowledge management: Are we missing something? In L. Brooks and C. Kimble (Eds.), *Proceedings of the 4th UKAIS Conference.* York, United Kingdom, April 7-9 (pp. 347-356). London: McGraw Hill.

Hildreth, P. M., Wright, P., and Kimble, C. (1999). Knowledge management: Are we missing something?, *Proceedings of the 4th KAIS Conference* (pp. 347-356). London: McGraw Hill.

Hinrichs, R. J. (1997). Intranet 101. *The Intranet Journal*. Retrieved July 16, 2003, from http://web.archive.org/web/19990428223232/http://www.intranetjournal.com/newbie.html).

Hlupic, V., Pouloudi, A., and Rzevski, G. (2002). Towards an integrated approach to knowledge management: 'Hard', 'soft', and 'abstract' issues. *Knowledge and Process Management, 9*(2), 90-102.

Horn, R. E. (2000). Information design: Emergence of a new profession. In R. Jacobson (Ed.), *Information Design* (pp. 15-34). Cambridge, Massachusetts: MIT Press.

Huber, G. P., and Daft, R. L. (1987). The information environments of organizations. In F. Jablin and L. L. Putnam (Eds.), *Handbook of organizational communications* (pp. 130-164). Newbury Park, CA: Sage Publications.

Hudson, W. (2000, May 3). *User-centered survey results*, [e-mail posting]. CHI-WEB@ACM.ORG.

Ingwersen, P. (1996). Cognitive perspectives of information retrieval interaction: Elements of a cognitive IR theory. *Journal of Documentation, 52*(1), 3-50.

Isakowitz, T., Bieber, M., and Vitali, F. (1998). Web information systems (special section). *Communication of the ACM, 41*(7), 78-80.

Jacob, E. K. (2003). Ontologies and the semantic web. *Bulletin of the American Society for Information Science, 29*(4), 19-22.

Jacobson, I., Ericsson, M., and Jacobson, A. (1995). *The object advantage*. Reading, MA: Addison-Wesley.

Jacobson, R. (2000). Introduction: Why information design matters. In R. Jacobson (Ed.), *Information Design* (pp. 1-10). Cambridge, Massachusetts: MIT Press.

Janes, J. W. (1991). Relevance judgments and the incremental presentation of document representations. *Information Processing and Management, 27*, 629-646.

Jennings, N., Sycara, K., and Wooldridge, M. (1998). A roadmap of agent research and development. *Autonomous Agents and Multi-Agent Systems, 1*(1), 275-306.

Johnson-Laird, P. N. (1989). Mental models. In M. I. Posner (Ed.), *Foundations of Cognitive Science* (pp. 469-499). Cambridge, MA: MIT Press.

Kahneman, D. (1973). *Attention and effort*. Englewood Cliffs, New Jersey: Prentice-Hall.

Kaplan, B., and Duchon, D. (1988). Combining qualitative and quantitative methods in information systems research: A case study. *MIS Quarterly, 12*(4), 571-587.

Karat, C., Campbell, R., and Fiegel, T. (1992). Comparison of empirical testing and walkthrough methods in user interface evaluation. In P. Bauersfeld, J. Bennett, and G. Lynch (Eds.), *Proceedings of the SIGCHI Conference on Human Factor in Computing Systems (CHI '92)*. Monterey, California, May 3-7 (pp. 397-404). New York: ACM.

Katzer, J., and Fletcher, P. T. (1992). The information environment of managers. In M. E. Williams (Ed.), *Annual Review of Information Science and Technology (ARIST)* (Vol. 27, pp. 227-263). Medford, New Jersey: Learned Information, Inc.

Keen, E. M. (1977). On the generation and searching of entries in printed subject indexes. *Journal of Documentation, 33*(1), 15-45.

Kensing, F., and Blomberg, J. (1998). Participatory design: Issues and concerns. *Computer Supported Cooperative Work, 7*, 167-185.

Kent, A., Betzer, J., Kurfeest, M., Dym, E. D., Shirey, D. L., and Bose, A. (1967). Relevance predictability in information retrieval systems. *Methods of Information in Medicine, 6*, 45-51.

Kidd, A. (1994a). The marks are on the knowledge worker. In B. Adelson, S. Dumais, and J. Olson (Eds.), *Proceedings of SIGCHI Conference on Human Factors in Computing Systems (CHI '94)*. Boston, Massachusetts (pp. 186-191). New York: ACM.

Kidd, A. (1994b). The marks are on the knowledge worker, *Proceedings of CHI '94, Human Factors in Computing Systems, Boston, Massachusetts* (pp. 186-191): ACM.

King, W. R., Marks, P. V., Jr., and McCoy, S. (2002). The most important issues in knowledge management. *Communications of the ACM, 45*(9), 93-97.

Kirk, J., and Miller, M. (1986). *Reliability and validity in qualitative research*. Newbury Park, CA: Sage.

Kotorov, R., and Hsu, E. (2001). A model for enterprise portal management. *Journal of Knowledge Management, 5*(1), 86-93.

Kuhlthau, C. C. (1991). Inside the search process: Information seeking from the user's perspective. *Journal of the American Society for Information Science, 42*(5), 361-371.

Kuhlthau, C. C. (1993). A principle of uncertainty for information seeking. *Journal of Documentation, 49*(4), 339-455.

Kuhn, S., and Muller, M. J. (1993). Introduction: Special issue on participatory design. *Communications of the ACM, 36*(4), 24-28.

Kuutti, K. (1996). Debates in IS and CSCW research: Anticipating system design for post-Fordist work. In W. J. Orlikowski, G. Walsham, M. R. Jones, and J. I. DeGross (Eds.), *Proceedings of the IFIP WG8.2 Working Conference on Information Technology and Changes in Organizational Work,* December 1995 (pp. 177-196). London: Chapman and Hall.

Labrou, Y., Finin, T., and Pong, Y. (1999). Agent communication languages: The current landscape. *IEEE Intelligent Systems, March/April*, 45-52.

Lamar, L. (2001). Introduction to a user interface design: Information architecture process for Web sites, *Proceedings of the IEEE International Professional Communication Conference (IPCC 2001).* Santa Fe, New Mexico, October 24-26 (pp. 185-198). Los Alamitos, CA: IEEE.

Lave, J., and Wenger, E. (1995). *Situated learning: Legitimate peripheral participation.* (Vol. first published in 1991). New York: Cambridge University Press.

Lee, A. S. (1989). A scientific methodology for MIS case studies. *MIS Quarterly, 13*(1), 33-52.

Leonard-Barton, D. (1998). *Wellsprings of knowledge: Building and sustaining the sources of innovation.* (paperback ed.). Boston, MA: Harvard Business School Press.

Leonidas, G. (2000). Information design: The missing link in information management? *International Journal of Information Management, 20,* 73-76.

Lieberman, H. (1995). Letizia: An agent that assists web browsing. In C. S. Mellish (Ed.), *Proceedings of the 14th International Joint Conference on Artificial Intelligence (IJCAI-95).* Montreal, Quebec, Canada, August 20-25 (pp. 924-929). San Mateo, CA: Morgan Kaufmann.

Lieberman, H. (1997). Autonomous interface agents. In S. Pemberton (Ed.), *Proceedings of the SIGCHI Conference on Human Factors in Computing Systems (CHI '97).* Atlanta, Georgia, March 22-27 (pp. 67-74). New York: ACM.

Lieberman, H., Fry, C., and Weitzman, L. (2001). Exploring the web with reconnaissance agents. *Communications of the ACM, 44*(8), 69-75.

Lieberman, H., Van Dyke, N., and Vivacqua, A. (1999). Lets browse: A collaborative browsing agent. *Knowledge Based Systems Journal, 12*, 427-431.

Lim, K. H., and Benbasat, I. (2000). The effect of multimedia on perceived equivocality and perceived usefulness of information systems. *MIS Quarterly, 24*(3), 449-471.

Lim, K. H., and Benbasat, I. (2002). The influence of multimedia on improving the comprehension of organizational information. *Journal of Management Information Systems, 19*(1), 99-127.

Lim, K. H., Benbasat, I., and Ward, L. M. (2000). The role of multimedia in changing first impression bias. *Information Systems Research, 11*(2), 115-136.

Lincoln, Y., and Guba, E. (1985). *Naturalistic inquiry.* Newbury Park, CA: Sage.

Lofland, J., and Lofland, L. (1995). *Analyzing social settings: A guide to qualitative observation and analysis.* (3rd ed.). Belmon, CA: Wadsworth.

Lovins, J. B. (1968). Developing of a stemming algorithm. *Mechanical translation and computational linguistics, 11*(1, 2), 11-31.

Luck, M., Griffiths, N., and d'Inverno, M. (1997). From agent theory to agent construction: A case study. In J. P. Muller, M. J. Wooldridge, and N. R. Jennings (Eds.), *Proceedings of the ECAI'96 Workshop on Agent Theories, Architectures, and Languages. Intelligent Agents III.* (pp. 49-63). Berlin: Springer-Verlag.

Lyytinen, K., Rose, G., and Welke, R. (1998). The brave new world of development in the internetwork computing architecture (InterNCA): Or how distributed computing platforms will change systems development. *Information Systems Journal, 8*(241-253).

Machlup, F. (1962). *The production and distribution of knowledge in the United States.* Princeton, NJ: Princeton University Press.

Mack, R., Ravin, Y., and Byrd, R. J. (2001). Knowledge portals and the emerging digital knowledge workplace. *IBM Systems Journal, 40*(4), 925-955.

MacMullin, S. E., and Taylor, R. S. (1984). Problem dimensions and information traits. *The Information Society, 3*(1), 91-111.

Maedche, A., Staab, S., Stojanovic, N., Studer, R., and Sure, Y. (2003). SEmantic portAL: The SEAL approach. In D. Fensel, J. Hendler, H. Lieberman, and W. Wahlster (Eds.), *Spinning the semantic web: Bringing the world wide web to its full potential* (pp. 317-359). Cambridge, Massachusetts: MIT Press.

Maes, P. (1994). Agents that reduce work and information overload. *Communications of the ACM, 37*(7), 30-40.

Maes, P. (1997). *CHI97 software agents tutorial.* Retrieved July 11, 2003 from http://pattie.www.media.mit.edu/people/pattie/CHI97/.

Maes, P. (1999). Smart commerce: The future of intelligent agents in cyberspace. *Journal of Internet Marketing, 13*(3), 66-76.

Maes, P. (2001). Smart commerce: The future of intelligent agents in cyberspace. In P. Richardson (Ed.), *Internet Marketing* (pp. 139-146). New York: McGraw-Hill.

Marchionini, G. (1992). Interfaces for end-user information seeking. *Journal of the American Society for Information Science, 43*(2), 156-163.

Marchionini, G. (1995). *Information seeking in electronic environments.* Cambridge, UK: Cambridge University Press.

Marchionini, G., and Komlodi, A. (1998). Design of interfaces for information seeking. In M. E. Williams (Ed.), *Annual Review of Information Science and Technology (ARIST)* (Vol. 33, pp. 89-130). Medford, New Jersey: Information Today.

Marcus, R. S., Kugel, P., and Benenfeld, A. R. (1978). Catalog information and text as indicators of relevance. *Journal of the American Society for Information Science, 29*, 15-30.

Marwick, A. D. (2001). Knowledge management technology. *IBM Systems Journal, 40*(4), 814-830.

McDermott, R. (1999). Why information technology inspired but cannot deliver knowledge management. *California Management Review, 41*(4), 103-117.

Meadow, C. T., Boyce, B. R., and Kraft, D. H. (2000). *Text information retrieval systems.* (2nd ed.). San Diego, CA: Academic Press.

Mellon, C. A. (1990). *Naturalistic Inquiry for Library Science.* Westport, CT: Greenwood Press.

Merriam, S. (1988). *Case study research in education: A qualitative approach.* San Francisco, CA: Jossey-Bass.

Miles, M. B., and Huberman, A. M. (1994). *Qualitative data analysis: A sourcebook of new methods*. Thousand Oaks, CA: Sage.

Millen, D. R., Fontaine, M. A., and Muller, M. J. (2002). Understanding the benefit and costs of communities of practice. *Communications of the ACM, 45*(4), 69-73.

Miller, E., and Swick, R. (2003). An overview of W3C semantic Web activity. *Bulletin of the American Society for Information Science, 29*(4), 8-11.

Miller, F. J. (2002). I = 0 (Information has no intrinsic meaning). *Information Research, 8*(1). Retrieved July 10, 2003, from http://InformationR.net/8-1/paper140.html.

Modjeska, D., and Chignell, M. (2003). Individual differences in exploration using desktop VR. *Journal of the American Society for Information Science and Technology, 54*(3), 216-228.

Montviloff, V. (1990). *National information policies: A handbook on the formulation, approval, implementation and operation of a national policy on information*. Paris: Unesco.

Muller, M. J., Carotenuto, L., Fontaine, M. A., Friedman, J., Newberg, H., Simpson, M., Slusher, J., and Stevenson, K. (1999). Social and computing solutions for voluntary communities of practice: Designing CommunitySpace. *Proceedings of the IEEE 8th International Workshop on Enabling Technologies: Infrastructure for Collaborative Enterprises (WET-ICE '99)*. (pp 271-278). Los Alamitos, CA: IEEE.

Murray, G. (1999). The portal is the desktop [Electronic version]. *Group Computing Magazine, 3*, 22-33. Retrieved July 10, 2003, from http://www.e-promag.com/eparchive/index.cfm?fuseaction=viewarticle&ContentID=166&websiteid=.

Myers, M. D. (2003). *Qualitative research in information systems*. ISWorld Net: MISQ Discovery (available at http://www.auchkland.ac.nz/msis/isworld).

Nardi, B. A., and O'Day, V. L. (1999). *Information ecologies: Using technology with heart*. Cambridge, Massachusetts: MIT Press.

Newell, S., Scarbrough, H., Swan, J., and Hislop, D. (1999). Intranets and knowledge management: Complex processes and ironic outcomes. In R. H. Sprague (Ed.), *Proceedings of the 32nd Annual Hawaii International Conference on System Sciences (HICSS-32)*. Maui, Hawaii, January 5-8 (pp. 7-17). Los Alamitos, CA: IEEE.

Nielsen, J., and Mack, R. L. (Eds.). (1994). *Usability inspection methods*. New York: John Wiley and Sons.

Nonaka, I. (1994). A dynamic theory of organizational knowledge creation. *Organization Science, 5*(1), 14-37.

Nonaka, I., and Nishiguchi, T. (2001). Social, technical, and evolutionary dimensions of knowledge creation. In I. Nonaka and T. Nishiguchi (Eds.), *Knowledge emergence: Social, technical, and evolutionary dimensions of knowledge creation* (pp. 286-289). New York: Oxford University Press.

Nonaka, I., and Takeuchi, H. (1995). *The knowledge-creating company: How japanese companies create the dynamics of innovation*. New York: Oxford University Press.

Norman, D. A., and Draper, S. W. (1986). *User-centered system design: New perspectives on human-computer interaction*. Hillsdale, New Jersey: Erlbaum.

Nwana, H. S., and Ndumu, D. T. (1999). A perspective on software agents research. *The Knowledge Engineering Review, 14*(2), 1-18.

O'Dell, C., and Grayson, C. J. (1998). If we only knew what we know: Identification and transfer of internal best practices. *California Management Review, 40*(3), 154-174.

Orlikowski, W. (1991). Integrated information environment or matrix of control? The contradictory implications of information technology. *Accounting, Management, and Information Technologies, 1*(1), 9-42.

Orlikowski, W. J. (1992). Learning from notes: Organizational issues in groupware implementation. In J. Turner and R. Kraut (Eds.), *Proceedings of CSCW '92, Toronto, Ontario, Canada, October 31-November 4* (pp. 362-369). New York: ACM Press.

Orlikowski, W. J. (1993). CASE tools as organizational change: Investigating incremental and radical changes in systems development. *MIS Quarterly, 17*(3), 309-340.

Orlikowski, W. J. (1995). *Evolving with Notes: Organizational change around groupware technology* (technical report available at http://ccs.mit.edu/CCSWP186.html). Cambridge, MA: Massachusetts Institute of Technology.

Orlikowski, W. J. (1996). Improvising organizational transformation over time: A situated change perspective. *Information Systems Research, 7*(1), 63-92.

Orlikowski, W. J., and Baroudi, J. J. (1991). Studying information technology in organizations: Research approaches and assumptions. *Information Systems Research, 2*(1), 1-28.

Ouellette, T. (1999). Opening your own portal [Electronic version]. *ComputerWorld, 33*(32). Retrieved July 4, 2003 from http://www.computerworld.com/home/print.nsf/all/990809B9F2.

Paice, C. D. (1990). Another stemmer. *SIGIR Forum, 24*(3), 56-61.

Paisley, W. J. I. (1968). Information needs and uses, *Annual Review of Information Science and Technology* (Vol. 3, pp. 1-30).

Paivio, A. (1971). Imagery and deep structure in the recall of English normalizations. *Journal of Verbal Learning and Verbal Behavior, 10*(1), 1-12.

Palys, T. (1997). *Research decisions: Quantitative and qualitative perspectives*. Toronto, Ontario: Harcourt Brace and Company.

Pao, M. L. (1989). *Concepts of information retrieval*. Englewood, Colorado: Libraries Unlimited.

Papazoglou, M. P. (2001). Agent-oriented technology in support of e-Business: Enabling the development of "intelligent" business agents for adaptive, reusable software. *Communications of the ACM, 44*(4), 71-77.

Passini, R. (2000). Sign-posting information design. In R. Jacobson (Ed.), *Information Design* (pp. 83-101). Cambridge, Massachusetts: MIT Press.

Perrin, C. (1991). Electronic social fields in bureaucracies. *Communications of the ACM, 34*(12), 75-82.

Peters, T. A. (1993). The history and development of transaction log analysis. *Library Hi Tech, 11*(2), 41-66.

Peters, T. A., Kurth, M., Flaherty, P., Sandore, B., and Kaske, N. K. (1993). An introduction to the special section on transaction log analysis. *Library Hi Tech, 11*(2), 38-40.

Pirolli, P., and Card, S. K. (1999). Information foraging. *Psychological Review, 106*, 643-675.

Plumtree. (1999). *Corporate portals: A simple view of a complex world* (White Paper): Plumtree Software.

Polanyi, M. (1966). *The tacit dimension*. London: Routledge and Kegan Paul.

Ponelis, S., and Fair-Wessels, F. (1998). Knowledge management: A literature overview. *South Africa Journal of Library Information Science, 66*(1), 1-10.

Ponzi, L., and Koenig, M. (2002). Knowledge management: Another management fad? *Information Research, 8*(1). Retrieved July 2, 2003, from http://InformationR.net/ir/8-1/paper145.html.

Port, O. (2002). The next web. *Business Week, 3772,* 96-102.

Porter, M. F. (1980). An algorithm for suffix stripping. *Program, 14,* 130-137.

Prusak, L. (2000). Plenary address. In R. H. Sprague (Ed.), *Proceedings of the 33rd Annual Hawaii International Conference on System Sciences (HICSS-33).* Maui, Hawaii, January 4-7. Los Alamitos, CA: IEEE.

Prusak, L. (2001). Where did knowledge management come from? *IBM Systems Journal, 40*(4), 1002-1007.

Quinn, J. B. (1992). *Intelligent enterprise: A knowledge and service based paradigm for industry.* New York: The Free Press.

Quinn, J. B., Anderson, P., and Finkelstein, S. (1996). Managing professional intellect: Making the most of the best. *Harvard Business Review, 74*(March-April), 71-80.

Ram, S. (2001). Intelligent agents and the world wide web: Fact or fiction? *Journal of Database Management, 12*(1), 46-47.

Raol, J. M., Koong, K. S., Liu, L. C., and Yu, C. S. (2002). An identification and classification of enterprise portal functions and features. *Industrial Management and Data Systems, 102*(7), 390-399.

Resnick, P., and Varian, H. R. (1997). Recommender systems. *Communications of the ACM, 40*(3), 56-58.

Rice, R. E. (1992). Task analyzability, use of new media, and effectiveness: A multi-site exploration of media richness. *Organization Science, 3,* 457-500.

Robinson, M. (1991). Computer supported co-operative work: Cases and concepts. In P. Hendriks (Ed.), *Groupware 1991: The potential of team and organisational computing* (pp. 59-75). P.O. Box 424, 3500 AK Utrecht, The Netherlands: Software Engineering Research Centre (SERC).

Roethlisberger, F. J. (1977). *The elusive phenomena.* Boston, Massachusetts: Harvard Business School, Division of Research.

Rogers, Y. (1994). Exploring obstacles: Integrating CSCW in evolving organizations. In R. Furuta and C. Neuwirth (Eds.), *Proceedings of CSCW '94, Chapel Hill, NC, October 22-26* (pp. 67-77). New York: ACM Press.

Rosenbaum, H. (1993). Information use environments and structuration: Towards an integration of Taylor and Giddens. In S. Bonzi (Ed.), *Proceedings of the 56th Annual Meeting of the American Society for Information Science, Columbus, OH* (Vol. 30, pp. 235-245). Medford, NJ: Learned Information.

Rosenbaum, H. (1996). *Managers and information in organizations: Towards a structurational concept of the information use environment of managers.* Unpublished Ph.D. dissertation, Syracuse University, Syracuse, New York.

Rosenbaum, H. (1999). Towards a theory of the digital information environment. In L. Woods (Ed.), *Proceedings of the 62nd Annual Meeting of the American Society for Information Science* (Vol. 36, pp. 705-712).

Rosenbaum, H. (2000). The information environment of electronic commerce: Information imperatives of the firm. *Journal of Information Science, 26*(3), 161-171.

Rosenfeld, L., and Morville, P. (1998). *Information Architecture for the World Wide Web.* Cambridge, Massachussets: O'Reilly.

Saffady, W. (1998). *Knowledge management: A manager's briefing.* Prairie Village, KS: ARMA International.

Saint-Onge, H., and Wallace, D. (2003). *Leveraging communities of practice for strategic advantage.* Boston: Butterworth-Heinemann.

Salton, G. (1989). *Automatic text processing: The transformation, analysis, and retrieval of information by computer.* Don Mills, Ontario: Addison-Wesley.

Salton, G., and McGill, M. J. (1983). *Introduction to modern information retrieval.* New York: McGraw-Hill.

Saracevic, T. (1969). Comparative effects of titles, abstracts and full text on relevance judgements, *Proceedings of the American Society for Information Science (ASIS) Conference* (Vol. 6, pp. 293-299).

Saracevic, T. (1971). Selected results from an inquiry into testing of information retrieval systems. *Journal of the American Society for Information Science, 22*, 126-139.

Scheepers, R. (1999). *Intranet implementation: Influences, challenges and role players.* Unpublished Ph.D. dissertation, R-99-5011, Aalborg University, Denmark.

Scheepers, R., and Rose, J. (2001). Organizational intranets: Cultivating information technology for the people by the people. In S. Dasgupta (Ed.), *Managing internet and intranet technologies in organizations: Challenges and opportunities* (pp. 1-20). Hershey, Pennsylvania: Idea Group.

Schmidt, K., and Bannon, L. (1992). Taking CSCW seriously: Supporting articulation work. *Computer Supported Cooperative Work, 1*, 7-40.

Schroeder, J. (2000). Enterprise portals: A new business intelligence paradigm. *MIS Quarterly, 23*(September), 124-126.

Schuler, D., and Namioka, A. (Eds.). (1993). *Participatory design: Principles and practices*. Hillsdale, New Jersey: Lawrence Erlbaum Associates.

Schultze, U. (1998). Investigating the contradictions in knowledge management. In T. J. Larsen, L. Levine, and J. I. DeGross (Eds.), *Proceedings of the IFIP WG8.2 and 8.6 Joint Working Conference on Information Systems: Current Issues and Future Changes*. Helsinki, Finland, December 10-13 (pp. 155-174). Laxenburg, Austria: IFIP.

Serenko, A., and Detlor, B. (2002). *Agent toolkits: A general overview of the market and an assessment of instructor satisfaction with utilizing toolkits in the classroom* (Working Paper 455). Hamilton, Ontario, Canada: Michael G. DeGroote School of Business, McMaster University.

Serenko, A., and Detlor, B. (2003a). Agent toolkit satisfaction and use in higher education. *Journal of Computing in Higher Education, 15*(1), 65-88.

Serenko, A., and Detlor, B. (2003b). Agent toolkits for eBusiness: Towards a typology. In M. Head and C. Bart (Eds.), *Proceedings of the 4th World Congress on the Management of Electronic Business*. Hamilton, Ontario: McMaster University.

Shadbolt, N., and O'Hara, K. (1997). Model based expert systems and the explanation of expertise. In P. J. Feltovich, K. M. Ford, and R. R. Hoffman (Eds.), *Expertise in context: Human and machine* (pp. 315-337). Cambridge, Massachusetts: AAAI Press / The MIT Press.

Shilakes, C. C., and Tylman, J. (1998). *Enterprise information portals* (White Paper). New York: Merrill Lynch.

Shoham, Y. (1997). An overview of agent-oriented programming. In J. M. Bradshaw (Ed.), *Sofware agents* (pp. 271-290). Menlo Park, California: American Association for Artificial Intelligence.

Skyrme, D. (1997). Knowledge management: Making sense of an oxymoron. *Management Insight, 22*. Retrieved July 5, 2003, from http://www.skyrme.com/insights/22km.htm.

Sloman, A. (1998). What's an AI toolkit for? In B. Logan and J. Baxter (Eds.), *Proceedings of AAAI-98 Workshop on Software Tools for Developing Agents*. Madison, Wisconsin (pp. 1-10). Menlo Park, CA: AAAI Press.

Smart, K. L., Cossell Rice, J., and Wood, L. E. (2000). Meeting the needs of users: Towards a semiotics of the Web, *Proceedings of the Technology and Teamwork Conference, Cambridge, MA* (pp. 593-605). New York: IEEE Press.

Smith, R. G., and Farquhar, A. (2000). The road ahead for knowledge management: An AI perspective. *AI Magazine, Winter*, 17-40.

Snis, U. (2000). Knowledge is acknowledged? A field study about people, processes, documents, and technologies. In R. H. Sprague (Ed.), *Proceedings of the 33rd Annual Hawaii International Conference on System Sciences (HICSS-33)*. Maui, Hawaii, January 4-7. Los Alamitos, CA: IEEE.

Snyder, C. A., and Wilson, L. T. (2002). Implementing knowledge management: Issues for managers. In D. White (Ed.), *Knowledge Mapping and Management* (pp. 154-165). Hershey, Pennsylvania: Idea Group.

Sonnenwald, D. H., and Iivonen, M. (1999). An integrated human information behavior research framework for information studies. *Library and Information Science Research, 21*(4), 429-457.

Sparck Jones, K. (1972). A statistical interpretation of term specificity and its application in retrieval. *Journal of Documentation, 28*(1), 11-21.

Sparck Jones, K., and Willet, P. (Eds.). (1997). *Readings in information retrieval*. San Francisco: Morgan Kaufmann.

Spinuzzi, C. (2002). A scandinavian challenge, a US response: Methodological assumptions in scandinavian and US prototyping approaches, *Proceedings of SIGDOC* (pp. 208-215). New York: ACM Press.

Staab, S., Angele, J., Decker, S., Erdmann, M., Hotho, A., Maedche, A., Schnurr, H. P., Studer, R., and Sure, Y. (2000). Semantic community web portals. *Computer Networks, 33*(1-6), 473-491.

Stehr, N. (1994). *Knowledge Societies*. Thousand Oaks: CA: Sage Publications.

Stenmark, D. (2001). The relationship between information and knowledge. In S. Bjornestad, R. E. Moe, M. A.I., and A. L. Opdahl (Eds.), *Proceedings of the 24th Information Systems Research Seminar in Scandinvia (IRIS24)*. Ulvik, Norway, August 11-14. Bergen, Norway: Bergen University.

Stenmark, D. (2002a). Information vs. knowledge: The role of intranets in knowledge management. In R. H. Sprague (Ed.), *Proceedings of the 35th Annual Hawaii International Conference of System Science (HICSS-35)*. Maui, Hawaii, January 7-10 (pp. 1326-1335). Los Alamitos, CA: IEEE.

Stenmark, D. (2002b). Intranet-supported knowledge creation: Factors and technology for organizational creativity, *Proceedings of the 3rd European Conference on Organizational Knowledge, Learning, and Capabilities (OKLC)*. Athens, Greece, April 5-7. Athens, Greece: ALBA (Athens Laboratory of Business Administration).

Stenmark, D. (2002c). Standardization vs. personalization: An alternate view of the problem of under-utilised corporate intranets. In K. Bodker, M. K. Pedersen, J. Norbjerg, J. Simonsen, and M. T. Vendelo (Eds.), *Proceedings of the 25th Information Systems Research Seminar in Scandinvia (IRIS25)*. Bautahoj, Denmark, August 10-13.

Stenmark, D. (2003). Intranet as formative context: A study of under-utilised corporate Webs. In N. C. Romano (Ed.), *Proceedings of the Americas Conference on Information Systems (AMCIS)*. Tampa, Florida, Aug 4-5.

Strauss, A., and Corbin, J. (1994). Grounded theory methodology: An overview. In N. Denzin and Y. Lincoln (Eds.), *Handbook of Qualitative Research* (pp. 273-285). Thousand Oaks, CA: Sage.

Strauss, A., and Corbin, J. (1998). *Basics of qualitative research: Techniques and procedures for developing grounded theory*. (2nd ed.). Thousand Oaks, CA: Sage.

Stryker, S., and Statham, A. (1985). Symbolic interaction and role theory. In G. Lindsay and E. Aronson (Eds.), *Handbook of social psychology* (3rd ed., Vol. 1, pp. 311-378). New York: Random House.

Suchman, L. A. (1987). *Plans and situated actions: The problem of human-machine communication*. New York: Cambridge University Press.

Suchman, L. (2000). Making a case: "Knowledge" and "routine" work in document production. In P. Luff, J. Hindmarsh, & C. Heath (Eds.), *Workplace studies: Recovering work practice and informing design* (pp. 29-45). Cambridge, MA: Cambridge University Press.

Sveiby, K. E. (1997). *The new organizational wealth: Managing and measuring knowledge-based assets.* San Francisco, CA: Berrett-Koehler.

Swan, W., Langford, N., Watson, I., and Varey, R. F. (2000). Viewing the corporate community as a knowledge network. *Corporate Communications: An International Journal, 5*(2), 97-106.

Tait, P., and Vessey, I. (1988). The effect of user involvement on system success: A contingency approach. *MIS Quarterly, 12*(1), 91-108.

Tate, A., Dalton, J., Levine, J., and Nixon, A. (2003). Task-achieving agents on the world wide web. In D. Fensel, J. Hendler, H. Lieberman, and W. Wahlster (Eds.), *Spinning the semantic web: Bringing the world wide web to its full potential* (pp. 431-458). Cambridge, Massachusetts: MIT Press.

Taylor, R. S. (1986). *Value-added processes in information systems.* Norwood, New Jersey: Ablex Publishing.

Taylor, R. S. (1991). Information use environments. In B. Dervin and M. J. Voigt (Eds.), *Progress in Communication Sciences* (Vol. 10, pp. 217-255). Norwood, New Jersey: Ablex Publishing.

Taylor, S., and Todd, P. A. (1995). Understanding IT usage: A test of competing models. *Information Systems Research, 6*(2), 144-176.

Terra, C., and Gordon, C. (2003). *Realizing the promise of corporate portals.* New York: Butterworth-Heinemann.

Tesch, R. (1990). *Qualitative research: Analysis types and software tools.* New York: Falmer.

Thomas, J. C., Kellogg, W. A., and Erickson, T. (2001). The knowledge management puzzle: Human and social factors in knowledge management. *IBM Systems Journal, 40*(4), 863-884.

Thuring, M., Hannemann, J., and Haake, J. M. (1995). Hypermedia and cognition: Designing for comprehension. *Communications of the ACM, 38*(8), 57-66.

Toffler, A. (1990). *Powershift: Knowledge, wealth and violence at the edge of the 21st century.* New York: Bantam Books.

Toms, E. G. (2002). Information interaction: Providing a framework for information architecture. *Journal of the American Society for Information Science and Technology, 53*(10), 855-862.

Toms, E. G., and Kinnucan, M. T. (1996). The effectiveness of the electronic city metaphor for organizing the menus of free-nets. *Journal of the American Society for Information Science, 47*, 919-931.

Tu, H.-C., and Hsiang, J. (2000). An architecture and category knowledge for intelligent information retrieval agents. *Decision Support Systems, 28,* 255-268.

Turoff, M., and Hiltz, S. R. (1998). Superconnectivity. *Communications of the ACM, 41*(7), 116.

Typanski, R. E. (1999). Creating an effective information environment: Management perspectives and personnel. *Information Systems Management, Spring,* 32-40.

van Dijk, T. A., and Kintsch, W. (1983). *Strategies of discourse comprehension.* Orlando, Florida: Academic Press.

Vaughan, M. W., and Schwartz, N. (1999). Jumpstarting the information design for a community network. *Journal of the American Society for Information Science and Technology, 50*(7), 588-597.

Venkatesh, V., and Davis, F. (1996). A model of the antecedents of perceived ease of use: Development and test. *Decision Sciences, 27*(3), 451-481.

Venkatesh, V., and Davis, F. (2000). A theoretical extension of the technology acceptance model: Four longitudinal field studies. *Management Science, 46*(2), 186-204.

Verity. (1999). *The Verity corporate portal: Organize your intranet the way you organize your business* (White Paper, Available at http://www.verity.com/solutions/cportal.html): Verity Inc.

Von Krogh, G. (1998). Care in knowledge creation. *California Management Review, 40*(8), 133-153.

Vredenburg, K., Mao, J.-Y., Smith, P. W., and Carey, T. (2002). A survey of user-centered design practice. In L. Terveen (Ed.), *Proceedings of the SIGCHI Conference on Human Factors in Computing Systems (CHI '02).* (pp. 471-478). New York: ACM.

Wallace, D., and Saint-Onge, H. (2003). Communities of practice: A strategic approach for generating knowledge capital. In C. Bart and N. Bontis (Eds.), *Proceedings of the 6th McMaster World Congress on the Management of Intellectual Capital and Innovation.* January 15-17, Hamilton, Ontario, Canada. Hamilton, Ontario: McMaster University.

Walsham, G. (1993). *Interpreting information systems in organizations.* Chichester: Wiley.

Wang, H., Mylopoulos, J., and Liao, S. (2002). Intelligent agents and financial risk monitoring systems. *Communications of the ACM, 45*(3), 83-88.

Weick, K. E., and Daft, R. L. (1983). The effectiveness of interpretation systems. In K. S. Cameron and D. A. Whetten (Eds.), *Organizational effectiveness: A comparison of multiple models* (pp. 71-93). New York: Academic Press.

Weill, P., and Broadbent, M. (1998). *Leveraging the new infrastructure: How market leaders capitalize on information*. Boston: Harvard Business School Press.

Wenger, E. (1998). *Communities of Practice: Learning, Meaning and Identity*. Cambridge: Cambridge University Press.

Wenger, E., and Snyder, W. (2000). Communities of practice: The organizational frontier. *Harvard Business Review, Jan-Feb*, 139-145.

Westbrook, L. (1993). User needs: A synthesis and analysis of current theories for the practitioner. *RQ, 32*, 541-549.

Wikstrom, S., and Normann, R. (1994). *Knowledge and value: A new perspective on corporate transformation*. New York: Routledge.

Wild, R. H., Griggs, K. A., and Downing, T. (2002). A framework for e-learning as a tool for knowledge management. *Industrial Management and Data Systems, 102*(7), 371-380.

Williams, F., Rice, R. E., and Rogers, E. M. (1988). *Research methods and the new media*. New York: The Free Press.

Wilson, T. D. (1997). Information behavior: An interdisciplinary perspective. *Information Processing and Management, 33*(4), 551-572.

Wilson, T. D. (1999). Models in information behaviour research. *Journal of Documentation, 55*(3), 249-270.

Winikoff, M., Padgham, L., and Harland, J. (2001). Simplifying the development of intelligent agents. In M. Stumptner, D. Corbett, and M. J. Brooks (Eds.), *Proceedings of 14th Australian Joint Conference on Artificial Intelligence*. Adelaide, Australia, December 10-14 (pp. 557-568). Berlin: Springer.

Woodruff, A., Rosenholtz, R., Morrison, J., Faulring, A., and Pirolli, P. (2002). A comparison of use of text summaries, plain thumbnails, and enhanced thumbnails for web search tasks. *Journal of the American Society for Information Science and Technology, 53*(2), 172-185.

Wooldridge, M., and Jennings, N. (1998). Pitfalls of agent-oriented development. In K. Sycara and M. Wooldridge (Eds.), *Proceedings of the 2nd International Conference on Autonomous Agents*. Minneapolis, Minnesota, May 9-13 (pp. 385-391). New York: ACM.

Wooldridge, M. J., and Ciancarini, P. (2001). Agent-oriented software engineering: The state of the art. In P. Ciancarini and M. J. Wooldridge (Eds.), *Agent-Oriented Software Engineering* (pp. 1-28). Berlin: Springer-Verlag.

Wuthnow, R., and Shrum, W. (1983). Knowledge workers as a "new class": Structural and ideological convergence among professional-technical workers and managers. *Work and Occupations, 10*, 471-487.

Yin, R. K. (1994). *Case study research, design and methods*. (2nd ed.). Newbury Park: Sage Publications.

Zack, M. (1999). Managing codified knowledge. *Sloan Management Review, 40*(4), 45-58.

Zhang, R. (2002). Web-based knowledge management. In D. White (Ed.), *Knowledge Mapping and Management* (pp. 131-143). Hershey, Pennsylvania: Idea Group.

Zuboff, S. (1988). *In the age of the smart machine*. New York: Basic Books.

NAME INDEX

Includes names of individuals, businesses, and institutions. For names of products and publications, see the Subject Index.

SUBJECT INDEX

The letters 'f' and 't' following page numbers denote figure and table respectively.